The Lakeside Classics

Pictures of
Gold Rush California

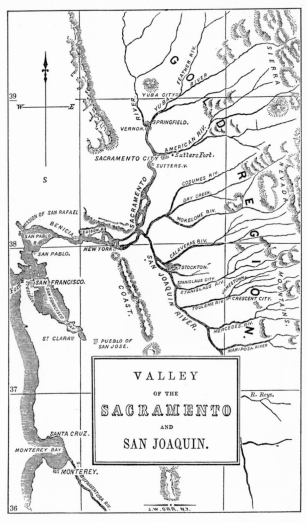

PRINCIPAL GOLD REGION IN 1849
Reproduced from Walter Colton's "The Land of Gold:
Three Years in California 1846–1849"

The Lakeside Classics

———

Pictures of
Gold Rush California

EDITED BY

M<small>ILO</small> M<small>ILTON</small> Q<small>UAIFE</small>

The Lakeside Press
R. R. D<small>ONNELLEY</small> & S<small>ONS</small> C<small>O.</small>
Christmas, 1949

Publishers' Preface

IN several previous volumes of The Lakeside Classics, the Publishers have presented to their readers narratives dealing
with the dangers and hardships of overland
journeys to the Far West. The volume published last year presented an account of such
a journey to California by a group of "forty-
niners."

This year California continues its celebration of the one hundredth anniversaries of
the discovery of gold and of its becoming
the thirty-first State. Although relatively
little has been written of the effects of these
events on the social and economic life of the
nation, there is a wealth of material depicting
life in California one hundred years ago.

The full texts of some of the contemporary
narratives are being republished by others.
For our volume this year we have selected a
series of extracts from famous contemporary
descriptions of various aspects of life in
California during the Gold Rush period.

We refer the reader to the historical introduction appearing on pages xv to xlv and
the notes prepared by Dr. Quaife, for many

Publishers' Preface

years the scholarly editor of these Classics. They bring out related additional information and give the selections a common perspective.

We are indebted to the Chicago Public Library and particularly to The Newberry Library for advice and for making available to us the material from which our selections were made. We are also grateful to the Chicago Historical Society for help in the selection of illustrations and for the privilege of reproducing them.

The company is completing another successful year of uninterrupted production. The postwar expansion of both buildings and equipment has been substantially completed. Our customers have provided for us a high level of activity and the gratifying cooperation of the entire organization has enabled us to make progress in coordinating improved practices and procedures.

We extend our best wishes for a Merry Christmas and a Happy and Prosperous New Year.

THE PUBLISHERS

Christmas, 1949

Contents

Historical Introduction

Historical Introduction

BURLY Sam Brannan rushed hatless
through the old San Francisco Plaza
waving aloft a bottle of gold dust and
bellowing lustily "Gold! Gold! Gold from
the American River!!!" Seldom in recorded
history have half a dozen words touched off
such a furor as the one which Brannan's performance aroused. Like the speech of Pope
Urban II at Clermont in the year 1096 they
started a veritable crusade. It was now the
end of May, 1848 and the gold discovery had
been made at Sutter's mill on the American
Fork over four months earlier. The news
had been published in the San Francisco
Californian on March 15 in a one-paragraph
announcement headed "GOLD MINE
FOUND." Since then numerous allusions
had been made to the subject, and for weeks
thereafter the youthful editor of Brannan's
own *California Star* had continued to ridicule
the reports. As late as May 29, but a few
hours before Brannan's earsplitting performance, he had denounced the discovery
as a "supurb take-in as was ever got up to
guzzle the gullible."

Historical Introduction

The truth seems to be that news is of no importance until the mind of the hearer is attuned to its significance. No one could long ignore Sam Brannan. His bull-throated bellowing galvanized the somnolent villagers to action, and with one accord they abandoned their accustomed ways to engage in a mad rush for the gold fields. Both *Star* and *Californian* suspended publication and their editors joined in the frantic rush. "The whole country," wrote the Editor of the latter journal, "from San Francisco to Los Angeles and from the seashore to the base of the Sierra Nevada resounds with the sordid cry of gold! Gold! Gold!!! while the field is left half-planted, the house half-built, and everything neglected but the manufacture of shovels and pickaxes, and the means of transportation to the spot."[1]

Such was the beginning of the Gold Fever. Before many weeks gold in important quantities began arriving at San Francisco. The magic news spread up and down the coast as

[1] On the general subject of the discovery, and the resultant spread of the news concerning it see Reuben C. Shaw, *Across the Plains in Forty-nine*, the Lakeside Classics volume for 1948, pp. XVIII–XX; Ralph P. Bieber, *Southern Routes to the Gold Mines* (Glendale, 1937), 17 ff. For Sam Brannan's career see James A. B. Scherer, *The First Forty Niner and the Story of the Golden Tea Caddy* (New York, 1925).

far as Portland and Valparaiso and across the Pacific to the Sandwich Islands, and everywhere it came men responded to the lure of gold to be had for the taking. Before the year closed several thousand adventurers had thronged to the mines.

No one from the settled eastern portion of America, however, was numbered among the Forty-Eighters. The story of the reception there of the news of the Gold Discovery curiously parallels the earlier and briefer story of its reception at San Francisco. Early in April, 1848 both San Francisco newspapers had issued somewhat extensive narrative surveys of the resources of California which included the statement that gold had been discovered on the American, but amid the assemblage of other data concerning the country's resources the significance of the statement had gone unnoticed. Even the *Californian's* brief initial announcement of the discovery, published on March 15, had concluded with the sweeping and largely untrue assertion that "California, no doubt is rich in mineral wealth . . . gold has been found in almost every part of the country." Two weeks later (April 1) the *Star* published a lengthy article on the resources of California and Proprietor Brannan dispatched a considerable number of copies eastward by special express over the overland route. They arrived on the Missouri about the end of July, but neither the St. Joseph nor the St. Louis papers, which published portions of the article, made any mention of the discovery of gold. A month later (September 1) the Washington *Daily Union* followed their example, omitting from its notice of the article all mention of the discovery of gold. In much the same fashion the journalists of half a century later were blind to the significance of the reported achievement of Orville and Wilbur Wright at Kitty Hawk.

Meanwhile Thomas O. Larkin, U.S. Consul at Monterey, inclosed in a dispatch to the Secretary of State a clipping of the *Californian's* March 15 report. Probably the bearer of this dispatch was Kit Carson, the famous scout, who arrived at Washington on August 2.[2] Like the Washington and St. Louis editors, the State Department did not perceive the significance of the discovery nor report it to the public.

Thus it remained for the New York *Herald* on August 19 to publish probably the first report in the East of the Gold Discovery. It consisted of an extensive narrative[3] dated at

[2] See *Kit Carson's Autobiography*, The Lakeside Classics volume for 1935, pp. 123–25.

[3] For it see *post*, chapter IV.

Historical Introduction

San Francisco, April 1, 1848 by a member of the New York Regiment of Volunteers which had been sent to California during the Mexican War, summarizing and restating the information current at that place concerning the resources of the newly-acquired province in general, together with definite mention of the discovery of gold on the American River. Like the earlier reports of the event, however, this one fell upon deaf ears. As earlier at San Francisco, neither newspaper editors nor general public manifested any interest in the news.

The public indifference on the subject continued until President Polk's annual message to Congress on December 5, 1848 was published. In it he stated that the reports concerning the discovery of gold were so extraordinary as to be unbelievable in the absence of official confirmation of their truth. Such confirmation he now supplied in the form of several documents which had been sent to the Government at Washington by responsible U.S. officials in California. Among them was a communication from Governor Richard B. Mason giving a detailed account of his visit to the mines, accompanied by the statement that there was more gold in the country than would be required to pay the expense of the Mexican War 100 times over.

Historical Introduction

Two days later (December 7) Lieutenant Loeser of the Third Artillery, who had been dispatched by Governor Mason, arrived at Washington bringing some 230 ounces of gold in a tea caddy. Specimens of it were exhibited at the White House and the War Department, and the remainder of the shipment was sent to the Philadelphia mint, which on December 12 announced it to be pure gold of great fineness. The Presidential message, quickly followed by the famous tea caddy, roused the eastern United States as Sam Brannan's spectacular performance had roused the denizens of San Francisco. Faster than the speed of a prairie fire the Gold Fever swept the country from Maine to Georgia and from the Atlantic to the Missouri. Everywhere, in obscure villages and teeming cities young men and old thrilled to the lure of fabulous wealth to be garnered in California. But winter was already at hand and the gold mines were more remote from the settled East than Tibet or Tasmania is to-day. So in hundreds of communities and thousands of homes the winter was devoted to making preparations for the great trek which the ensuing summer season was to witness.

Such was the dawn of the Era of the Forty-niners. Although the Gold Rush drew its votaries from the entire civilized world, in what follows our attention will be centered upon the role played by Americans in it. To reach California a variety of routes and combinations of routes might be followed, depending upon the starting point of the adventurers, their individual resources and preferences, their state of information, and other pertinent factors. Broadest distinction of all lay between the choice of travel by sea or overland (Various combinations of the two will presently appear). Probably the majority of adventurers living close to the Atlantic seaboard and more or less accustomed to the idea of ships and sea voyages elected to go to California by sea. Inland dwellers were more inclined to journey overland to California, although exceptions to both generalizations were numerous. Parties from Ohio embarked at New York for the voyage by sea and others from New Hampshire or Virginia journeyed to Independence to embark upon the Overland Crossing.

Those who elected to follow the sea route commonly shipped from such ports as Boston, New York, New Orleans, or other coastal cities for a voyage around South America to San Francisco. Provided the vessel was adequate and the captain and crew competent, the journey was made in relative ease and safety, chief objections to it being the cost of the passage and the great amount of time consumed in the voyage.

The shorter sea routes by way of the Isthmus of Panama and Nicaragua were followed by other thousands of argonauts, while still others who started by sea landed at various Texan and Mexican ports to pursue the further journey overland. All of these routes entailed, of course, land passages more or less arduous and dangerous. For those fortune hunters who elected to travel overland to California several leading routes were available, and the number of variations and combinations of them which individual argonauts made defies generalization.

Best-known, probably, of all the continental crossings was the famous Oregon-California Road. From various starting points as widely separated as New Hampshire, Virginia, and Wisconsin gold-seekers converged in spring or early summer upon such Missouri River points as Independence, St. Joseph, and Council Bluffs. From them, they launched their schooners upon the Plains as early in the season as the growing grass upon which their animals must subsist would permit. All who followed the California Road journeyed by way of the Platte and Sweetwater rivers to South Pass. Some continued to follow the Oregon Road as far as Fort Hall on the Snake, near present-day Pocatello, Idaho. Others turned southward to seek the upper Humboldt by way of Salt Lake City or by some variant cut-off. Descending the Humboldt to the vicinity of the dreaded "Sink," most of the travelers crossed thence to the Carson or the Truckee and surmounted the Sierras by way of the Carson or Truckee passes. Many, however, sought to find an easier route to the Sacramento by turning westward from the Humboldt at the Great Bend and making their way across the no less dreadful intervening desert to the upper Sacramento.

Estimates (perhaps "guesses" would be the more accurate word to use) of the number who traveled the Oregon-California Road in 1849 run to 25,000 or 30,000. During much of the 2000-mile journey from St. Joseph or Independence to California trains were constantly in sight of the traveler. Frequently they moved in solid procession extending as far as the eyesight reached and the clouds of dust stirred up were a sore affliction to the men and animals alike. More serious still was the consumption of the available supply of grass along the route, without which the animals would perish, leaving their owners to shift as best they might.

Historical Introduction

Many who followed the Oregon-California Road utilized the steamboats on the Mississippi and Missouri to travel as far as Independence. Those who congregated here could either take the Oregon-California Road or follow the famous Santa Fe Trail southwestward to Santa Fe. Still others—apparently several thousand in all—started their Plains journey from Fort Smith in Arkansas or Fort Gibson in Oklahoma and ascended the Canadian River Valley and thence onward to Santa Fe.

Westward from this point a choice of several routes was again presented. One was the old Spanish Trail which, with numerous variants, ran northwestward into and across southern Utah and thence southwestward to the Mohave Desert and Los Angeles. Other routes led southward from Santa Fe to converge by several variants upon the valley of the Gila. Descending this to the Colorado at Yuma, they turned northward toward Los Angeles. By whatever way this point was reached there still remained, of course, a journey of several hundred miles to reach the mines on the Sacramento.

Still other gold-seekers might journey by sea from New Orleans to such Texas ports as Galveston or Brownsville. From such points the Overlanders traveled by various routes across Texas and Mexico, many of them converging eventually by way of the Guadalupe Pass and the Pima Indian villages upon the Gila Valley, where they joined the routes leading from Santa Fe to this vicinity. Still others continued across Mexico to Mazatlan on the Gulf of California, where they continued by sea to San Francisco.[4]

By whatever route they sought to reach California the Gold Seekers were moved by one common impulse whose significance seems largely to have gone unnoticed by most commentators. Americans of Anglo-Saxon lineage have a practically universal instinct for formal group organization. When the Pilgrim Fathers prepared to land in the Massachusetts wilderness they adopted the famous Mayflower Compact to provide regulations to govern their future conduct. In like fashion the Gold Seekers, whether five in number or twenty times as many, before setting out upon their hegira organized themselves into companies and adopted more or less elaborate sets of rules to govern their conduct. Some of these agreements were de-

[4] For these various routes see Ralph P. Bieber, "The Southwestern Trails to California in 1849" in *Mississippi Valley Historical Review*, XII, 342–77 (December, 1925); *Southern Routes to the Gold Mines* (Glendale, 1937), 17 ff.

signed to last only for the duration of the
journey to California. Others, especially
those groups that went by sea, adopted regulations intended to cover their entire stay in
the mines and their return therefrom. Practically always the basis of organization was
highly democratic, although from necessity
practically always a captain was chosen,
whose directions his followers were pledged
to obey.

Since all alike were in advance ignorant of
the conditions and trials they were about to
undergo, and since the organizations possessed no power to coerce a delinquent member, secessions, reorganizations, and dissolu-
tions of the associations en route were frequent. For obvious reasons the larger
companies were more liable to experience
such discords than were the smaller ones.
The very size of the larger companies produced problems which the smaller ones
were likely not to encounter. A group of
half a dozen men traveling with perhaps
two or three wagons possessed greater freedom of action, and commonly greater co-
hesion of membership than it was possible for
companies numbering scores of men and
wagons to attain. Human nature was op-
erative on these journeys as everywhere else
in life, and under the stress of the crossing

and the intimate associations it enforced unexpected traits of character were likely to
become disclosed. When feelings of dislike
or motives of supposed self-interest arose, the
obvious solution was for the dissatisfied ones
to secede from the company, sometimes to
unite with another organization, at other
times to continue onward alone.

Individual illustrations of all generalizations, as well as individual exceptions to all
of them, can readily be cited. Commonly all
argonauts bound for California provided
themselves with excessive equipment and
stores of supplies. Those who went by sea
frequently invested in stocks of food or other
merchandise which they hopefully anticipated selling at a profit in the mines. Many
individuals, too, equipped themselves with
strange and useless contrivances for mining
and shipping the gold they confidently expected to acquire. Commonly both goods
and equipment were abandoned upon reaching San Francisco.

Overland travelers almost universally provided too heavy wagons for the journey and
commonly loaded them to capacity with supplies of food and other equipment. Unbridged
rivers had to be crossed, sandy deserts traversed, and hills and mountains ascended and
descended. For those who followed the

Oregon-California Road, the earlier portion of the journey, from Independence or St. Joseph up the Platte, was comparatively easy and the animals at the start were, of course, in good condition. Soon, however, they began to fail under hard driving and the burden of the overloaded wagons. Correspondingly, as early as arrival at Fort Kearney (now Grand Island, Nebraska) the owners began to reduce their loads, and the farther west they went the more equipment, including even wagons, was jettisoned. Since commonly there were no purchasers for the discarded supplies they were simply abandoned to the Indians or the elements. Even here human nature's traits were disclosed. One argonaut might post a sign on his property inviting any later comer to help himself to it. Another might purposely despoil his belongings before leaving them, by destroying the equipment or pouring kerosene over the food.

In the main, however, the property was simply left behind. Where animals were failing or dying, or stolen, or strayed beyond recovery, one or more wagons, their contents shifted to the others, might be left behind. Thereby the animals required to pull them were released to reinforce those hauling the wagons that were retained. From Fort

Historical Introduction

Kearney to the Sierra passes the highway was strewn with clothing, furniture, tools, and food supplies of almost every kind. It was strewn, too, with the carcasses of oxen and mules, whose decaying odor polluted the atmosphere for miles around. The terrible trek down the Humboldt, which animals and humans entered upon worn down by the hardships and toil already endured, was especially marked by the bodies of dead animals and the graves of the people who perished.

Those who survived to the end of the journey commonly presented a distressing appearance. Roughened and tanned by desert winds and sun, with clothing in tatters and heads and beards unshorn, even the men were no Adonises. One of them who had not looked in a glass for months has recorded his dismayed surprise upon gazing at his shocking reflection in a mirror. Much harder, of course, was the lot of the women who crossed the Plains. Blackened by sun and grime and worn down by exposure and toil, they often arrived in California looking more like the natives of the desert than like the civilized persons who had left their eastern homes only a few months before.

When the Overlanders departed from the Missouri border they entered a land where

xxix

the agencies of civilized law and order were non-existent. Yet seldom in American history has the native genius for improvising methods of social control manifested itself more clearly. Where thousands of men and women are congregated, offenses against person and property are bound to be committed. Frequently, of course, these went unpunished, but in numerous instances a rude and summary justice was dispensed. In some extreme cases impromptu trials of culprits ended with the award of the death sentence, when a convenient wagon-tongue might be converted to serve the purpose of a gallows. A somewhat amusing case of a milder offense and punishment is recorded by one overland journalist. The writer had served his turn as camp guard during the earlier half of the night. When it ended he roused the man who was to relieve him and himself went to bed. It was a stormy night, however, and the relief guard, instead of turning out, resumed his broken slumber. In the morning his delinquency was discovered, and for several days his companions taunted him unmercifully. At length, to escape their ridicule he abandoned the party to attach himself to another one near-by. The diarist concludes by stating that he was really a good man, whose companions wished him well and regretted their conduct in ribbing him so severely.

Upon reaching the mines the fortune seekers commonly scattered to whatever points chance or expectant hope might dictate. In many instances men who had lived in most intimate association throughout the months of the journey parted never to meet again. In the mines as on the Plains there was at first no organized local government. Until its agencies should be established the miners made shift to create and enforce their own laws. The native American genius for political action which has already been noted did not fail them. Rules governing the tenure and extent of mining claims were quickly established and commonly scrupulously observed. Since the miner had practically no facilities for safeguarding his property, consisting chiefly of gold dust, persons guilty of stealing were accorded prompt and severe punishment.

In like fashion crimes of violence met with swift retribution, and within hours the guilty wretch was likely to be suspended from some convenient tree. If contemporary evidence can be trusted, criminal conduct was comparatively rare in the mines in 1849. In the following years, when formal local governments and courts had been established offenses were much more common. Probably the real reason for this lay in the fact that many men of criminal inclinations had now been attracted to the mines, although the Forty-niner was wont to maintain, and probably to believe, that the coming of lawyers and law courts was responsible for the change. Quite probably, too, the Forty-niner tended, as the years passed, to idealize the state of halcyon innocence which he fondly believed had characterized the life of the mines in its earlier period.

The task of mining gold was extraordinarily severe. Commonly the miner was wholly without previous experience of mining and knowledge of mining methods. Commonly, too, his shelter was of the rudest sort. Some camped out under a convenient tree. Sooner or later, unless they migrated in search of better "diggings," they erected a structure which with more or less accuracy was denominated a cabin. An occasional miner found shelter in an empty cask. The food upon which they subsisted was commonly as atrocious as it was expensive.

In the beginning most mining was done by the panning process. This involved stooping in a cold mountain stream, more or less constantly exposed to water and the elements. No labor union or eight or ten hour day concept prescribed the hours of toil, which were limited only by the sun and the miners' powers of endurance. When resort was had to the cradle, the long tom, and the damming of streams to divert them from their beds the hazards and hardships undergone were not appreciably lessened.

The gold was found in the form of dust, flakes, or nuggets, where it was deposited in the beds and adjoining "bars" of rivers. Because of its high specific gravity it commonly worked its way down to the rock foundation and was overlain by one or several feet of gravel, clay or other soil and the miner's first task was that of prospecting a claim or location. This he sampled for its gold-bearing promise by "panning" some of the soil in the river. This called for a certain expertness which could only be acquired by practice. Perhaps half a dozen pans of soil could be washed in an hour, and if the pan disclosed fifty cents worth of dust the claim was well worth holding. Commonly the return was much less than this sum, although oftentimes it was vastly more.

The mining of gold as followed by the Forty-niners was as precarious a gamble as sensible men ever indulged in. Occasionally the rewards achieved were rich but more commonly they were pitifully meager. In return

for absenting himself from home and friends
to live in a distant wilderness under conditions of hardship and hazards to health and
life which prudent men commonly refuse to
undergo, most gold seekers obtained the
meagerest of daily earnings, whose value was
largely offset by the unusual cost of living in
the mines. If at the end of one or more years
the miner was able to return home with any
surplus over the expenses entailed by his
journey to and from California he was luckier
than most of his fellow argonauts. Thousands, of course, lacked the means of paying
the cost of the return journey. Other thousands established business or other connec-
tions which induced them to remain in the
land of gold. And thus American California
was born.

The financial rewards achieved by the
miners have commonly been grossly exaggerated. When a Gutenberg Bible sells for
$100,000 or a Button Gwinnett autograph
for $20,000 or more, all over the land unin-
formed dreamers begin to imagine that the
manuscript or printed contents of their own
attics should sell for similar sums. So, too,
when a lucky Forty-niner chanced upon an
extraordinary nugget thousands of other
miners were spurred on by the dream of enjoying like success. In sober reality but few

of them ever did, and the multitude toiled for mere existence wages.

Although precise statistics are lacking, the following data concerning the output of gold in 1850 are enlightening. The *Illustrated London News* of December 26, 1850 reprinted an article from the Sacramento *Placer Times* of Oct. 26, wherein the editor of the California publication sought to estimate the season's output of gold and the number of miners engaged in producing it.

Although precise information was difficult to obtain, he presented these figures for the several leading mining districts: Feather River, 7,000 miners, average daily return $6; for 5 months, estimating 24 days monthly labor, total income per miner was $600 and total for the district $5,400,000; Yuba River, 30,000 miners, average daily earnings $4, total for 5 months, $14,400,000; Bear River, 3,000 miners, average daily earnings $4, total for 5 months, $1,440,000; American River, 16,000 miners, average daily earnings $5, total for 5 months, $8,000,000.

In all, 57,000 miners earned $30,240,000, an individual average of $530. If we arbitrarily assume that the actual season lasted two months longer, the total yearly individual income would be increased to $742. Of the entire 57,000 miners, 33,000—over one-half—earned $4 a day; 16,000 earned $5, and the remaining 7,000 earned $6. Since these averages include the more fortunate few who made larger incomes, the earnings of the great mass of miners were correspondingly less.

The Editor states that the districts reported upon were supposed to comprise two-thirds of the total mining output of the State, and concludes with this observation: "This sum, we believe, is as near an average of the produce of the mines upon the rivers named for the past five months as can be ascertained at the present time."

His conclusions concerning the earnings of the individual miner find support in the data supplied by Daniel B. Woods, author of *Sixteen Months at the Gold Diggings*. Along with examples of remarkable successes achieved, he supplies sobering information concerning the returns of the average miner. Four out of five river damming operations, he declares, ended in failure. Of 14 such companies for whose operations figures were obtained, several found no gold at all. One relatively small company obtained $20.37 per day's labor expended. All fourteen companies obtained $113,633 from 35,876 days' labor; an average of $3.16 per day.

These earnings, it will be noted, average much lower than the estimates supplied by the Editor of the *Placer Times*. Evidently the latter were much too high or else the returns from damming operations were much less profitable than the labor of miners engaged in individual operations. Whichever the case may be in this respect, the figures cited suffice to squeeze the water out of the exaggerated statements which are frequently made concerning the earnings of the gold miners.

Regardless of individual bonanzas or misfortunes, the Era of the Forty-niners opened a new page in American and world history. Overnight, as it were, the Commonwealth of California was born. At last America had spanned the Continent, and in so doing had achieved a new and broader concept of her destiny as a world power. In his leading article for August 10, 1850 the sapient editor of the *Illustrated London News* undertook to unroll the scroll of the future. Through the discovery of gold a land hitherto barren and almost unknown, lying at the extreme west of America and fronting the extreme east of Asia, had suddenly become populated by the vigorous, restless, daring, and unscrupulous American race.

Before many years millions of men would occupy the new country and not forever would they be content to confine their energy to mining gold. A new civilized state had been created in close proximity to the ancient nations of China and Japan. Before long the restless Americans would seek to open a trade with these oriental kingdoms, and failing, would pick a quarrel with them. The factor of remoteness alone had enabled China and Japan to maintain the seclusion from the western world which until now they had observed. Now this safeguard had suddenly been removed, and California, "teeming with life, ambition, and daring" would not permit a generation to pass before taking the measure of the flowery kingdoms and opening them to the civilization of the world.

In all this, save for details of time sequence, the Editor prophesied with amazing prescience. Instead of a generation, only four years had elapsed when the menacing cannon of Matthew Perry's fleet in Yedo Bay extorted a treaty of trade and amity from the Emperor of Japan, inducing the people over whom he ruled to embark upon a breath-taking program of westernization and to become within half a century an industrial and military world power. Not until the bombs fell upon Pearl Harbor in 1941, however, did the editorial forecast of 1850 find its further realization.

Such, briefly and inadequately sketched, has been one of the consequences of the chance discovery of some flakes of gold in the mill-race at Coloma on January 24, 1848. The many others, both at home and abroad, a volume would not suffice to describe.

This is the centennial year of the Forty-niners and it is fitting that the occasion should arouse widespread interest throughout America. One form of expression which this interest takes is the publication of commemorative articles and volumes upon California and the Gold Rush. To readers of *The Lakeside Classics* series the subject is far from novel. Beginning with Manly's *Death Valley in '49*, published in 1927, some half dozen volumes have been issued dealing with early California and its adjacent area. *Death Valley* was followed by the narratives of John Bidwell and John Steele in 1928 and by James Ohio Pattie's *Personal Narrative*, dealing with the Spanish California of the Twenties, in 1929. In 1934 Zenas Leonard's fine narrative of Great Basin-California exploration in 1833 was issued. The following year marked the first authoritative publication of Kit Carson's tersely thrilling autobiography. Mrs. Sumnerhayes' charming *Vanished Arizona*, published in 1939, supplies vivid descriptions of the Lower Colorado, Gila River, and other areas which the Gold Hunters who went by the southern overland routes had traversed a quarter of a century earlier. Finally, Reuben Cole Shaw's *Across the Plains in '49*, issued in 1948, provides another valuable Gold Seeker's narrative, this one dealing with the Oregon-California Road by way of the Platte, South Pass, and the Humboldt.

For the current volume, the Publisher has adopted a different plan than the one usually followed in *The Lakeside Classics* series. Instead of providing the reader with a single narrative or journal, as commonly heretofore, the design has been adopted of presenting a considerable number of selections from various sources, chosen with the view of providing a somewhat general conspectus of the entire Gold Rush episode.

In pursuance of this conception, selections dealing with three of the most important routes to California followed by the Gold Seekers are first presented; a narrative of the voyage from New York around Cape Horn by Hinton R. Helper; another of the journey by sea and across the Isthmus of Panama by J. D. Borthwick; and one by Daniel B. Woods, an argonaut who sought to reach

California by sea and the overland journey across Mexico.[5]

With the reader thus vicariously conducted to California, Chapter IV supplies a comprehensive contemporary survey of the region on the eve of the advent of the Gold Rush, written by some unidentified California correspondent of the New York *Herald* in the spring of 1848 and published in the August 19 issue of that journal. Although this announced the discovery of gold on the American River, the single paragraph of information devoted to the subject was accompanied by so much additional data about the mineral wealth of California, quicksilver, copper, coal, silver and "asphaltum" that it did not impress the reader as it might have done if standing alone. However the wealth of optimistic data about the resources of California might well have inspired the desire to migrate thither even if the mention of gold had been omitted.

[5] The reader will no doubt note that no narrative of the overland route by way of the famed Oregon-California Road is presented in the present volume. In view of the fact that *The Lakeside Classics* volume for 1948 (Reuben C. Shaw's *Across the Plains in Forty Nine*) was wholly devoted to the narrative of a caravan which followed this route, the Publisher has deemed it unnecessary to devote space in the present volume to another description of its passage.

Chapter V depicts the magic transformation of San Francisco into the roaring metropolis of the mines, together with certain of the sorrier consequences attendant upon this development; the selections reprinted are taken from Bayard Taylor's *El Dorado*.

The effect of the news of the discovery of gold upon the residents of California is interestingly described in Rev. Walter Colton's *The Land of Gold; or, Three Years in California* from which our selection in Chapter VI is taken. One of Dame Shirley's lively letters, originally published in the *Pioneer*, California's first literary magazine, describing "Three Weeks in a Mining Camp" provides the material for Chapter VII. Chapter VIII follows with a detailed description of mining methods, reprinted from an article entitled "How we got gold in California," originally published in *Harper's Magazine* for April, 1860.

Gold Rush California contained about as thorough a mixture of racial groups, congregated from all over the earth, as may be found in present-day Chicago or Detroit. Lack of space, along with lack of narratives suitable for reprinting, makes it impossible to supply the reader with descriptions of more than a few of these alien groups. The Yankee gold seeker from the States viewed them all with lofty contempt and, himself a newcomer, with superb absence of humor regarded even the native Californians as "aliens." Selections from J. D. Borthwick, *Three Years in California* and from Alonzo Delano, *Life on the Plains and Among the Diggings* provide the reader with descriptions of the way of life of the Mexican, Chinese, and native Indian racial groups.

The miners were not wholly devoid of sources of amusement, nor were they entirely lacking in means of organizing social action. Helper's description of a bear and bull fight, reprinted in Chapter X, illustrates one type of amusement open to them. Commoner far, of course, were the gambling saloons. In more recent years the open saloon has often been defended as being the "poor man's club." The gambling saloons of the early mining era were emphatically every man's club, the common resort of almost all miners in their hours of freedom from toil.

Most miners, too, sought recreation in dancing, whether by themselves in the mining camps, in the saloons and gambling houses, or at the Mexican Fandangoes. The selection from Woods, *Sixteen Months at the Gold Diggings*, reprinted in Chapter X, provides a picture of the saloons and gambling houses; the letter of Dame Shirley reprinted in the same chapter pictures the recreations of dancing and other diversions.

Finally, our series of Gold Rush pictures is concluded with an account of self-government in the mines. The selections presented are from Woods, *Sixteen Months at the Gold Diggings;* from the manuscript diary of Abiel Easter Brooks; and from the narrative of Professor John B. Parkinson of the University of Wisconsin.

The literature of the Gold Rush Era is extensive and its volume increases yearly. California, unique in various respects, is probably also unique in this one, that the beginnings of no other Commonwealth have been so extensively documented. The drama of the Discovery of Gold commanded the attention of the civilized world and among the thousands who rushed to the mines were men of every conceivable trade, profession, and talent. Seldom, if ever, too, has the world witnessed such an outburst of overflowing energy as the argonauts of '49 exhibited. Out of it all came a volume of written and printed reports excelling in quantity and comprehensiveness, perhaps, the comparable records of any earlier era.

Obviously not all of the desirable material can be compressed within the covers of one small volume. Vastly more, indeed, must be ignored than can be utilized. In *Pictures of Gold Rush California* The Lakeside Press provides its readers with representative narratives depicting a considerable variety of aspects of the lives of the Gold Seekers. If their perusal shall inspire them with the desire and the determination to read more widely on the subject, Publisher and Editor will alike be gratified.

MILO M. QUAIFE

Detroit, Michigan
June, 1949

Pictures of
Gold Rush California

Pictures of
Gold Rush California

Chapter 1*

TO CALIFORNIA VIA CAPE HORN

FROM the pier of Wall Street, New York, on Friday, January 31st, [1851], seven passengers, myself amongst the number, embarked for San Francisco on board the clipper ship *Stag Hound*, under command of Capt. Josiah Richardson. The wind blowing from the north-east afforded us a favorable opportunity for standing out from land; of this, however, we did not avail ourselves until about four o'clock in the afternoon; for, although our vessel was towed out early in the morning, and every thing seemed to be in readiness for our final departure, yet, through some unavoidable delay, we were obliged to cast anchor off Staten Island, where it became necessary for us to remain until the time above men-

*For the editor's introductory note to this chapter, see Appendix pages 349–52.

tioned. We then weighed anchor, set sail, and in a few minutes our noble ship was gliding over the blue waves with swan-like grace.

It was truly a magnificent sight as we headed off so smoothly and so majestically from the shore and made our way out farther and farther upon the dark blue deep; we spent the greater part of the evening promenading the quarter-deck, and admiring the enchanting scene. But our reverie and conversation were not altogether undisturbed by melancholy thought. We had just started upon a long, uncertain and monotonous voyage. Old associations had been broken up. We had bid adieu to our native homes, our nearest relations and dearest friends, probably for three or four years—possibly for ever. All before us then was an unknown world—an untrodden path, and phantom-faces of doubt and fear would loom up from the obscurity of the future.

The next morning I began to feel symptoms of that most intolerable of all sensations, seasickness. Of this malady I had had some little experience once before, while on my way from Philadelphia to New York via Cape May; but I never entertained the least idea that it was half so depressing as I now found it. For three weeks and more

I could scarcely eat a mouthful. It really seemed to me at times that eating was the most abominable occupation men could engage in; and when I looked upon dishes of which I had often freely partaken before coming on board the vessel, I either found it difficult to reconcile myself to the opinion that I was not dreaming, or came well nigh detesting myself for having ever been addicted to so gross a habit.

The monotony of our daily life was without variety for the next four or five days. The wind had been somewhat favorable, and we were making good progress until the evening of the fifth day, when suddenly the wind changed and we shortly after found ourselves in the midst of as nice a hurricane as ever sunk a ship or leveled a forest. The wind howled and shrieked in such a manner that I could compare it with nothing earthly; the sea, too, had assumed, by this time, a most formidable appearance; the rain was falling in perfect torrents—the lightning flashed incessantly, and such deafening thunder-peals mortal man never heard before. It appeared as if the elements, for the last five days or so, had been nursing their wrath for this particular occasion, and were determined that we, poor devils of passengers, should be made thoroughly acquainted

5

with the comforts of a crowded ship in a tornado at sea.

The poor affrighted passengers (myself among the rest) despaired of the ship long before the severest part of the tempest was felt, and prayers and promises were offered up without stint for our salvation, by many that never prayed before and I suppose have never done so since. When morning dawned it seemed as if the fury of the storm increased—sea and sky were apparently as one; every thing and every body appeared helpless, hopeless, panic-stricken. Most of our canvas had been taken in or closely furled, yet the ship dashed along with the speed of a racehorse. Things that were not well secured rolled about in the greatest disorder and confusion. The heavy seas which she had already shipped, and the still heavier ones she was then shipping, increased, if possible, the consternation inspired by the awful scene. In fact, things began to wear such a threatening aspect that a speedy change of some sort was looked forward to with the greatest anxiety, not only by the passengers, but by the captain and crew, when, to complete our terrors, topgallant masts, royals, and maintop-masts, with their appendages, came down with a crash that was heard above the howling of the storm. By this

6

time the day had been spent and night considerably advanced; with fear and trembling we retired to our state-rooms, doubting whether we should ever be permitted to see the light of another day. For myself, I suppose I was quite as indifferent about the matter as any one else; for, when a person gets to be as much under the influence of nausea as I was at the time, any change is desirable, even though it carry him to the bottom of the deep. The night passed, and we found that the storm was beginning to abate, so that in about forty-eight hours thereafter its violence had entirely ceased, and fine weather attended us across the equator.

The loss of our masts in this severe gale, at once threw a damper on our high hopes of a quick passage; but, fortunately for us, we had extra masts on board; and, through the indefatigable exertions and perseverance of our vigilant captain, we succeeded in getting all the wreck cleared away and jury masts rigged. The shattered timbers and torn sails opened an unusually large field of labor for our carpenter and sail-maker. We kept on our course, which had been very nearly south east ever since we started, until we passed the Cape Verde Islands, about four degrees to the west, when we steered due south and crossed the equator between twenty-nine and thirty degrees west longitude.

The next interesting event that happened to us occurred off the coast of Brazil, in latitude 22° 25'—longitude 38° 29', Sunday, March 2d. It was about six o'clock in the morning, and I had just left my state-room and gone on deck to take a bath when a sailor by my side, pointing over the starboard bow, cried out, "Boat ahoy! boat ahoy! with men in it." In an instant, as if by electricity, the news was conveyed to every ear on board, and at the same time the starboard rail was lined fore and aft with anxious sailors and half-dressed passengers. As we drew near them (they had been rowing towards us all the while as hard as they could pull) they commenced waving their hands and handkerchiefs, beckoning to us and calling out in an unintelligible language, as if imploring us to receive them on board. At the time, the sea was running moderately high, and we were gliding along at the rate of five or six knots per hour, so that in a few minutes we had them directly astern of us; but we were not so destitute of humanity as to pass them by and leave them to certain death. Our sympathies were quickly and enthusiastically aroused in their behalf, and as soon as our captain could get his ship under proper

8

command he hove her to and waited for them to row along side. Pretty soon they came close under the lee of our vessel, and their weather-beaten features and nautical garb at once gave evidence that they were not unacquainted with the life of sea-faring men.

A rope was thrown to them and they were all able to pull themselves on board by it, except one, whom we afterwards ascertained to be their captain. He, poor fellow, was so much exhausted that he could not help himself, and we were obliged to hoist him in. Their story was the next thing to be learned; for, as yet, not a word they said had been understood. This difficulty was removed, however, as soon as we got our men collected; for, among our polyglot assemblage of men, representing nearly forty different nations, we quickly found an interpreter in the person of an old Swede, whose translation of their story was, in substance, as follows: They were Swedes and belonged to the Russian brig *Sylphide*, which had been to Rio and taken in a cargo of eighteen hundred and twenty-five bags of coffee, with which they had set sail for Helsingfors, Finland; when five days out from Rio, a severe storm, or rather squall, came upon them, and so completely and suddenly wrecked their vessel that they had barely time to escape in one

of the little boats with their lives—not even
having an opportunity to procure so much
as a bottle of water or a mouthful of food.
So precipitate and unexpected was the ca-
lamity which thus overtook them, that they
had to quit their brig without any preparation whatever, and abandon their carpenter,
who happened to be in his berth sick at the
time, to a watery grave.

They had been out three days and nights
in this condition, with nothing to eat or
drink, save the legs of their captain's boots,
which they said they had been chewing to
sustain life. Exposed as they were to the
burning rays of a tropical sun, without any
thing to eat or drink, it is not reasonable to
suppose that they would have lived more
than three days longer at farthest, if we had
not picked them up, or if they had not been
otherwise providentially relieved. We received the captain in our own cabin, and at
our own table, and entertained him as hos-
pitably and agreeably in every way as it was
possible for us to do. His men went before
the mast, and proved a very acceptable addition to our crew, especially in doubling
Cape Horn, for they could endure the cold
much better than our own seamen. That
day, in commendation of the act we had performed in the morning, our captain, who, by

the by, was a very exemplary and devout scion of an orthodox Yankee house, read, during divine service, the parable of the Good Samaritan.

About three o'clock in the afternoon of the same day, a little circumstance came under my observation which, though it may seem quite a trivial affair in the eyes of many, may nevertheless serve to illustrate in some degree the barbarity of man and his utter indifference in regard to the lives of inferior animals. The subject of the incident was a small land bird, very much resembling our hedge sparrow, which was discovered resting upon one of the larboard main braces. A gust or blast of wind had probably driven it out to sea, and it could not find its way back to the shore. It was so weak that it could scarcely fly, and looked as if it was almost dead. On seeing it, I ran below and got a few crumbs of bread and strewed them along over the life-boat nearest to it. But just at that moment the Swedish captain, who had now begun to resuscitate, came up on deck; and spying the distressed little wanderer, he walked up as boldly and deliberately to the rope upon which it was sitting as if it had been some noxious intruder, and shook it violently. Thus frightened, the bird flew off some distance from the ship, but soon returned and alighted in the very same place; again the captain shook the rope as he had done at first, and again the bird did just as it had done before. This same thing was repeated for the third time, when the wearied little creature, apparently disgusted with the brutality of the man, who but a few hours before was himself in a forlorn and helpless condition, dropped down upon the water and was seen no more.

Keeping along down the South American coast, we passed between Patagonia and the Falkland Islands; and on the morning of the 21st of March were within twenty miles of Staten Land. This was the first land we had seen since leaving home, and we feasted our eyes upon it, until our ship bore us so far distant that it had dwindled down to a mere speck. When we were near enough to Staten Land, I could see with the aid of the captain's spy-glass nothing but rugged and sterile mountains, the highest peaks of which were covered with snow, and presented quite a picturesque appearance. No vegetation nor living thing of any kind could be discerned. But a young Bostonian, whom we afterwards saw in Valparaiso, told us he passed so near the shore of some of the land lying at the southern extremity of Patagonia that he could see the natives, who, he said,

were a gigantic people, about eight feet high!
He also said they ran along on the shore
abreast of his vessel, whooping and yelling
at him like a set of ferocious savages.[1] On
Sunday following we saw Cape Horn, the
most notorious of all places upon the high
seas for rough weather and contrary winds.

Up to this time we had been congratulat-
ing ourselves upon the auspicious season in
which we had happened to reach the Cape,
and upon the quick run we were going to
make around it. Delightful weather and
favorable winds had cheered us since leaving
the latitude of the La Plata river, and we
were in high hopes that we had just hit upon
the right time to sail safely round the dangerous Cape in one or two days, instead of
being kept there six or eight weeks, as is
sometimes the case. But we were doomed
to sad disappointment. Towards night that
terror of all navigators, a downright Cape
Horn tempest, assailed us, and for seven
successive days and nights kept us almost
completely submerged. During the whole of

[1] Although the sailor exaggerated somewhat, there
was considerable warrant for his story. According to
the *Britannica*, Magellan, who discovered the land in
1520, gave it the name "Tierra de Patagones" from
observing the large footprints made by its inhabitants.
The natives, now practically extinct, are said to have
averaged 6 feet to 6 feet 4 inches in stature.

this time the wind, which was so intolerably cold and piercing that it seemed to be charged with icicles, blew right in our teeth, and brought hail, sleet, rain or snow with it every hour. Owing to this hard and continued blowing of the wind, the size and power of the waves became perfectly appalling; indeed they ran so heavy and so high that each one looked like a little ocean of itself, and frequently they would strike the ship with such tremendous force that she quivered and groaned as if she were going to pieces; in fact, I often expected to see her shivered into fragments, and could hardly believe otherwise than that we were all destined to become food for the fierce monsters of the deep. We succeeded, however, in getting fairly around the Cape, much to the gratification of all, and especially to the relief of our worn-out seamen, who had been up working with all their might, day and night, for a whole week.

While in the neighborhood of the Cape, we saw great numbers of the albatross, gull, petrel, and other birds; by means of a fish-hook tied to the end of a long line and baited with a piece of fat bacon, which we let out some eight or ten rods from the stern of the vessel, we caught several of a species which the sailors called the Cape Hen. On measuring one of them from the tip of its right wing to the tip of its left, I found it to be seven feet across. The albatross is about twice as large as the Cape Hen. Here, too, while in this latitude, we had our fairest views of the great Southern Cross and the Magellan Clouds, constellations of as much notoriety in the southern hemisphere as the Pleiades and Belt of Orion are in the northern.

It seems that the Atlantic and Pacific oceans are ever at war with each other off Cape Horn, where their waters are continually coming into mad collision, as if no friendship existed between them. But we will now bid adieu to this aquatic battle field, this bleak, dreary region of storms and hurricanes, and look forward to a more congenial clime.

Finding our water was now beginning to give out, and that we should have to procure a fresh supply before we could reach San Francisco, we bent our course towards Valparaiso, upon the coast of Chili, south of the city and harbor to which we were then bound; and as we passed along up the shore, we had a most magnificent view, not only of its own long range of barren hills, but also of the lofty and towering heights of the Andes at the distance of one hundred and forty-five miles in the interior. To add to

15

the grandeur of this spectacle on land, another now presented itself on the ocean around us, in the form of great whales—the first we had seen. We saw many of these huge creatures that day and the next; one of them came within two or three rods of the stern of the ship, and spouted the water with a noise something like that of a high pressure Mississippi steamboat.

We had scarcely dropped our anchor in the harbor of Valparaiso before we were surrounded with little boats filled with natives and foreigners, who had come out, as they said, to talk with us and to see our ship. From these men we learned that four days previously a severe earthquake had been felt, and that all the houses in the city had been more or less injured—a part of the city completely destroyed, and some few persons killed. It was also reported by some of them, that it had laid a great portion of Santiago, the capital, in ruins; but, as yet, no definite news had been received from any of the inland cities or towns; and it was not positively ascertained what amount of damage had been sustained in any place, save only here. Late that evening, about half an hour before sundown, we passengers made our entrance into the city; but it was then too late in the day to see or learn any thing of interest, so we returned directly to our own quarters aboard the ship, and waited in suspense for the coming morn.

Immediately after an early breakfast, Wednesday morning, we put off in a small boat for the shore, and were not a little surprised on arriving there to find every thing so new and so different from what we had supposed. Crowds of the natives, dressed in their peculiar costume, were collected upon the wharves, and were making a great hubbub with their clamorous tongues and noisy actions. They appeared to be an inoffensive, simple-hearted sort of people; but they were inexcusably ignorant and abominably filthy.

Scarcely had we been in the city half an hour that morning when I stepped into a barbershop to have the superfluous hair removed from my head and face. While in the very act of shaving me, the barber very suddenly sprang aghast from me towards the door; and the first thing I knew, the whole earth, houses and every thing around me, were quivering in the most terrific manner; but, fortunately for the timid, helpless creatures, the vacillation continued but a few seconds, and no very serious consequences resulted from it. Just at the moment the rumbling and quaking commenced, I could not for my life think what it was; but the

17

barber seemed to understand it immediately, for he had been the unwilling spectator of a much more destructive earthquake only five days before; and consequently, he knew well enough what the matter was. On retiring from the shop, just as I entered the street, a similar shock was experienced, and instantaneously the whole population rushed headlong out of their houses into the thoroughfares, apparently in the greatest distress, and frightened half out of their wits. I observed several of the women particularly, who, upon running into the streets, immediately placed themselves in an attitude of prayer, by falling upon their knees, crossing their hands upon their breasts, and casting their eyes towards heaven. There was something really beautiful and touching in the unfeigned humility with which these awe-struck mortals resigned themselves to the will of Him who alone is able to convulse worlds, or command tranquillity throughout the universe.

Both of these tremors were slight, and neither did much mischief. But the one that occurred four days previous to our arrival came very near laying the whole city in ruins. The custom house, churches, stores, and nearly all the principal buildings were cracked so badly that many of them were considered dangerous. The people were engaged in pulling down some entirely, and repairing others as best they could. The ground was terribly rent in many places; and while on a stroll beyond the limits of the city, I saw one crevasse which was about five inches in width, and so long and so deep that I could find neither end nor bottom to it. We remained in Valparaiso till the afternoon of Saturday, but did not feel any other shock. For myself, I was satisfied with what I saw then, and having been since shaken by them two or three times during my sojourn in California, I hope I shall never feel another.

As for the city itself, we saw nothing that was really beautiful about it. The majority of the residences were built of mud and straw, and covered with tiles; and were, I think, upon the whole, rather inferior to the negro huts upon a southern plantation. The immense sterile hills all round, about, and through the city, presented quite a dreary and desolate appearance, and prevented us from seeing more than half the number of its buildings at the same time. One of the merchants, a New Orleans man, informed me that the population was estimated at from 60,000 to 65,000.[2] Speaking of this merchant

[2] Valparaiso, the chief commercial port on the Pacific side of South America, occupies a narrow beach on Val-

reminds me of a remarkable instance of stupidity which came under my observation one morning while visiting his store. He had just received fifty barrels of pork, which the drayman had left before his door, and which he wished to have stowed in his cellar. His regular porter being sick, he hired two doltish countrymen to perform the job. It was stipulated that they should receive a certain sum of money for removing the pork from the street into the cellar; and the bargain being fairly understood on both sides, they began to fulfil their part of the contract by *lifting* the barrels instead of rolling them. We allowed them to pursue this toilsome system of labor until they had finished about one-fifth of their task, when we interposed and explained to them the easier method of accomplishing it. It is a fact, according to

paraiso Bay, extending inland and upwards along the steep slopes of the enclosing hills, which rise to a height of 1,400 feet. The city was founded in 1536 but while it belonged to Spain free commerce was prohibited and as late as 1819 it numbered but 5,000 population. Sir Francis Drake captured the town in 1578 and Sir John Hawkins in 1596. It was sacked by a Dutch fleet in 1600 and in 1866 was in large part destroyed by a Spanish fleet. Earthquakes have been frequent. One in 1908 once more destroyed a large part of the city, whose modernization dates from this time. In 1939 its estimated population was 263,000.

their own confession, that they had not sense enough to avail themselves of the rotundity of the barrels.

Valparaiso surpasses San Francisco in the abruptness of its surface and the barrenness of its soil. There is no plant within sight of the town, except here and there in the little vales and hollows. The inhabitants have to bring all their supplies from beyond the coast range, a distance of nine or ten miles; and as the hills are so large and so steep that they cannot be traversed with vehicles, every thing must be transported upon the backs of mules. The interior of Chili is represented to be a very beautiful and productive country; and, to use the language of her historian, "all the fruits of the earth grow there in the greatest abundance." Towards noon that day we chartered some donkeys and rode out about two miles, to a garden called the Vale of Paradise, in the upper part of the city. This was one of the most charming spots I ever beheld, and, with the exception of two or three other little places like it, the only level and fertile piece of ground we saw during the whole time we were there. Here, on the 9th of April, we got apples, pears, peaches, pomegranates, pine apples, quinces, oranges, lemons, figs, bananas, mangoes and melons to our hearts' content.

On Thursday, having wandered from my comrades, I began to perambulate the streets alone, determined to see and learn as much of the city as practicable. At last I found I had wandered very nearly to its northern outskirts, when I came to a little winding path, which I followed up till it led me to the opened gate of a beautiful, palisaded inclosure. Upon looking in I observed a long, clean, level walk in the midst of the most delectable garden I ever saw. All the way overhead, from one end of the walk to the other, there were large, luscious clusters of grapes, hanging down in the richest profusion; while on either side there seemed to be an actual rivalry in growth and luxuriance between the various fruits and vegetables. About half way up the walk, in a well shaded place, two middle-aged men, dressed in long robes, and with books in their hands, were sitting on a bench, reading. Still I continued to stand at the gate, admiring the fascinating scenery before me, being seen by nobody, and seeing no one myself, except the two gownsmen, whose attention seemed to be wholly absorbed by their books. To go in I feared would not only be an interruption to the quietude and serenity which pervaded those elysian grounds, but also an intrusion upon the privacy of gentlemen whom I had no right to disturb. However, hoping to frame a reasonable excuse by offering to purchase some fruit, I stepped in, and slowly approaching the literary group, inquired, "Do you speak English?" Scarcely had the words fallen from my tongue, when the one who sat farthest from me arose, and having replied in the affirmative, extended his hand towards me in a very cordial manner, and then asked me a long question in Latin, not a word of which I understood except the termination, which was "St. Patrick?" Manifesting by my looks, as well as I could, my ignorance of his ecclesiastical salutation, interrogation, or whatever it was, he immediately dropped his classical lore and conversed with me freely in English—both of us, in the meantime, promenading up and down the lovely arbor. From him I learned that the adjoining buildings were occupied as a Roman Catholic college, and that this garden was exclusively for the use and benefit of the priests, of whom he was one, as well as a professor in the institution. He informed me that it was the largest and most popular college in Chili, and that they had students from nearly all the republics and provinces of the continent. He himself was a native of Belgium, but had emigrated to South America as a missionary some fifteen years prior to the time I saw him. The book he then held in his hand was a Spanish history of the United States; and as he asked me a great many questions concerning our country, I inferred that he felt a good deal of interest in it. Upon the whole, he appeared to be a very kind-hearted and well-disposed man. Just before leaving, he presented me with a mammoth bunch of delicious grapes, and at parting, gave my hand a courteous and sincere shake.

At this place we parted with the wrecked crew we had picked up five weeks before, leaving them in the hands of the Russian consul. But before bidding a final adieu to the captain, we purchased a gold ring and inclosed it in a sympathizing epistle to his wife, condoling with her in her husband's misfortunes. When we committed the letter and little keepsake to his charge, he seemed to be very much affected, and acknowledged himself under a thousand obligations to us.

Little occurred on our passage from Valparaiso to San Francisco worthy of note, except the myriads of fish of various kinds which we saw between the tropics, the sublime sunrises and sunsets, the enchanting moonlight evenings, and the phosphorescent phenomena of the ocean at night. The Pacific far surpasses the Atlantic in beauty and diversity of ocean scenery. Its gentle gales and placid waves inexpressibly charm the heart of the sailor. Almost every species of fish, from the tiny pilchard to the monstrous whale, may be found in its waters; while countless numbers of aquatic birds, from the diminutive petrel to the ponderous albatross, swim lazily upon its bosom.

Six days after leaving Valparaiso we passed within a short distance of the St. Felix Islands, which rise alone out of the world of water. We could see nothing that had life in it about them, nor any thing that was inviting or pleasing to the eye. On the morning of the 5th May, we again crossed the equator, in longitude 114°.

This voyage afforded us an excellent opportunity for reading; but it may well be supposed that, in traveling seventeen thousand miles upon the water, we were sometimes overcome with ennui. As a refuge from this monotony of "life on the ocean wave," we betook ourselves to games of euchre, whist, chess, backgammon and solitaire. Our ship being very large, perfectly new, beautifully and comfortably finished, and furnished with the very best accommodations, eatables and drinkables, we enjoyed ourselves remarkably well, except while sea-sick, or when dashed and beaten about by ill-bred storms and hurricanes. As there were only six passengers besides myself, we had abundance of room; and being together so long, and secluded from all other society, we became as sociable and familiar as if we had all been members of the same household. A very amiable and estimable young lady, the sister of a passenger, and the only female on board, contributed in an eminent degree to the pleasure of the trip.

We arrived in San Francisco on the 25th of May, having made the passage in one hundred and thirteen days from New York. This was a very quick run, considering the misfortunes we met with off the Bermudas. If we had not been dismasted, we would probably have reached our destination twelve or fifteen days earlier. The *Flying Cloud*, clipper-modeled, and built almost exactly like the *Stag Hound*, ran from New York to San Francisco in eighty-nine days, which is the shortest voyage that has yet been made by a sailing vessel between the two ports. Many of the old-fashioned ships crawl along for seven or eight months; and I know one blunt, tub-like carac which consumed three hundred and seventy days in the passage.[3]

[3] The era of the Clipper Ships was approximately the quarter century beginning in 1843. They gave to the world its ultimate development of the sailing ship in

speed and beauty. The tea brought from China quickly deteriorated in the hold of a ship, and the Clippers were built with an eye single to speed, at the sacrifice of cargo capacity. Upon the discovery of gold in California a new demand for this type of vessel was created, and much larger ships were built. The first of these vessels was the *Stag Hound*, whose maiden voyage Helper describes. She was launched from the yard of Donald McKay at East Boston, December 7, 1850 and despite the cold weather, which froze the cotton on the ways, 15,000 people are said to have witnessed the sight.

At the time freights were high in the California trade and prices depended upon the speed of delivery. Many of the vessels paid for themselves on their first voyage. The *Flying Cloud*, built in 1851, made the voyage in 89 days, 20 hours. In 1854 she lowered this time to 89 days, 8 hours, a record never equaled save once by the *Andrew Jackson*, which in 1860 made the voyage in 4 hours less time.

The *Stag Hound's* loss of her masts was a characteristic Clipper Ship incident. The *Flying Cloud* lost hers on her famous initial voyage of 1851. The masts of the Clippers were unusually high (the *Flying Cloud's* mainmast towered 200 feet) and so eager were the captains to attain the utmost possible speed that they sometimes locked the sails to prevent the crew from lowering them without orders. Races between rival Clipper Ships were commonplace. England, too, was building Clippers, and when in 1852 the *Illustrated London News* stated that two English Clippers had beaten two American ships, several United States ship owners organized the American Navigation Club and issued a challenge for a race to China and back between an English-built and manned ship and an American vessel for 10,000 pounds a side. This challenge was never accepted.

In 1863 the *Stag Hound* burned and sunk off the coast of Brazil.

Chapter 2*

ABOUT the beginning of the year 1851 the rage for emigration to California from the United States was at its height. All sorts and conditions of men, old, young, and middle-aged, allured by the hope of acquiring sudden wealth, and fascinated with the adventure and excitement of a life in California, were relinquishing their existing pursuits and associations to commence a totally new existence in the land of gold.

The rush of eager gold-hunters was so great that the Panama Steamship Company's office in New York used to be perfectly mobbed for a day and a night previous to the day appointed for selling tickets for their steamers. Sailing vessels were despatched for Chagres almost daily, carrying crowds of passengers, while numbers went by the different routes through Mexico, and others chose the easier, but more tedious, passage round Cape Horn.

The emigration from the Western States was naturally very large, the inhabitants

*For the editor's introductory note to this chapter, see Appendix, page 352.

being a class of men whose lives are spent in clearing the wild forests of the West, and gradually driving the Indian from his hunting-ground.

Of these western-frontier men it is often said that they are never satisfied if there is any white man between them and sundown. They are constantly moving westward; for as the wild Indian is forced to retire before them, so they, in their turn, shrinking from the signs of civilisation which their own labors cause to appear around them, have to plunge deeper into the forest in search of that wild border-life which has such charms for all who have ever experienced it.

To men of this sort the accounts of such a country as California, thousands of miles to the westward of them, were peculiarly attractive; and so great was the emigration that many parts of the Western States were nearly depopulated.[4] The route followed by

[4] The author's comments disclose a great lack of understanding of the character of the gold seekers who crossed the Plains. A very small minority of them were undoubtedly raw frontiersmen, but the overwhelming majority were not. Instead they were people from every walk of life—merchants, farmers, and professional men— from practically every part of the country. One couple were the parents of Professor Josiah Royce, famous Harvard philosopher. A young college student from Madison, Wisconsin, who made the overland crossing

these people was that overland, across the plains, which was the most congenial to their tastes and the most convenient for them, as, besides being already so far to the westward, they were also provided with the necessary wagons and oxen for the journey. For the sake of mutual protection against the Indians, they travelled in trains of a dozen or more wagons, carrying the women and children and provisions, accompanied by a proportionate number of men, some on horses or mules and others on foot.

In May, 1851 I happened to be residing in New York, and was seized with the California fever. My preparations were very soon made, and a day or two afterwards I found myself on board a small barque about to sail for Chagres with a load of California emigrants. Our vessel was little more than two hundred tons, and was entirely devoted to the accommodation of passengers. The ballast was covered with a temporary deck, and the whole interior of the ship formed a saloon, round which were built three tiers of berths: a very rough extempore table and

was Lucius Fairchild, subsequently Civil War General, Governor of Wisconsin, and U. S. Minister to Spain. These are random illustrations of the fact that among the Overlanders of 1849 and subsequent years all gradations of American life were represented.

benches completed the furniture. There was no invidious distinction of cabin and steerage passengers—in fact, excepting the captain's room, there was nothing which could be called a cabin in the ship. But all were in good spirits, and so much engrossed with thoughts of California that there was little disposition to grumble at the rough-and-ready style of our accommodation. For my own part, I knew I should have to rough it in California, and felt that I might just as well begin at once as wait till I got there.

We numbered about sixty passengers, and a nice assortment we were. The majority, of course, were Americans, and were from all parts of the Union; the rest were English, French, and German. We had representatives of nearly every trade, besides farmers, engineers, lawyers, doctors, merchants, and nondescript "young men."

The first day out we had fine weather, with just sea enough to afford the uninitiated an opportunity of discovering the difference between the lee and the weather side of the ship. The second day we had a fresh breeze, which towards night blew a gale, and for a couple of days we were compelled to lay to.

The greater part of the passengers, being from the interior of the country, had never seen the ocean before, and a gale of wind was a thing they did not understand at all. Those who were not too sick to be able to form an opinion on the subject, were frightened out of their senses, and imagined that all manner of dreadful things were going to happen to the ship. The first night of the gale I was awakened by an old fool shouting frantically to the company in general to get up and save the ship, because he heard the water rushing into her, and we should sink in a few minutes. He was very emphatically cursed for his trouble by those whose slumbers he had disturbed, and told to hold his tongue and let those sleep who could, if he were unable to do so himself.

It was certainly, however, not very easy to sleep that night. The ship was very crank, and but few of the party had taken the precaution to make fast their luggage; the consequence was, that boxes and chests of all sizes, besides casks of provisions and other ship's stores which had got adrift, were cruising about promiscuously, threatening to smash up the flimsy framework on which our berths were built, and endangering the limbs of any one who should venture to turn out.

In the morning we found that the cook's galley had fetched way, and the stove was rendered useless; the steward and waiters—landlubbers who were only working their passage to Chagres—were as sick as the sickest, and so the prospect for breakfast was by no means encouraging. However, there were not more than half a dozen of us who could eat anything, or could even stand on deck; so we roughed it out on cold beef, hard bread, and brandy and water.

The sea was not very high, and the ship lay to comfortably and dry; but in the evening some of the poor wretches below had worked themselves up to desperation, being sure, every time the ship laid over, that she was never coming up again. At last one man, who could stand it no longer, jumped out of his berth, and, going down on his knees, commenced clapping his hands and uttering the most dismal howls and groans, interspersed with disjointed fragments of prayers. He called on all hands to join him; but it was not a form of worship to which many seemed to be accustomed, for only two men responded to his call. He very kindly consigned all the rest of the company to a place which I trust none of us may reach, and prayed that for the sake of the three righteous men—himself and the other two—the ship might be saved. They continued for about an hour, clapping their hands as if applauding, and crying and groaning most piteously—so bereft of sense, by fear, that they seemed not to know the meaning of their incoherent exclamations. The captain, however, at last succeeded in persuading them that there was no danger, and they gradually cooled down, to the great relief of the rest of the passengers.

The next day we had better weather, but the sicklist was as large as ever, and we had to mess again on whatever raw materials we could lay our hands on—red herrings, onions, ham, and biscuit.

We deposed the steward as a useless vagabond, and appointed three passengers to fill his place, after which we fared a little better —in fact, as well as the provisions at our command would allow. No one grumbled, excepting a few of the lowest class of men in the party, who had very likely never been used to such good living ashore.

When we got into the trade winds we had delightful weather, very hot, but with a strong breeze at night, rendering it sufficiently cool to sleep in comfort. The all-engrossing subject of conversation and of meditation was, of course, California, and the heaps of gold we were all to find there. As we had secured our passage only as far as Chagres, our progress from that point to San Francisco was also a matter of constant discussion. We all knew that every steamer to leave Panama for months to come was already full, and that hundreds of men were waiting there to take advantage of any opportunity that might occur of reaching San Francisco; but among our passengers there were very few who were travelling in company; they were mostly all isolated individuals, each "on his own hook," and every one was perfectly confident that he, at least, would have no trouble in getting along, whatever might be the fate of the rest of the crowd.

We added to the delicacies of our bill of fare occasionally by killing dolphins. They are very good eating, and afford capital sport. They come in small shoals of a dozen or so, and amuse themselves by playing about before the bows of the vessel, when, getting down into the martingale under the bowsprit, one takes the opportunity to let drive at them with the "grains," a small five-pronged harpoon.

The dolphin, by the way, is most outrageously and systematically libelled. Instead of being the horrid, big-headed, crookedbacked monster which it is generally represented, it is the most elegant and highly-finished fish that swims.

For three or four days before reaching Chagres all hands were busy packing up, and firing off and reloading pistols; for a revolver and a bowie-knife were considered the first items in a California outfit. We soon assumed a warlike appearance, and though many of the party had probably never handled a pistol in their lives before, they tried to wear their weapons in a negligé style, as if they never had been used to go without them.

There were now also great consultations as to what sort of hats, coats, and boots should be worn in crossing the Isthmus. Wondrous accounts constantly appeared in the New York papers of the dangers and difficulties of these few miles of land-and-river travel, and most of the passengers, before leaving New York, had been humbugged into buying all manner of absurd and useless articles, many of them made of india rubber, which they had been assured, and consequently believed, were absolutely necessary. But how to carry them all, or even how to use them, was the main difficulty, and would indeed have puzzled much cleverer men.

Some were equipped with pots, pans, kettles, drinking cups, knives and forks, spoons, pocket filters (for they had been told that the water on the Isthmus was very dirty), india rubber contrivances which an ingenious man with a powerful imagination and

36

strong lungs could blow up and convert into a bed, a boat, or a tent—bottles of "cholera preventive," boxes of pills for curing every disease to which human nature is liable; and some men, in addition to all this, determined to be prepared to combat danger in every shape, bade defiance to the waters of the Chagres River by buckling on india rubber life preservers.

Others of the party, who were older travellers, and who held all such accoutrements in utter contempt, had merely a small valise with a few necessary articles of clothing, an oil-skin coat, and, very probably, a pistol stowed away on some part of their person, which would be pretty sure to go off when occasion required, but not before.

At last, after twenty days' passage from New York, we made Chagres, and got up to the anchorage towards evening.[5] The scenery was very beautiful. We lay about three-

[5] The port of Chagres, at the mouth of the Chagres River, was discovered by Columbus in 1502. The route by way of the Chagres River to Panama on the Pacific side of the Isthmus was opened in the sixteenth century. In the eighteenth, Chagres became the chief Atlantic port on the Isthmus. Completion of the Panama Railroad in 1855 diverted the cross-Isthmian travel to Colon, eight miles distant, and Chagres went into a permanent decline. It is now an unimportant town of about 1,000 population.

quarters of a mile from shore in a small bay enclosed by high bluffs, completely covered with dense foliage of every shade of green.

We had but little time, however, to enjoy the scenery that evening, as we had scarcely anchored when the rain began to come down in true tropical style; every drop was a bucketful. The thunder and lightning were terrific, and in good keeping with the rain, which is one of the things for which Chagres is celebrated. Its character as a sickly wretched place was so well known that none of us went ashore that night; we all preferred sleeping aboard ship.

It was very amusing to watch the change which had been coming over some of the men on board. They seemed to shrink within themselves, and to wish to avoid being included in any of the small parties which were being formed to make the passage up the river. They were those who had provided themselves with innumerable contrivances for the protection of their precious persons against sun, wind, and rain, also with extraordinary assortments of very untempting-looking provisions, and who were completely equipped with pistols, knives, and other warlike implements. They were like so many Robinson Crusoes, ready to be put ashore

38

on a desert island; and they seemed to imagine themselves to be in just such a predicament, fearful, at the same time, that companionship with any one not provided with the same amount of rubbish as themselves might involve their losing the exclusive benefit of what they supposed so absolutely necessary. I actually heard one of them refuse another man a chew of tobacco, saying he guessed he had no more than what he could use himself.

The men of this sort, of whom I am happy to say there were not many, offered a striking contrast to the rest in another respect. On arriving at Chagres they became quite dejected and sulky, and seemed to be oppressed with anxiety, while the others were in a wild state of delight at having finished a tedious passage, and in anticipation of the novelty and excitement of crossing the Isthmus.

In the morning several shore boats, all pulled by Americans, came off to take us ashore. The landing here is rather dangerous. There is generally a very heavy swell, causing vessels to roll so much that getting into a small boat alongside is a matter of considerable difficulty; and at the mouth of the river is a bar, on which are immense rollers, requiring good management to get over them in safety.

39

We went ashore in torrents of rain, and when landed with our baggage on the muddy bank of the Chagres River, all as wet as if we had swam ashore, we were immediately beset by crowds of boatmen, Americans, natives, and Jamaica niggers, all endeavoring to make a bargain with us for the passage up the river to Cruces.

The town of Chagres is built on each side of the river, and consists of a few miserable cane-and-mud huts, with one or two equally wretched-looking wooden houses, which were hotels kept by Americans. On the top of the bluff, on the south side of the river, are the ruins of an old Spanish castle, which look very picturesque, almost concealed by the luxurious growth of trees and creepers around them.[6]

The natives seemed to be a miserable set of people, and the few Americans in the town were most sickly, washed-out-looking objects, with the appearance of having been steeped for a length of time in water.

After breakfasting on ham and beans at one of the hotels, we selected a boat to con-

[6] The castle of Lorenzo, destroyed by the pirate Henry Morgan when he captured the town in 1671, and subsequently rebuilt by the Spaniards. Admiral Vernon, for whom Lawrence Washington, elder brother of George, named Mount Vernon, also captured Chagres in 1740.

vey us up the river; and as the owner had no crew engaged, we got him to take two sailors who had run away from our vessel, and were bound for California like the rest of us.

There was a great variety of boats employed on the river—whale boats, ships' boats, skiffs, and canoes of all sizes, some of them capable of carrying fifteen or twenty people. It was still raining heavily when we started, but shortly afterwards the weather cleared up, and we felt in better humor to enjoy the magnificent scenery. The river was from seventy-five to a hundred yards wide, and the banks were completely hidden by the dense mass of vegetation overhanging the water. There was a vast variety of beautiful foliage, and many of the trees were draped in creepers, covered with large flowers of most brilliant colors. One of our party who was a Scotch gardener was in ecstacies at such a splendid natural flower show, and gave us long Latin names for all the different specimens. The rest of my fellow passengers were a big fat man from Buffalo, two young Southerners from South Carolina, three New Yorkers, and a Swede. The boat was rather heavily laden, but for some hours we got along very well, as there was but little current. Towards the afternoon, however, our two sailors, who had been pulling all the time, began to flag, and at last said they could go no farther without a rest. We were still many miles from the place where we were to pass the night, and as the banks of the river presented such a formidable barricade of jungle as to prevent a landing, we had the prospect of passing the night in the boat, unless we made the most of our time; so the gardener and I volunteered to take a spell at the oars. But as we ascended the river the current became much stronger, and darkness overtook us some distance from our intended stopping place.

It became so very dark that we could not see six feet ahead of us, and were constantly bumping against other boats coming up the river. There were also many boats coming down with the current at such a rate that if one had happened to run into us, we should have had but a poor chance, and we were obliged to keep shouting all the time to let our whereabouts be known.

We were several times nearly capsized on snags, and, as we really could not see whether we were making any way or not, we came to the determination of making fast to a tree till the moon should rise. It was now raining again as heavily as ever, and having fully expected to make the station that evening, we had taken no provisions with us. We were all very wet, very hungry, and more or less inclined to be in a bad humor. Consequently, the question of stopping or going ahead was not determined without a great deal of wrangling and discussion. However, our two sailors declared they would not pull another stroke—the gardener and myself were in favor of stopping—and as none of the rest of our number were at all inclined to exert themselves, the question was thus settled for them, although they continued to discuss it for their own satisfaction for some time afterwards.

It was about eight o'clock, when, catching hold of a bough of a tree twelve or fifteen feet from the shore, we made fast. We could not attempt to land, as the shore was so guarded by bushes and sunken branches as to render the nearer approach of the boat impossible.

So here we were, thirteen of us, with a proportionate pile of baggage, cramped up in a small boat, in which we had spent the day and were now doomed to pass the night, our miseries aggravated by torrents of rain, nothing to eat, and, worse than that, nothing to drink, but, worse than all, without even a dry match wherewith to light a pipe. If ever it is excusable to chew tobacco, it surely is on such an occasion as this. I had worked a good deal at the oar, and from the frequent alternations we had experienced of scorching heat and drenching rain, I felt as if I could enjoy a nap, notwithstanding the disagreeableness of our position; but, fearing the consequences of sleeping under such circumstances in that climate, I kept myself awake the best way I could.

We managed to get through the night somehow, and about three o'clock in the morning, as the moon began to give sufficient light to let us see where we were, we got under way again, and after a couple of hours' hard pulling, we arrived at the place we had expected to reach the evening before.

It was a very beautiful little spot—a small natural clearing on the top of a high bank, on which were one or two native huts, and a canvas establishment which had been set up by a Yankee, and was called a "Hotel." We went to this hotel, and found some twenty or thirty fellow travellers, who had there enjoyed a night's rest, and were now just sitting down to breakfast at a long rough table which occupied the greater part of the house. The kitchen consisted of a cooking stove in one corner, and opposite to it was the bar, which was supplied with a few bottles of bad brandy, while a number of canvas shelves, ranged all round, constituted the dormitory.

44

We made up for the loss of our supper by eating a hearty breakfast of ham, beans, and eggs, and started again in company with our more fortunate fellow travellers. The weather was once more bright and clear, and confined as we were between the densely wooded and steaming banks of the river, we found the heat most oppressive.

We saw numbers of parrots of brilliant plumage, and a great many monkeys and alligators, at which there was a constant discharge of pistols and rifles, our passage being further enlivened by an occasional race with some of the other boats.

The river still continued to become more rapid, and our progress was consequently very slow. The two sailors were quite unable to work all day at the oars; the owner of the boat was a useless encumbrance; he could not even steer; so the gardener and myself were again obliged occasionally to exert ourselves. The fact is, the boat was overloaded; two men were not a sufficient crew; and if we had not worked ourselves, we should never have got to Cruces. I wanted the other passengers to do their share of work for the common good, but some protested they did not know how to pull, others pleaded bad health, and the rest very coolly said that having paid their money to be taken to Cruces, they expected to be taken there, and would not pull a stroke; they did not care how long they might be on the river.

It was evident that we had made a bad bargain and if these other fellows would not lend a hand it was only the more necessary that some one else should. It was rather provoking to see them sitting doggedly under their umbrellas, but we could not well pitch them overboard, or put them ashore, and I comforted myself with the idea that their turn would certainly come, notwithstanding their obstinacy.

After a tedious day, during which we had, as before, deluges of rain, with intervals of scorching sunshine, we arrived about six o'clock at a native settlement, where we were to spend the night.

It was a small clearing, with merely two or three huts, inhabited by eight or ten miserable-looking natives, mostly women. Their lazy listless way of doing things did not suit the humor we were in at all. The invariable reply to all demands for something to eat and drink was *poco tiempo* (by-and-by), said in that sort of tone one would use to a troublesome child. They knew very well we were at their mercy—we could not go anywhere else for our supper—and they took it easy accordingly. We succeeded at last in getting supper in instalments—now a mouthful of ham, now an egg or a few beans, and then a cup of coffee, just as they could make up their minds to the violent exertion of getting these articles ready for us.

About half a dozen other boat loads of passengers were also stopping here, some fifty or sixty of us altogether, and three small shanties were the only shelter to be had. The native population crowded into one of them, and, in consideration of sundry dollars, allowed us the exclusive enjoyment of the other two. They were mere sheds about fifteen feet square, open all round; but as the rain was again pouring down, we thought of the night before and were thankful for small mercies.

I secured a location with three or four others in the upper story of one of these places—a sort of loft made of bamboos about eight feet from the ground, to which we climbed by means of a pole with notches cut in it.

The next day we found the river more rapid than ever. Oars were now useless— we had to pole the boat up the stream; and at last the patience of the rest of the party was exhausted and they reluctantly took their turn at the work. We hardly made twelve miles, and halted in the evening at a place called Dos Hermanos, where were two native houses.

Here we found already about fifty fellow travellers, and several parties arrived after us. On the native landlord we were all dependent for supper; but we, at least, were a little too late, as there was nothing to be had but boiled rice and coffee—not even beans. There were a few live chickens about, which we would soon have disposed of, but cooking was out of the question. It was raining furiously, and there were sixty or seventy of us, all huddled into two small places of fifteen feet square, together with a number of natives and Jamaica negroes, the crews of some of the boats. Several of the passengers were in different stages of drunkenness, generally developing itself in a desire to fight, and more particularly to pitch into the natives and niggers. There seemed a prospect of a general set-to between black and white, which would have been a bloody one, as all the passengers had either a revolver or a bowie knife—most of them had both—and the natives were provided with their *machetes*—half knife, half cutlass—which they always carry, and know how to use. Many of the Americans, however, were of the better class, and used their

48

influence to quiet the more unruly of their countrymen. One man made a most touching appeal to their honor not to "kick up a muss," as there was a lady "of their own color" in the next room, who was in a state of great agitation. The two rooms opened into each other, and were so full of men that one could hardly turn round, and the lady of our own color was, of course, a myth. However, the more violent of the crowd quieted down a little, and affairs looked more pacific.

We passed a most miserable night. We lay down as best we could, and were packed like sardines in a box. All wanted to sleep; but if one man moved, he woke half a dozen others, who again in waking roused all the rest; so sleep was, like our supper, only to be enjoyed in imagination, and all we could do was to wait intently for daylight. As soon as we could see, we all left the wretched place, none of us much improved in temper or in general condition. It was still raining, and we had the pleasure of knowing that we should not get any breakfast for two or three hours.

We had another severe day on the river—hot sun, heavy rain, and hard work; and in the afternoon we arrived at Gorgona, a small village, where a great many passengers leave the river and take the road to Panama.

Cruces is about seven miles farther up the river, and from there the road to Panama is said to be much better, especially in wet weather, when the Gorgona road is almost impassable.

The village of Gorgona consisted of a number of native shanties, built, in the usual style, of thin canes, between any two of which you might put your finger, and fastened together, in basket fashion, with the long woody tendrils with which the woods abound. The roof is of palm leaves, slanting up to a great height, so as to shed the heavy rains. Some of these houses have only three sides, others have only two, while some have none at all, being open all round; and in all of them might be seen one or more natives swinging in a hammock, calmly and patiently waiting for time to roll on, or, it may be, deriving intense enjoyment from the mere consciousness of existence.

There was a large canvas house on which was painted "Gorgona Hotel." It was kept by an American, the most unwholesome looking individual I had yet seen; he was the very personification of fever. We had here a very luxurious dinner, having plantains and eggs in addition to the usual fare of ham and beans. The upper story of the hotel was a large loft, so low in the roof that one could not stand straight up in it. In this there were sixty or seventy beds, so close together that there was just room to pass between them; and as those at one end became tenanted the passages leading to them were filled up with more beds, in such a manner that, when all were put up, not an inch of the floor could be seen.

After our fatigues on the river, and the miserable way in which we had passed the night before, such sleeping accommodation as this appeared very inviting; and immediately after dinner I appropriated one of the beds, and slept even on till daylight. We met here several men who were returning from Panama, on their way home again. They had been waiting there for some months for a steamer, by which they had tickets for San Francisco, and which was coming round the Horn. She was long overdue, however, and having lost patience, they were going home, in the vain hope of getting damages out of the owner of the steamer. If they had been very anxious to go to California, they might have sold their tickets, and taken the opportunity of a sailing vessel from Panama; but from the way in which they spoke of their grievances, it was evident that they were homesick, and glad of any excuse to turn tail and go back again.

We had frequently, on our way up the river, seen different parties of our fellow passengers. At Gorgona we mustered strong; and we found that, notwithstanding the disadvantage we had been under of having an overloaded boat, we had made as good time as any of them.

A great many here took the road for Panama, but we determined to go on by the river to Cruces, for the sake of the better road from that place. All our difficulties hitherto were nothing to what we encountered in these last few miles. It was one continued rapid all the way, and in many places some of us were obliged to get out and tow the boat while the rest used the poles.

We were all heartily disgusted with the river, and were satisfied, when we arrived at Cruces, that we had got over the worst of the Isthmus; for however bad the road might be, it could not be harder travelling than we had already experienced.

Cruces was just such a village as Gorgona, with a similar canvas hotel, kept by equally cadaverous looking Americans.

In establishing their hotels at different points on the Chagres River, the Americans encountered great opposition from the natives, who wished to reap all the benefit of the travel themselves; but they were too many centuries behind the age to have any chance in fair competition; and so they resorted to personal threats and violence, till the persuasive eloquence of Colt's revolvers and the overwhelming numbers of American travellers, convinced them that they were wrong, and that they had better submit to their fate.

One branch of business which the natives had all to themselves was mule-driving, and carrying baggage over the road from Cruces to Panama, and at this they had no competition to fear from any one. The luggage was either packed on mules, or carried on men's backs, being lashed into a sort of wickerwork contrivance, somewhat similar to those used by French porters, and so adjusted with straps that the weight bore directly down on the shoulders. It was astonishing to see what loads these men could carry over such a road; and it really seemed inconsistent with their indolent character that they should perform, so actively, such prodigious feats of labor. Two hundred and fifty pounds weight was an average load for a man to walk off with, doing the twenty-five miles to Panama in a day and a half, and some men carried as much as three hundred pounds. They were well made, and muscular though not large men, and were apparently more of the Negro than the Indian.

The journey to Panama was generally performed on mules, but frequently on foot; and as the rest of our party intended to walk, I determined also to forego the luxury of a mule; so, having engaged men to carry our baggage, we set out about two o'clock in the afternoon.

The weather was fine, and for a short distance out of Cruces the road was easy enough, and we were beginning to think we should have a pleasant journey; but we were very soon undeceived, for it commenced to rain in the usual style, and the road became most dreadful. It was a continual climb over the rocky beds of precipitous gullies, the gully itself perhaps ten or twelve feet deep, and the dense wood on each side meeting over head, so that no fresh air relieved one in toiling along. We could generally see rocks sticking up out of the water, on which to put our feet, but we were occasionally, for a considerable distance, up to the knees in water and mud.

The steep banks on each side of us were so close together that in many places two packed mules could not pass each other; sometimes, indeed, even a single mule got jammed by the trunk projecting on either side of him. It was a most fatiguing walk. When it did not rain, the heat was suffocating; and when it rained, it poured.

There was a place called the "Half-way House," to which we looked forward anxiously as the end of our day's journey; and as it was kept by an American, we expected to find it a comparatively comfortable place. But our disappointment was great when, about dark, we arrived at this half-way house, and found it to be a miserable little tent, not much more than twelve feet square.

On entering we found some eight or ten travellers in the same plight as ourselves, tired, hungry, wet through, and with aching limbs. The only furniture in the tent consisted of a rough table three feet long, and three cots. The ground was all wet and sloppy, and the rain kept dropping through the canvas over head. There were only two plates and two knives and forks in the establishment, so we had to pitch into the salt pork and beans two at a time, while the rest of the crowd stood round and looked at us; for the cots were the only seats in the place, and they were so rickety that not more than two men could sit on them at a time.

More travellers continued to arrive; and as the prospect of a night in such a place was so exceedingly dismal, I persuaded our party to return about half a mile to a native hut which we had passed on the road, to take our chance of what accommodation we could get there. We soon arranged with the woman, who seemed to be the only inhabitant of the house, to allow us to sleep in it; and as we were all thoroughly soaked, every sort of waterproof coat having proved equally useless after the few days' severe trial we had given them, we looked out anxiously for any of the natives coming along with our trunks.

In the meantime I borrowed a towel from the old woman of the shanty; and as it was now fair, I went into the bush, and got one of our two sailors, who had stuck by us, to rub me down as hard as he could. This entirely removed all pain and stiffness; and though I had to put on my wet clothes again, I felt completely refreshed.

Not long afterwards a native made his appearance, carrying the trunk of one of the party, who very generously supplied us all from it with dry clothes, when we betook ourselves to our couches. They were not luxurious, being a number of dried hides laid on the floor, as hard as so many sheets of iron, and full of bumps and hollows; but they were dry, which was all we cared about, for we thought of the poor devils sleeping in the mud in the half-way house.

The next morning, as we proceeded on our journey, the road gradually improved as the country became more open. We were much refreshed by a light breeze off the sea, which we found a very agreeable change from the damp and suffocating heat of the forest; and about mid-day, after a pleasant forenoon's walk, we strolled into the city of Panama.

On our arrival we found the population busily employed in celebrating one of their innumerable *dias de fiesta*. The streets presented a very gay appearance. The natives, all in their gala dresses, were going the rounds of the numerous gaudily-ornamented altars which had been erected throughout the town; and mingled with the crowd were numbers of Americans in every variety of California emigrant costume. The scene was further enlivened by the music, or rather the noise, of fifes, drums, and fiddles, with singing and chanting inside the churches, together with squibs and crackers, the firing of cannon, and the continual ringing of bells.

The town is built on a small promontory, and is protected on the two sides facing the sea by batteries, and on the land side by a high wall and a moat. A large portion of the town, however, lies on the outside of this.[7]

Most of the houses are built of wood, two stories high, painted with bright colors, and with a corridor and veranda on the upper story; but the best houses are of stone, or sun-dried bricks plastered over and painted.

The churches are all of the same style of architecture which prevails throughout Spanish America. They appeared to be in a very neglected state, bushes, and even trees, growing out of the crevices of the stones. The towers and pinnacles are ornamented with a profusion of pearl-oyster shells, which, shining brightly in the sun, produce a very curious effect.

On the altars is a great display of gold and silver ornaments and images; but the

[7] Panama, the oldest European town on the mainland of America was founded in 1519. In the sixteenth century, except for Cartagena it was the strongest Spanish fortress in the New World. Its importance was due to the fact that gold and silver from Peru were brought by sea to Panama for transportation overland to Chagres on the Atlantic side of the Isthmus. The city was destroyed by Henry Morgan in 1671, and was rebuilt on a new site about five miles west of the old one in 1673. At this time a great granite wall was built around the city, whose remains, noted by Borthwick, may still be seen.

interiors, in other respects, are quite in keeping with the dilapidated uncared-for appearance of the outside of the buildings.

The natives are white, black, and every intermediate shade of color, being a mixture of Spanish, Negro, and Indian blood. Many of the women are very handsome, and on Sundays and holidays they dress very showily, mostly in white dresses, with bright-colored ribbons, red or yellow slippers without stockings, flowers in their hair, and round their necks gold chains, frequently composed of coins of various sizes linked together. They have a fashion of making their hair useful as well as ornamental, and it is not unusual to see the ends of three or four half-smoked cigars sticking out from the folds of their hair at the back of the head; for though they smoke a great deal, they never seem to finish a cigar at one smoking. It is amusing to watch the old women going to church. They come up smoking vigorously, with a cigar in full blast, but when they get near the door they reverse it, putting the lighted end into their mouth, and in this way they take half a dozen stiff pulls at it, which seems to have the effect of putting it out. They then stow away the stump in some of the recesses of their "back hair," to be smoked out on a future occasion.

The native population of Panama is about eight thousand, but at this time there was also a floating population of Americans, varying from two to three thousand, all on their way to California; some being detained for two or three months waiting for a steamer to come round the Horn, some waiting for sailing vessels, while others, more fortunate, found the steamer for which they had tickets ready for them on their arrival. Passengers returning from San Francisco did not remain any time in Panama, but went right on across the Isthmus to Chagres.

The Americans, though so greatly inferior in numbers to the natives, displayed so much more life and activity, even in doing nothing, that they formed by far the more prominent portion of the population. The main street of the town was densely crowded, day and night, with Americans in bright red flannel shirts, with the universal revolver and bowie knife conspicuously displayed at their backs.

Most of the principal houses in the town had been converted into hotels, which were kept by Americans, and bore, upon large signs, the favorite hotel names of the United States. There were also numbers of large American stores or shops, of various descriptions, equally obtruding upon the attention of the public by the extent of their English signs, while, by a few lines of bad Spanish scrawled on a piece of paper at the side of the door, the poor natives were informed, as a mere matter of courtesy, that they also might enter in and buy, if they had the wherewithal to pay. Here and there, indeed, some native with more enterprise than his neighbors intimated to the public—that is to say, to the Americans—in a very modest sign, and in very bad English, that he had something or other to sell; but his energy was all theoretical, for on going into his store you would find him half asleep in his hammock, out of which he would not rouse himself if he could possibly avoid it. You were welcome to buy as much as you pleased; but he seemed to think it very hard that you could not do so without giving him at the same time the trouble of selling.

Although all foreigners were spoken of as *los Americanos* by the natives, there were among them men from every country in Europe. The Frenchmen were the most numerous, some of whom kept stores and very good restaurants. There were also several large gambling saloons, which were always crowded, especially on Sundays, with natives and Americans gambling at the Spanish game of monte; and, of course, specimens were not wanting of that great American institution, the drinking saloon, at the bars of which a brisk business was done in brandy-smashes, whisky-skins, and all the other refreshing compounds for which the Americans are so justly celebrated.

Living in Panama was pretty hard. The hotels were all crammed full; the accommodation they afforded was somewhat in the same style as at Gorgona, and they were consequently not very inviting places. Those who did not live in hotels had sleeping quarters in private houses and resorted to the restaurants for their meals, which was a much more comfortable mode of life.

Ham, beans, chickens, eggs, and rice were the principal articles of food. The beef was dreadfully tough, stringy, and tasteless, and was hardly ever eaten by the Americans, as it was generally found to be very unwholesome.

There was here at this time a great deal of sickness, and absolute misery, among the Americans. Diarrhœa and fever were the prevalent diseases. The deaths were very numerous, but were frequently either the result of the imprudence of the patient himself or of the total indifference as to his fate on the part of his neighbors, and the consequent want of any care or attendance whatever. The heartless selfishness one saw and heard of was truly disgusting. The principle of "every man for himself" was most strictly followed out, and a sick man seemed to be looked upon as a thing to be avoided, as a hindrance to one's own individual progress.

There was an hospital attended by American physicians, and supported to a great extent by Californian generosity; but it was quite incapable of accommodating all the sick; and many a poor fellow, having exhausted his funds during his long detention here, found, when he fell sick, that in parting with his money he had lost the only friend he had, and was allowed to die as little cared for as if he had been a dog.

An American characteristic is a weakness for quack medicines and specifics, and numbers of men here fell victims to the national mania, chiefly Yankees and Western men. Persons coming from a northern climate to such a place as Panama are naturally apt at first to experience some slight derangement of their general health, which, with proper treatment, is easily rectified; but these fellows were all provided with cholera preventive, fever preventive, and boxes of pills for the prevention and the cure of every known disease. The moment they imagined that there was anything wrong with them they became alarmed and dosed themselves with all the medicines they could get hold of, so that when they really were taken ill, they were already half poisoned with the stuff they had been swallowing. Many killed themselves by excessive drinking of the wretched liquor which was sold under the name of brandy, and others by eating ravenously of fruit, green or ripe, at all hours of the day, or by living, for the sake of economy, on gingerbread and spruce beer, which are also American weaknesses, and of which there were several enterprising Yankee manufacturers.

The sickness was no doubt much increased by the outrageously filthy state of the town. There seemed to be absolutely no arrangement for cleanliness whatever, and the heavy rains which fell, and washed down the streets, were all that saved the town from being swallowed up in the accumulation of its own corruption.[8]

[8] From time immemorial until the American government cleaned up the town when entering upon construction of the Panama Canal four decades ago, Panama was a hotbed of diseases, especially yellow fever. Although the city is outside the Canal Zone, the United States still administers its sanitation. In all other respects it is governed by the Republic of Panama.

Among the Americans en route for California were men of all classes—professional men, merchants, laborers, sailors, farmers, mechanics, and numbers of long gaunt Western men, with rifles as long as themselves. The hotels were too crowded to allow of any distinction of persons, and they were accordingly conducted on ultra democratic principles. Some faint idea of the style of things might be formed from a notice which was posted up in the bar-room of the most fashionable hotel. It ran as follows: "Gentlemen are requested to wear their coats at table, if they have them handy." This intimation, of course, in effect amounted to nothing at all, but at the same time there was a great deal in it. It showed that the landlord, being above vulgar prejudices himself, saw the necessity, in order to please all his guests, of overcoming the mutual prejudices existing between broadcloth and fine linen, and red flannel with no linen—sanctioning the wearing of coats at table on the part of the former by making a public request that they would do so, while, of the shirt-sleeve gentlemen, those who *had* coats, and refused to wear them could still glory in the knowledge that they were defying all interference with their individual rights; and in behalf of the really coatless, those who could not call a coat their own, the idea was kindly suggested that that garment was only absent, because it was not "handy."

As may be supposed, such a large and motley population of foreigners confined in such a place as Panama, without any occupation, were not remarkably quiet or orderly. Gambling, drinking, and cock-fighting were the principal amusements; and drunken rows and fights, in which pistols and knives were freely used, were of frequent occurrence.

The 4th of July was celebrated by the Americans in great style. The proceedings were conducted as is customary on such occasions in the United States. A procession was formed, which, headed by a number of fiddles, drums, bugles, and other instruments, all playing "Yankee Doodle" in a very free and independent manner, marched to the place of celebration, a circular canvas structure, where a circus company had been giving performances. When all were assembled, the Declaration of Independence was read and the orator of the day made a flaming speech on the subject of George III and the Universal Yankee nation. A gentleman then got up and, speaking in Spanish, explained to the native portion of the assembly what all the row was about; after which the meeting dispersed, and the further celebration of the day was continued at the bars of the different hotels.

I met with an accident here which laid me up for several weeks. I suffered a good deal, and passed a most weary time. All the books I could get hold of did not last me more than a few days, and I had then no other pastime than to watch the humming-birds buzzing about the flowers which grew around my window.

As soon as I was able to walk, I took passage in a barque about to sail for San Francisco. She carried about forty passengers; and as she had ample cabin accommodation, we were so far comfortable enough. The company was, as might be expected, very miscellaneous. Some were respectable men, and others were precious vagabonds. When we had been out but a few days a fever broke out on board, which was not, however, of a very serious character. I got a touch of it, and could have cured myself very easily, but there was a man on board who passed for a doctor, having shipped as such: he had been physicking the others, and I reluctantly consented to allow him to doctor me also. He began by giving me some horrible emetic, which, however, had no effect; so he continued to repeat it, dose after dose, each dose half a tumblerful, with still no effect, till at last he had given me so much of it that he began to be alarmed for the consequences. I was a little alarmed myself, and putting my finger down my throat, I very soon relieved myself of all his villainous compounds. I think I fainted after it. I know I felt as if I was going to faint, and shortly afterwards was sensible of a lapse of time which I could not account for; but on inquiring of some of my fellow passengers, I could find no one who had so far interested himself on my account as to be able to give me any information on the subject.

I took my own case in hand after that and very soon got rid of the fever, although the emetic treatment had so used me up that for a fortnight I was hardly able to stand. We afterwards discovered that this man was only now making his *début* as a physician. He had graduated, however, as a shoemaker, a farmer, and I don't know what else besides; latterly he had practised as a horse dealer, and I have no doubt it was some horse medicine which he administered to me so freely.

We had only two deaths on board and in justice to the doctor I must say he was not considered to have been the cause of either of them. One case was that of a young man who, while the doctor was treating him for fever, was at the same time privately treating himself to large doses, taken frequently, of bad brandy, of which he had an ample stock stowed away under his bed. About a day and a half settled him. The other was a much more melancholy case. He was a young Swede—such a delicate, effeminate fellow that he seemed quite out of place among the rough and noisy characters who formed the rest of the party. A few days before we left Panama a steamer had arrived from San Francisco with a great many cases of cholera on board. Numerous deaths had occurred in Panama, and considerable alarm prevailed there in consequence. The Swede was attacked with fever like the rest of us, but he had no force in him, either mental or bodily, to bear up against sickness under such circumstances; and the fear of cholera had taken such possession of him, that he insisted upon it that he had cholera, and that he would die of it that night. His lamentations were most piteous, but all attempts to reassure him were in vain. He very soon became delirious and died raving before morning. None of us were doctors enough to know exactly what he died of, but the general belief was that he frightened himself to death. The church service was read over him by the supercargo, many of the passengers merely leaving their cards to be present at the ceremony, and as soon as he was launched over the side, resuming their game where they had been interrupted; and this, moreover, was on a Sunday morning. In future the captain prohibited all card-playing on Sundays, but throughout the voyage nearly one-half of the passengers spent the whole day, and half the night, in playing the favorite game of Poker, which is something like Brag, and at which they cheated each other in the most barefaced manner, so causing perpetual quarrels, which, however, never ended in a fight—for the reason, as it seemed to me, that as every one wore his bowie knife the prospect of getting his opponent's knife between his ribs deterred each man from drawing his own, or offering any violence whatever.

The poor Swede had no friends on board; nobody knew who he was, where he came from, or anything at all about him; and so his effects were, a few days after his death, sold at auction by order of the captain, one of the passengers who had been an auctioneer in the States officiating on the occasion.

Great rascalities were frequently practised at this time by those engaged in conveying passengers in sailing vessels from Panama to San Francisco. There were such numbers of men waiting anxiously in Panama to take the first opportunity that offered of reaching California that there was no difficulty in filling any old tub of a ship with passengers; and, when once men arrived in San Francisco, they were generally too much occupied in making dollars to give any trouble on account of the treatment they had received on the voyage.

Many vessels were consequently despatched with a load of passengers, most shamefully ill supplied with provisions, even what they had being of the most inferior quality; and it often happened that they had to touch in distress at the intermediate ports for the ordinary necessaries of life.

We very soon found that our ship was no exception. For the first few days we fared pretty well, but by degrees one article after another became used up; and by the time we had been out a fortnight we had absolutely nothing to eat and drink but salt pork, musty flour, and bad coffee—no mustard, vinegar, sugar, pepper, or anything of the sort, to render such food at all palatable. It may be imagined how delightful it was, in recovering from fever, when one naturally has a craving for something good to eat, to have no greater delicacy in the way of nourishment than gruel made of musty flour *au naturel*.

There was great indignation among the passengers. A lot of California emigrants are not a crowd to be trifled with, and the idea of pitching the supercargo overboard was quite seriously entertained; but, fortunately for himself, he was a very plausible man, and he succeeded in talking them into the belief that he was not to blame.

We would have gone into some port for supplies, but of such grub as we had there was no scarcity on board, and we preferred making the most of it to incurring delay by going in on the coast, where calms and light winds are so prevalent.

We killed a porpoise occasionally, and ate him. The liver is the best part, and the only part generally eaten, being something like pig's liver, and by no means bad. I had frequently tasted the meat at sea before; it is exceedingly hard, tough, and stringy, like the very worst beefsteak that can possibly be imagined; and I used to think it barely eatable, when thoroughly disguised in sauce and spices, but now, after being so long under a severe salt pork treatment, I thought porpoise steak a very delicious dish, even without any condiment to heighten its intrinsic excellence.

We had been out about six weeks when we sighted a ship many miles off, going the same way as ourselves, and the captain determined to board her and endeavor to get some of the articles of which we were so much in need. There was great excitement among the passengers; all wanted to accompany the captain in his boat, but to avoid making invidious distinctions he refused to take any one unless he would pull an oar. I was one of four who volunteered to do so, and we left the ship amid clamorous injunctions not to forget sugar, beef, molasses, vinegar, and so on—whatever each man most longed for. We had four or five Frenchmen on board, who earnestly entreated me to get them even one bottle of oil.

We had a long pull, as the stranger was in no hurry to heave-to for us; and on coming up to her, we found her to be a Scotch barque bound also for San Francisco, without passengers, but very nearly as badly off as ourselves. She could not spare us anything at all, but the captain gave us an invitation to dinner, which we accepted with the greatest pleasure. It was Sunday, and so the dinner was, of course, the best they could get up. It only consisted of fresh pork (the remains of their last pig) and duff; but with mustard to the pork and sugar to the duff it seemed to us a most sumptuous banquet; and, not having the immediate prospect of such another for some time to come, we made the most of the present opportunity. In fact, we cleared the table. I don't know what the Scotch skipper thought of us, but if he really could have spared us anything the ravenous way in which we demolished his dinner would surely have softened his heart.

On arriving again alongside our own ship, with the boat as empty as when we left her, we were greeted by a row of very long faces looking down on us over the side; not a word was said, because they had watched us with the glass leaving the other vessel, and had seen that nothing was handed into the boat; and when we described the splendid dinner we had just eaten, the faces lengthened so much, and assumed such a very wistful expression, that it seemed a wanton piece of cruelty to have mentioned the circumstance at all.

But, after all, our hard fare did not cause us much distress: we got used to it, and besides, a passage to California was not like a passage to any other place. Every one was so confident of acquiring an immense fortune there in an incredibly short time that he was already making his plans for the future enjoyment of it, and present difficulties and hardships were not sufficiently appreciated.

The time passed pleasantly enough; all were disposed to be cheerful, and amongst so many men there are always some who afford amusement for the rest. Many found constant occupation in trading off their coats, hats, boots, trunks, or anything they possessed. I think scarcely any one went ashore in San Francisco with a single article of clothing which he possessed in Panama; and there was hardly an article of any man's wardrobe which, by the time our voyage was over, had not at one time been the property of every other man on board the ship.

We had one cantankerous old Englishman on board who used to roll out, most volubly, good round English oaths, greatly to the amusement of some of the American passengers, for the English style of cursing and swearing is very different from that which prevails in the States. This old fellow was made a butt for all manner of practical jokes. He had a way of going to sleep during the day in all sorts of places; and when the dinner bell rang, he would find himself tied hand and foot. They sewed up the sleeves of his coat, and then bet him long odds he could not put it on and take it off again within a minute. They made up cigars for him with some powder in the inside; and in fact the jokes played off upon him were endless, the great fun being, apparently, to hear him swear, which he did most heartily. He al-

ways fancied himself ill, and said that quinine was the only thing that would save
him; but the quinine, like everything else on
board, was all used up. However, one man
put up some papers of flour and salt, and
gave them to him as quinine, saying he had
just found them in looking over his trunk.
Constant inquiries were then made after the
old man's health, when he declared the quinine was doing him a world of good and that
his appetite was much improved.

He was so much teased at last that he used
to go about with a naked bowie knife in his
hand, with which he threatened to do awful
things to whoever interfered with him. But
even this did not secure him much peace,
and he was such a dreadfully crabbed old
rascal that I thought the stirring-up he got
was quite necessary to keep him sweet.

After a wretchedly long passage, during
which we experienced nothing but calms,
light winds, and heavy contrary gales, we
entered the Golden Gate of San Francisco
harbor with the first and only fair wind we
were favored with, and came to anchor before
the city about eight o'clock in the evening.

Chapter 3*

ON the 1st of February, 1849 we embarked at the foot of Arch Street, Philadelphia, on board the barque *Thomas Walters*, under command of Captain Marshman, for Tampico, thence intending to cross Mexico, and, re-embarking at Mazatlan, to proceed up the Pacific Coast to San Francisco. Our company consisted of about forty persons, known as the Camargo Company. There were among them men from all the professions and pursuits in life —young and old, grave and gay, married and unmarried.

After the usual amount of adventures, sea sickness, and home sickness, we arrived at Tampico[9] on the 21st of February, where we were most happy to exchange the monotony, the junk and other salt provisions, and the green waves of a sea life for the pleasing

*For the editor's introductory note to this chapter, see Appendix, pages 353–54.

[9] Tampico remained a relatively unimportant town until the beginning of the twentieth century when as the outlet of the country's principal oil fields it rapidly became the most important port of Mexico. As late as 1900 its population was about 10,000. In 1940 it was

variety, the delicious fruits and vegetables, and the beautiful fields of a tropical climate.

We must take our readers with us, first to the theater of Tampico, where we went, not as spectators, but as actors upon its boards. The first night after our arrival we appeared upon its stage, performing our parts in the celebrated farce, the California Gold Diggers —a play which has since been performed a thousand times, and with unabated interest. To explain myself, our quarters while in the city were in the old theater, the various rooms of which we occupied as sleeping and eating apartments.

This city is pleasantly located upon an elevated promontory, being almost an island, having the River Panuco on the one side and a lake upon the other. It contains about seven thousand inhabitants, many of whom are Americans. There are several large plazas or public squares, and some pleasant houses. The American Consul, Captain Chase, took us to the spot where his heroic wife raised the American flag, and main-

81,000. For some years it was the greatest oil port in the world. The summers are hot and humid and the poor section of the city stands on low ground subject to inundations. Prior to the twentieth century epidemics were frequent. The Forty-niners were fortunate when the insect pests did no more damage than to torment them temporarily.

tained it in spite of the threats of the Mexicans.

The furnishing of such a company as ours with all the horses and mules necessary for a journey of about eight hundred miles was not to be accomplished at once. On the morning of the 8th of March, and the fifteenth day after our arrival, we were mounted on mustangs, a small and hardy horse peculiarly adapted to the mountains over which we were to travel, our provisions and clothing being on the backs of mules. All being ready, we slowly filed out from the hacienda of Mr. Laffler, a large farmer from Ohio, who was under contract to supply us with animals to Mazatlan. We had spent some days here preparing for the march, and amusing ourselves in spearing fish, and in shooting deer and alligators, being ourselves, likewise, the sport of innumerable swarms of mosquitoes, ticks, fleas, and jiggers. This latter insect, though very small; is the occasion, at times, of great inconvenience and suffering. These tropical insects handled us so cruelly that we were compelled to write, eat, and sleep with gloves. To avoid them at night, I encased myself in a bag made of cotton, which I drew up over my whole body, then bringing it around my head. This arrangement proved so much to my advantage that I continued it during the whole time of my absence.

Upon the march, a Caballero, mounted upon his mule, took the lead, followed by the whole train of draft mules and the attendants. Then came the guide and the company, sometimes drawn up, under our military captain, in regular order of march, and sometimes extended out over the trail as far as the eye could reach. We were advised to keep well together, and never to dispense with the night guard, on account of the guerillas, who would ever be on the watch for an opportunity to attack us.

For several days our march lay across the level plains of the Tierra Caliente, the region of perpetual spring, and clothed with verdure. Having reached the foothills of the Sierra Madre, or Andes of Mexico, one day's travel brought us up into the temperate region. This was the lower table land. The landscape was no longer gay with flowers, but abounded in immense forests. Here were found the varieties of the mesquite, the stately cypress, and the banyan. The whole undergrowth was a thorny thicket, in which the prickly pear and the cactus predominated. After traveling a day over this region we came to a valley, into which we descended, and where, in the midst of a fertile country, we entered Villa de Vallee. This town contains a cathedral in ruins, which, like those of many of the towns of Mexico, were partially destroyed at the time of the revolution and have never since been repaired. One of the wings was occupied as a chapel, while the residence of the Padre was in a kind of shed behind.

A letter from Bishop Kendrick of Philadelphia, which he kindly sent me as I was about leaving home, procured me every attention here. This general letter of introduction, written in the Latin language, gained for me much valuable information from the priests of Mexico. The assistance, and in some cases the protection, which it secured to our whole company, can not be overrated.[10]

The houses of Villa de Vallee were of one story, and generally made of mud-bricks dried in the sun. The people seemed all poor and very indolent, the women, as is the case through Mexico, being far superior to the men in industry and intelligence. We remained here several days to have our animals shod, a necessary preparation for cross-

[10] The letter of commendation is printed at this point in the original edition. It supplies the information that Woods was a native of Massachusetts who had been living for some years in Philadelphia.

ing the mountains. The day before we left, the padre invited me to dine with him.

After the animals were made ready, we proceeded over the plains toward the mountains, some of the peaks of which we could see. Before we reached these we crossed the Tomwin River at a small town where we passed the night. The place for the entertainment of travelers was near the banks of the river, and late in the afternoon we walked out to the stream, where were gathered men, women, and children, floundering and bathing in the water. Nor was it long before several of our company were joining in their wild and gleeful sports.

For some time reports of a revolution in the country about us reached our ears, and hearing from some villagers that, if we kept on our course, we should meet the insurgents the next day, we concluded to turn aside at once into the mountains, though we should thus be compelled to ascend by a path which is seldom attempted. We were three days in climbing the mountains and clambering over the rocks—such as I hope not to see again. Its precipices were fearful. We would sometimes wind our way up or down the face of a mountain by paths cut in the side, over which a person might be let down many hundred feet by ropes. It was a volcanic country, and its conical peaks were surrounded for miles with scoria and pumice stone, which tore the shoes from the feet of our animals, rendering it almost impossible to travel. This was a country fitted for the ladrones and guerillas. And the frequent crosses planted by the path told of murders which had been committed here, and where the traveler was, if so disposed, to offer up prayers for the repose of the souls of the murdered. We were cautioned to be on our guard, and to maintain a constant watch at night. But, notwithstanding such cautions, we were often tempted, for the sake of avoiding the dust, to travel in advance of the train. In company with a gentleman who was armed as well as myself I started on, not expecting to meet our companions again till we halted for the night. We were about three miles in advance of the train, and, as we rode around the angle of a large rock near the path, six or seven men, who were lying there apparently watching for us, started suddenly to their feet and sprung to our side. Our guns were fortunately in our hands, and in a position that we could use them; we were also armed with revolvers and knives at our belts. Seeing that we were not intimidated by their violent gestures, but were calm and ready, they soon dropped behind us, and after a time disappeared. These robbers never attack travelers if every chance is not in their favor. A small party of five persons belonging to our company were placed in greater danger even than ours. They were traveling some days before us, and not far from this same spot. They had been warned at the last town that a party of twenty guerillas had gone out early in the morning for the purpose of attacking them. As they rode slowly on, they came in sight of the robbers, who had chosen well their positions, and were waiting for them. Five of the twenty-one robbers were stationed in the path, while the others were divided up into small gangs on each side and in the rear. All these were mounted but one, who was employed as a runner between the different parties. The Americans halted, newly capped their rifles and revolvers, and slowly proceeded on their way. With pale faces, but undaunted hearts, they rode up to the Mexicans, who, as they came on, retired and allowed them to pass. When they reached the summit of a hill a half mile distant, and looked back, the robbers were still in the same position. The knowledge, on their part, of the certainty, in case of an encounter, of the death of some of their number, daunted them.

84

At length we reached the summit of the tableland, eight thousand feet above the level of the sea, which spread out a vast plain before us, from which many lofty volcanic peaks sprung up, attaining to an elevation of fourteen thousand feet.

Excepting in the valleys, there is but little vegetation upon these plateaus. And we could not imagine where the supplies for the markets of the cities could be obtained. For several days our path lay through palm and palmetto groves. The parasol shade of their small tops was no shelter from the heat of the sun at noon, but rather increased its intensity. And the whole day long would come, screaming over us, the never-ending flocks of parrots. Their cry, to a weary traveler, is almost intolerable. The cactus, Mexico's national flower, and emblazoned upon her coat of arms and stamped upon her coin, is found here in a thousand varieties. The beautiful flower itself is often three feet in height. After leaving these palm groves we entered upon a very barren and desolate region. It was a desert of sand and dust, almost without water. Our mules would raise such a cloud of dust, especially if there was any wind, as to be nearly suffocating. The great elevation to which we had attained caused the most disagreeable sensations. On lying down at night or rising in the morning there would be a painful giddiness. The skin became parched and dry, and the spirits were oppressed. While traveling over this region we were overtaken one day by a dust storm, which was as novel as it was oppressive. It was near night. We saw before us, which after a time spread out all around us, many wild whirlwinds which extended up into the sky, carrying with them apparently solid conical masses of clouds. We counted upward of sixty cones formed and forming at the same time. As the sun was setting, these extended at the top, opening something in the form of an umbrella, the cones still continuing to play up their heaving masses into its expanding bosom, which presented a most unearthly and terrific appearance. It was the *blackness of darkness*, which suddenly became illuminated by the lurid flashes of lightning darting through it, and forming a picture of that wrath which, we may suppose, broods and bursts over the bottomless pit. Suddenly its edges closed down around us, snatching away the remaining light of day, and shrouding us in darkness like that of Egypt, through which we groped, calling and shouting to each other, yet not able to see a yard before us.

86

Again a rush was heard, which came nearer and more near, filling us with dread, till it struck us with the suddenness of a blow. It was as though all those cones had drawn closer and closer together, till they were piled into one consolidated mountain of dust, pressed down by the mass in the air upon our heads. For a time all our efforts to see or to speak were vain. We could hardly breathe. If we moved at all, it was by setting our backs against the elements and pushing with all our strength. There was not a drop of rain; it was a storm of dust—a *sirocco*. Fortunately for us we were near the *meson*, which we entered after being half an hour exposed to its fury, and as it was abating. Every thing was penetrated by it, and it seemed as though water could not clean our eyes or our throats.

In the *mesons*, the various apartments for travelers, the stables, the eating room, and all the offices, are built around a spacious paved court, upon which all the windows and doors open. A large gate forms the entrance, which is closed and bolted at night. The rooms for travelers, often twenty feet square, are entirely unfurnished. He is to supply his own bed and bedding, which he spreads out upon a floor which seems never to have been swept. For his meals he must go to the *fonda* and order what he may choose or what they may have. One dish at a time is spread upon the bare table, which is often furnished with plates, but not often with knives, forks, or spoons. A variety of soups made hot with red pepper and a slice of bread, forms the first course. Then follows rice, with thin Indian cakes. Sometimes squash fried in lard is added. A favorite dessert is the Mexican custard, made of rice or chocolate. Coffee, wine, or pulque, a drink made of the maguey, closes the entertainment. There are distilleries in the country where the pulque is converted into a most hateful species of whisky.

In the morning the horses and mules are led out into the court, every preparation is made, and the travelers take their leave, throwing behind them their hasty adieus. These *mesons* in city and country are very filthy, and much infested with vermin. In one instance we saw a number of *tarantulas* —the venomous black spider of the tropics— hanging upon the walls of our room after we had slept upon its floor.

On the 22d of March we entered San Luis Potosi.[11] This is a large city, possessing con-

[11] San Luis Potosi is a railway and commercial center about 215 miles northwest of Mexico City. The city was founded in 1586 and in the colonial period was an

siderable wealth. It is near the silver mines, and contains a mint.

We saw here, for the first time, a stage-coach. It was up from the city of Mexico, distant about three hundred miles, which journey is accomplished in six days, at an expense of $25 for a seat. The coach consists of a large unwieldy frame, upon which is swung the body, which is comparatively small.

The ignorance of the Mexicans is equal to their superstition. We were amused at an instance afforded us in the case of a schoolmaster. While describing to him the modes of traveling in America, we told him about the steamers, at which he was not much surprised, having heard of them before; but when we told him of the railroad, he listened with the same incredulity with which the King of Siam heard the missionaries describe ice; but when we told him of the telegraph, he slowly arose, wrapped his *serapi* around him, and moved off, without deigning us a word or a look.

We were present at a cock fight, one of the favorite amusements of the Mexicans in general, and of Santa Anna in particular.[12] A

important center of administration. In 1937 it had a population of 92,000.

[12] Antonio Lopez de Santa Anna, born about 1795, was a leader in Mexican governmental affairs for about

low fence inclosed the pit, within which were the attendants exhibiting the game cocks, and the owners who were taking the bets of the spectators. Among these were several padres, always known by their peculiar dress. The crowd around exhibited no excitement. Gambling with the Mexicans is a regular pursuit, and not a means of diversion or excitement. There was no difference in their appearance, whether they were at church or at their cock fights. After all the betting was done, long steel spears, made very sharp and three inches in length, were fastened upon the legs of the cocks, and they were pitted to fight. In the first encounter one cock thrust his spear into the breast of the other, which died very soon after. In the second, two fine cocks were pitted, and more interest than usual was felt and deeper betting elicited. In less than half a minute one was lying dead, the spear of the other being thrust so far through his head that is was with difficulty withdrawn.

half a century. In American memory he figures most prominently as the victor who perpetrated the massacre of the Alamo (March, 1836) and as the General who was repeatedly defeated by the armies of Scott and Taylor in the war of 1846–1848. He subsequently lived in the United States for a time, and died, poor and neglected, at Mexico City in June, 1876.

In one of our rambles through the city we were accosted in the most remarkable manner by a well-dressed and beautiful signorita. She was seated at a window of one of the houses of the wealthy. As we caught her piercing black eye, she smiled a cordial greeting, to which one of the party responded by a respectful *"Buenos dias, signorita!"* Her reply was a terrible oath, and a most obscene expression in English, and yet there was that about her manner and tone which denoted that she meant to say that which was very civil and kind. We were told, when relating the incident afterward to an Englishman residing in the city, that some American soldiers very basely amused themselves, while pretending to teach the signoritas our language, by making them repeat just the expressions we had heard, and other similar ones, as forms of polite salutation.

We spent two days in the city to give rest to our animals and then proceeded on our way toward Guadalajara. Between these two cities the country is more uneven. The scenery is often very beautiful. We received many cautions to be on our guard, as we were to pass through a part of the country where many depredations and murders had been committed. We were told of travelers who had been suddenly dragged from their horses by the lasso, and murdered. One day we witnessed an instance of the surprising skill of the Mexicans in the use of the lasso. One of the horses threw his rider and went galloping off across the plain. In a moment a muleteer had spurred his mule forward in pursuit, coiling up his rope as he went. Presently the coil darted through the air and fell with unerring aim over the head of the horse, bringing him at once to a pause.

The most beautiful city we saw in Mexico was Santa Maria de los Lagos. Its cathedral was grand, towering high above its houses, and as we rode through the streets was inviting, by its chimes, to vespers. This town appeared to be more thriving and prosperous than any we had seen. The remark has often been made that the views of the city and its environs, from the tower of the cathedral, are similar to those of Jerusalem. San Juan de los Lagos, another city a day's journey from the former, was almost equal in beauty. Its cathedral was even more splendid. The first object which caught our attention as we were crossing the plaza on which it fronted was a woman creeping on her knees toward the steps of the cathedral, probably as a penance.

It was not without some apprehension, after having heard so much of guerilla parties, that we saw before us, the day after we left the last town, a company of armed men coming toward us. We were ordered to examine our arms and have them ready for use. They proved to be government troops, which were marching to meet the insurgents in Tamaulipas County. At their head were several American deserters, but not Americans, who were leading along some females by the hand. We also met a company of "Volunteers," who had just been "pressed" into service. They were chained together in gangs of ten or more and were driven along—the most desperate-looking wretches.

On the 2d of April, 1849 we reached Guadalajara.[13] This is the second city in Mexico, and contains a population of 125,000. Some of the cathedrals have cost millions. Many of the public buildings and squares, and the palaces of the wealthy, are very beautiful. The interiors of the cathedrals glistened with their silver shrines, chandeliers, and railings. The rude floors were covered with kneeling

[13] Guadalajara, capital of the state of Jalisco, in 1930 had a population of 184,000. It has a university, a mint, a government palace, and numerous government buildings. Its cathedral, built between 1571 and 1618, is one of the finest in Mexico. The city was founded in 1531 and became the seat of a bishopric in 1549.

worshipers. The tones of the bells are very clear and sonorous. This is probably owing to the large amount of silver used in their composition. This, like the city of Mexico, is very compact, the streets straight, broad, and well paved. The houses, with their heavy grated windows upon the streets, and their huge doorways in the center, gave them the appearance of so many fortresses. It is behind these walls and gates that the Mexican is luxurious and extravagant. His house is most gayly furnished, nor does he spare any expense in procuring that which will please his fancy. The women never wear bonnets. The covering for the head is called the *reboso*. This is a kind of scarf some six feet long and three wide which covers the head and is drawn closely down over the face, and then crosses in front. It is a very common practice with the Mexican women to smoke the *cigarrito*.

On the 4th of April we left Guadalajara, having received notice from an officer of government that no travelers were permitted to enter or to leave the city during the Easter solemnities. In a few hours we entered the wild passes of a very picturesque and mountainous country. The first time for many days our road led us along over many fine mountain streams and through forests where we began to find our own pine and oak. "A song for the brave old oak" was heartily responded to by all. As night set in we pitched our camp in a narrow defile, surrounded by high peaks, which we were to ascend on the morrow. The inhabitants seemed as wild as their country. Every hour our guides were coming to us with stories of recent robberies and murders, and committed upon the very spot, perhaps, where we then were. In one deep gorge of the mountains into which we were passing, we were told that three hundred armed guerillas awaited us. And in another place, a few days previous, some government soldiers had met a large company of robbers and had dispersed them after shooting several of the most desperate. In corroboration of these stories, we suddenly came upon a scene so fearfully in keeping with our own excited state of feeling and the wild character of the country around us that we shall never lose the impression left upon our imaginations. In the midst of a field charred and blackened by a fire which had passed over it stood out in bold relief a gallows, upon which were hanging three mangled and distorted bodies. There they had hung about six weeks, after having murdered twenty persons. Over the gallows, which was a painted one, were printed these words of warning: *Asi Castiga La Ley Al Ladron Y Al Asesino.*[14]

Magdalena is a pleasant town, situated among the mountains, on the banks of a beautiful lake. Here we saw the first of the dramatic street representations of the closing scenes in the life of our Savior. These consisted in enacting each day in their order the events recorded in Scripture. Most of the day and one entire night were devoted to these exhibitions, in which all the people participated. In Magdalena the procession paraded the streets during the night, with torches, and accompanied by a band performing solemn music. The image of the Savior, which was Spanish in its features, like all the sacred images of Mexico, had a bandage over the eyes, and was led away by a band of ruffians, as if for trial. At a distance the image of the Virgin Mary was borne along by weeping females. We saw nothing more —not again entering any town—till the third night, when we reached Tocotes. At this stage in the series the Savior was represented as borne by the centurions and soldiers to the tomb. The image was placed in a glass coffin strewed with flowers. This was borne by men. At a distance was the image of Mary led by women, her hands folded in an

[14] Thus the law rewards robbers and murderers.

attitude of grief. The cathedral was decorated with a profusion of flowers, in the midst of which was the tomb. These tragical scenes were followed, at the close, by a fandango, which is a dance peculiar to the country. It is a lazy shuffle, accompanied by music upon the guitar, varied occasionally by a song, in the chorus of which all present join.

During one evening of Easter, soon after we had arrived at the *meson*, some one came rushing in, informing us that the guerillas had surrounded us. Seizing our arms, we hastened to the court, where all was confusion. There were thirty robbers outside the walls. They said that they were government soldiers, and loudly demanded admittance, asserting that they came from the alcalde. The proprietor told them they were ladrones, and refused to admit them. They left soon after, threatening to return. The alcalde came in much alarmed, and told us that they were robbers; that the troops of government never traveled during Easter, and if they did they were bound to report themselves to him. We mutually pledged ourselves, in case of an attack during the night upon the town or upon our quarters, to aid the citizens or they us, as the case might be. We made our preparations for defense, and slept with our arms at our sides. Nothing more was heard of the robbers. In the vicinity of To-cotes we crossed over a remarkable mountain. For several hours we were ascending by zigzag paths, each turn bringing us higher among the clouds. When we had reached the summit point we were several thousand feet above many of our companions and all the mules, a distance of more than two miles by the road, but in a direct line not more than one quarter of a mile, for we could distinctly hear the loud talking of the company and the shouts of the mule-drivers. We looked over the edge of the precipice and watched our companions as they wound their way slowly up. The view was very grand, though it produced a painful giddiness. Soon after ascending this mountain, our way led us through the crater of an old volcano. There were the pumice stone, the scoria, and the charred and blackened rocks as though they had but just issued, boiling and bursting, from the bowels of the earth. We could imagine that we smelt the sulphurous vapor and felt the volcanic heat arising from the pent-up fires below, so fresh did the whole field of desolation and ruin appear, and our imaginations were carried back to the fearfully terrific scenes which had been enacted here. The descent from the table land down to the shores of the Pacific is abrupt and steep. On the 12th of April we reached San Blas, a dull and unhealthy sea port.[15] At this place our company, which had hung together in fragments, was dissolved. Men alone are not social beings; and the numerous attempts to bind them together in California gold-mining associations are as vain as the attempt to make a rope of sand.

After some delay in making our preparations, we embarked at San Blas on the 12th of April in the *San Blasiña*, a schooner of twenty-three tons—being thirty-six feet long and twelve wide—for San Francisco. In this miserable, unseaworthy craft thirty-eight of us took passage. It was represented to us that the Pacific was so quiet that it would be safe to go up in open boats. Alas for our error! Yet it was only too common. In some instances emigrants, in their extreme anxiety to proceed on their way, have embarked in whale boats at Panama, hoping to reach San Francisco. Our voyage to Mazatlan was most disagreeable. We were so cramped for room on deck, the hold being filled with bananas, that three of us slept in a canoe hewed from a log, which was made secure on deck. The portion of it which I

[15] This description still suffices to characterize the town.

occupied was two and a half feet long and three and a half wide. There I slept for eight nights. On the 20th of April we reached Mazatlan, after having been put upon an allowance of water, and the last day having no water at all. This is an important sea port and a fine city.[16] Though it possesses no public buildings of note, many of the dwelling houses are spacious and pleasant. Its fine bathing ground forms its principal attraction. A small and inferior chapel is the only place of worship, while the amphitheater for the bull fights is a spacious inclosure, capable of accommodating many hundred persons. This *"Plaza de los Toros,"* as it is called, is an amphitheater covering about one quarter of an acre. Around this the seats are arranged in tiers. On one side are the pens for the bulls, on the other the elevated seat of the manager, fancifully decorated. Large show bills state the number and qualifications of the various animals, brute and human, to be brought forward, and invite all who are so disposed to be present. The Sabbath is generally the day selected for the spectacle, and on the morning of that day a procession of the valiant

[16] Mazatlan, situated at the entrance of the Gulf of California, is still an important commercial center. In 1926 it had a population of 28,000.

and brave, already equipped for the encounter, and accompanied by martial music, parade the streets. During the pauses in the music a crier, in a loud voice, boasts the victories they expect to achieve. Many of the spectators are females. Nothing but unmingled disgust and loathing can be excited by the scene. It is a disgraceful and cowardly butchery, in which the poor animal has not even one chance of defense or escape.

A great number of Americans were waiting at this place for opportunities to go to San Francisco. Many of them had exhausted their means, and were engaging in various employments to raise money to take them through.

We took our departure from Mazatlan on May 4th, having spent two weeks in litigation respecting the schooner, which resulted in favor of the passengers and made us, the first time in our lives, ship owners. The whole had been an unfortunate operation, and we had already paid more for our passage than the schooner was worth. The owners had lost the money which had been advanced to them and were unable to comply with the terms of the contract by putting the schooner in sailing order in Mazatlan. Papers were accordingly made out giving us undisputed possession of twenty-three tons burden of shipping. Our captain, a very old man, had not been to sea for twenty years before this memorable voyage. I shall presently have to relate an account of the adroit manner in which he upset a boat-load of us to pass half an hour among the sharks and waves before we could get to land. Our mate was a Frenchman, and the only skillful sailor among us. He knew that we were proceeding on a wrong course, and as it was mutiny to put the vessel on a right course by daylight, as soon as it was dark enough he would put the ship about, so that what we lost in the day we gained in the night. The rest of the crew were sailors drafted from the passengers. We were again short of water, and having been unable to procure a supply along the coast we anchored off San José, a small town near the Cape.[17] The captain requested me to accompany him on shore. The waves ran very high and it was dangerous to attempt a landing, unless under the guidance of one who understood "surfing" a boat. After every third wave which breaks upon the shore there is a lull, short indeed, but of sufficient length to permit a boat which follows instantaneously upon it to get beyond the reach of the first

[17] The "Cape" was the Cape of San Lucas, the southerly tip of the Lower California Peninsula.

wave of the next series. The only method is to row nearly to the line where the waves show a long white crest before they break upon the shore, and then to rest upon the oars. As soon as the third wave has passed, the rowers must urge the boat promptly and vigorously in. If this one rule is neglected, the "swamping" of the boat must inevitably be the result. The captain explained this so accurately that we could not doubt his skill. We had four stout rowers, breathlessly awaiting the signal upon the brink of the breakers. But, unfortunately, the signal came between the second and third waves. We were a hundred yards from the landing. Suddenly we heard the warning roar, like the low tone of the distant thunder. I looked behind, and the wave was moving toward us like an impending wall, six feet above the boat. Suddenly it broke, showing the white crest rapidly extending itself along as far as the eye could reach. Its first approach tossed the boat, like a straw on one side, and instantly the whole wave came toppling down upon us, burying the boat and three of those who were in it beneath the rushing tides. I had risen from my seat and the wave struck me many feet toward the shore, crushing my hat over my face and eyes, so that some moments and several waves passed

over me before I could again see. When I
was able to look around me the captain and
one of my companions were swimming for
land. The others were clinging to the keel of
the boat, after having been buried beneath
it till they were nearly strangled. Those who
were swimming were soon on shore, the captain so completely exhausted that he sank
down into the water, and was dragged back
to the dry sand. In half an hour all were
safe on the beach, grateful for so remarkable
a deliverance. Our danger was greatly increased by the fact that the place was infested with sharks. The next day, as we
were walking along the shore, two fish darted
out of the water and were instantly followed
by two large sharks, which pursued them
high upon the beach. We made several attempts to double the Cape and proceed on
our way, but were driven back each time by
heavy head winds. In our third attempt we
were becalmed, and spent the most of the
day in rowing our schooner along, which we
did at the rate of three miles an hour. After
we had turned in and were sleeping upon
some water and provision casks in the hold,
made level by laying down sticks of wood
and boards between them, a severe gale
sprang up and drove us at a fearful rate
from our course. The sails were rent and

flapped wildly in the wind. No one but the mate dared to approach them. He was at the helm, which he lashed down while he drew in and furled the refractory sails. Our danger was great, and during the long hours of that night there was little sleep among us. Eight, each unknown to the others, formed a resolution, that if we lived to reach the land, we would never again risk our lives in the *San Blasiña*. Near the close of the next day we anchored in a narrow roadstead off the Cape. The mate and many of the passengers went on shore, which was half a mile distant, taking the torn sails to be mended. The boat was also hauled up on the beach and turned over to be caulked. It was near night of the following day and we were all scattered over the beach and in the village when alarm guns from the schooner arrested our attention. To our surprise the vessel had changed her position, having dragged her only anchor. She was already nearly two miles distant, those on board having lost much time in ineffectual attempts to bring her back to anchorage. By the time the mate and a crew daring enough to venture out could be found she was almost at sea, and already pitching about over the waves. Soon a dark, cloudy night obscured the schooner and the boat alike from our view. We kindled a large beacon fire on the beach and, wrapping ourselves in our blankets, anxiously awaited the return of our companions. In the morning the schooner was safely moored near the shore.

At this place our ship's company was divided, a part being determined to proceed on their journey by sea while another part intended to walk up to San Francisco, a distance of twelve hundred miles, over a barren country, and uninhabited except by Indians. Of these latter, a portion started by an almost imperceptible path, which led them toward the Atlantic Coast, while the remaining four of us expected to proceed up the Gulf Coast.[18] As we ascended the hills behind the village, we caught a last look of

[18] Unless the author intended to say "Pacific Coast," instead of Atlantic, the distinction is unintelligible. Apparently one group proposed traversing the Pacific Coast of the Peninsula and the other (to which Woods belonged) the eastern or Gulf Coast. The fate of the members of the former party is recorded by H. H. Bancroft in *California Inter Pocula*, 191. They made their way on foot as far as Todos Santos where they procured mules and on May 24 set out for La Paz, suffering greatly en route from lack of food and water. On August 11 they fell in with the party of Lieutenant William H. Emory, who was surveying the boundary between the United States and Mexico determined by the recent war. The *San Blasiña*, which they had deserted, had meanwhile ended her voyage at Monterey on July 1.

the schooner, already out some distance at sea. When we reached San José, to our joy we found the Scottish barque *Collooney*, Capt. Livingston, for San Francisco, anchored there, having put in for water. We were received on board and on May 25th weighed anchor and were again on our way. The *Collooney* was from Panama, having on board two hundred passengers, with accommodations for twenty. At the time for meals two assistant stewards, mounted upon the long boat near the two galleys, called over the names of the passengers belonging to their divisions. As his name was called, each one walked up if it was calm, and reeled up if it was rough, to the galleys and received in a tin plate and dipper his allowance. It was a tedious voyage of thirty-five days from the Cape to San Francisco. On several Sundays I was invited to preach upon the quarter-deck. On these occasions we were sometimes favored with original hymns from the pen of T. G. Spear, of Philadelphia, who was a passenger on board.

June 25th, 1849, we reached San Francisco, seventy-four days from San Blas and one hundred and forty-five days from Philadelphia. This wonderful city is an uninviting spot. There is but a small strip of level land, crowded down to the bay, surrounded by high, sandy hills, covered with short bushes, while not a tree is to be seen. The city is composed chiefly of tents. Each day regularly at about ten o'clock there arrives in the city, coming down with a rush over the bleak and barren hills, a cold, chilling wind, which takes one at once from the summer to the winter solstice. Fires are comfortable, and cloaks or serapis are necessary. Gambling seems to be universal. Rents are held at the most exorbitant prices. I almost fear to risk my credibility by stating that the Parker House rents at $150,000 a year. On the afternoon of the second day after our arrival, the 27th of June, our luggage being transferred from the *Collooney* to a river schooner which was taken alongside, we set sail up the bay.

We spent the first night at Benicia,[19] anchoring near the landing. Taking our blan-

[19] Benicia, on the north shore of Carquinas Strait, was founded by General Mariano G. Vallejo and his partner, Robert Semple, and was named Francisca, in honor of Vallejo's wife. After the townsmen of Yerba Buena, across San Francisco Bay appropriated its name, Vallejo gave his wife's second name, Benicia, to the town. In 1849 it was an important point on the highway to the mines and a few years later it was made the State Capital. Despite this and numerous other advantages dreams of becoming the metropolis of San Francisco Bay gradually faded as the town was outdistanced by its more fortunate rival and it still remains but a small town.

VIEW OF THE STEAM-BOAT LANDING SACRAMENTO CITY, FROM K STREET

From Chicago Historical Society Collections

kets, as we would our umbrellas at home, we called upon the Rev. Mr. W. and were introduced by him to a trader, who kindly permitted us to sleep in a large unfinished room, while in another part of the same room were a party consisting of a Mexican master and his peons, on their way to the mines.

June 29th. Arrived at Sacramento City, the present of which is under canvas and the future on paper. Every thing is new except the ground and trees and the stars, beneath a canopy of which we slept. Quarreling and cheating form the employments, drinking and gambling the amusements, making the largest pile of gold the only ambition of the inhabitants. As each one steps his foot on shore he seems to have entered a magic circle, in which he is under the influence of new impulses. The wills of all seem under control of some strong and hidden agency. The city is every day newly filled, then emptied but to be filled again. The crowd ever presses on, elate with hope, excited by expectations, which it would be impossible to define or realize. The world-renowned Sutter's Fort, which is two miles from the landing, is a rude structure made of sun-dried bricks, about five hundred feet long and two hundred wide. It is now used for other purposes, a part of it being fitted up as a hospital.

July 2d. Walked from Sacramento to Mormon Island, a distance of twenty-nine miles; and the next day, each one having forty pounds of baggage upon his back, consisting of a cradle, tools for mining, provisions, blankets, &c., walked eight miles farther up the south fork of the American River to Salmon Falls, there to commence our mining operations.

Chapter 4[*]

AFFAIRS IN OUR NEW TERRITORY. *Interesting Narrative of the Voyage to California, by a New York Volunteer—Commodore Stockton, General Kearny, Colonel Fremont—San Francisco—Customs —Religion—Cattle—Produce—Press—Inhabitants, &c., &c.*

San Francisco, Alta California, April 1, 1848

BEING a subscriber to and constant reader of your invaluable paper in New York, and from its vast circulation, its love of truth, its political independence, and generally the first to give publicity to foreign and important news, I take the liberty of addressing you these lines, which, if not important to you, will be satisfactory to numbers of your subscribers who have friends in this far-distant clime. We sailed from New York in October, 1846 in the *Thomas H. Perkins*, as one of the 1st regiment New York Volunteers; and on the 6th March, 1847, came to anchor in San Francisco Bay, or what was called

[*]For the editor's introductory note to this chapter, see Appendix, pages 354–55.

the Bay of Sir Francis Drake, in the Pacific, in north latitude 37 47. On our arrival here the regiment was divided up and down the coast—two companies remaining here, one about 60 miles north, at a town called Sonoma, three to Monterey, distant 120 miles from here, two to Santa Barbara, farther south, and the residue farther south still, to Puebla de los Angeles, I being attached to one of the companies stationed here as hospital steward, under Assistant Surgeon R. C. Parker, with whom I had lived in Center Street, New York for some time previous to our departure.

On making inquiry after landing, we learned to our regret that the fighting in the two Californias was over—that there had been some well-contested skirmishes and battles fought only a few weeks previous to our landing, between the Mexicans (or Californians, rather) and Commodore Stockton and his men, he having commanded personally in the field, and reinforced by detachments under General Kearny and Fremont: and from the united bravery and skill of the officers, together with the hardiness and intrepidity of the volunteers and marines, the enemy was completely defeated; and since that time the Californias remained tranquil until about a month since, when some of our men had a few skirmishes at La Paz and Puebla de los Angeles, one of our men belonging to company B being killed, and two wounded—the enemy not daring to encounter them in fair field fighting, but kept up a continual firing at the little gallant band in the town for two days and upwards; however, they were dispersed and scattered from their hiding places, their flag captured, and many of them killed and wounded, and now we are again in tranquillity.

To give you any account of the war and movements of the army is useless, as the greater part of our information is derived from United States papers, as the communication by Mazatlan is uncertain and difficult, and by Panama tedious; however, we learned last night by private information that a proposal has been made by the Mexican government to Gen. Scott to surrender to the Americans the Californias, New Mexico and some other places of value on condition that he would protect the tottering government for a few years, til the intestine wars and sanguinary parties would be extirpated; which, we understand, is likely to meet the approbation of our government in Washington, as their object is not to annihilate the government of Mexico, but conquer a peace.[20]

This portion of the globe may in a future time become valuable in mercantile affairs, as well as the immense wealth which commerce, industry, and speculation may reap from the mines of gold, silver, quicksilver, saltpeter, coal, &c., &c., which abound in these districts. If the roads were in such state as to afford emigrants the means of travelling with facility and with more despatch, so as to avoid the hardships some encounter in travelling over snow—as has been experienced by the unfortunate sufferers last year, when some of them subsisted for a number of days on hides and venison flesh[21] then would this country be

[20] As frequently in the history of warfare, President Polk found it easier to start the war with Mexico than it proved to be to end it. A Peace Commissioner, Nicholas P. Trist, armed with authority to negotiate a treaty of peace, accompanied Scott's invading army. Following the capture of Mexico City and the collapse of Mexican armed opposition a treaty was negotiated by Trist at Guadalupe Hidalgo near Mexico City on February 2, 1848. Apparently the news which had been brought to San Francisco dealt with some of the prior negotiations between General Scott and Santa Anna.

[21] Apparently the allusion is to the disaster which overtook the Donner party in its attempt to cross the Sierras in the winter of 1846–47. Unable to advance, 47 of the party of 87 perished. The *California Star* of April 10, 1847 published an account of it.

worth contending for. The bay of San Francisco is one of the best harbors in America, or perhaps in the world; the entrance is good and safe, and inside a deep, wide bay, extending upwards of 100 miles, sheltered from all winds, an excellent anchorage, and as healthy as any port of the Union.

The town of San Francisco (formerly "Yerba Buena")[22] which had only a few shanties or camp-like cabins when we arrived, with the exception of half a dozen houses built of adobes or sun baked brick, now exhibits

---

[22] On August 26, 1846 Captain John B. Montgomery of the U.S. Ship *Portsmouth* appointed Lieutenant Washington A. Bartlett Alcalde of Yerba Buena and ordered an election for the office to be held on September 15. Bartlett won the election, and continued to hold the office. Not long afterward Mariano G. Vallejo and Robert Semple formed a project for founding the town which is now Benicia, which Vallejo proposed to name in honor of his wife the City of Francisca. The contract between Semple and Vallejo was executed on December 23, 1846. When it was presented to Alcalde Bartlett of Yerba Buena for recording, his fear that the name, closely resembling that of the Bay of San Francisco, might give the new town an advantage led him to issue an ordinance on January 30, 1847 decreeing that thereafter the name San Francisco instead of Yerba Buena should be used on all official documents and communications. Vallejo and Semple protested this act, but their protest was ignored, whereupon they renamed their town Benicia, from another of Mrs. Vallejo's baptismal names.

a pleasing prospect—upwards of 150 houses, some of which vie with our American cities for elegance and accommodation. Town lots which cost only $16, are now selling for $100 to $200, and some at $600. Wharves are building, streets formed clear over the hills, and great taste evinced in the improvements. We have an excellent barrack, and adjoining it is the custom house, under the skilful direction of Captain Folsom, Quartermaster. There are two excellent hotels, billiard rooms, and an extensive lumber yard. Lumber is very dear, $50 per M. for boards, &c., on account of the distance they are brought; but now we receive a supply from Oregon of lumber, as well as wheat and dry goods, which tend to lower the prices.

All kinds of merchandise were exceedingly dear when we first landed, and until lately; but now the place is well supplied, and instead of 300 per cent profit they are now content to sell at cent per cent over New York prices current. The brig *Sabine* of Boston, Capt. Vincent, is now discharging a valuable cargo from Boston, and we have many arrivals from the Sandwich Islands, China, and southern ports, as well as from the United States. We are accumulating a revenue; goods of all kinds, lumber excepted, pays a duty of 20 per cent on the valuation here. Liquor sells dear. Brandy, gin, rum, and aguardiente are sold at $150 per barrel, and retailed at one rial per glass. Wine the same; they have some Californian wines that they sell cheaper, but it is of rather inferior quality. Boots are $8 to $10 per pair; shoes $3. Black and blue cloths very dear, as well as ready made clothing—tailors' work being very high. Tea from $1 to $2 per lb., that is, good souchong, or green; but the inferior kind is cheap. Butter is four rials or half a dollar per lb., notwithstanding the vast number of cows; but the Californians, who own the principal part, are too indolent to milk or churn.

Cows are large, and good milkers, and sell from $12 to $16 each. Horses are very numerous, but not very large, a few exceptions only, and sell from $8 to $50 each. You can get a serviceable mare for $8, and a horse for $15, but they are very skittish, and till broken down, difficult for Americans to catch. The Mexicans, however, have no difficulty, it being their chief employment, lassoing and taming wild horses. Most of our men have purchased horses; their saddle, bridle and spurs are all different from ours; strong and heavy; their enormous long spurs rattle like chains, and some have little bells attached. The natives never ride without the riata, or raw hide rope or lasso, and at which they are very expert; they will throw the noose on a horse's head or neck at the distance of twenty yards, at full speed, and the pummel of their saddles are so fashioned as to take a turn of the riata round it and bring up a wild horse, cow or ox.

The men are generally lazy, fond of riding, dancing and gambling. Their chief game is called monte; it is a mere game of chance, and it is not unusual to see $200 staked on the turn up of a single card. The women will gamble as well as the men. The men are mostly addicted to liquor. The women are, or may be generally considered handsome, with dark, fascinating eyes and good features; the better kind very courteous, but, in general, indolent; they dress rich and costly, are addicted to fandangoing and gallantry, but not much coquetry; sociable, kind, and good-natured, beautiful and extravagant, and chiefly over-kind; but of this I am no judge.

Both males and females are not so religious as the French. They are fond of ceremony, but the dreadful intestine feuds, and tyranny exercised by the military com-

manders and despotic rulers over the lower
class render them generally revengeful and
irreligious. The missions owned by the
clergy in former times were mostly ran-
sacked previous to the present war, and
clerical influence at present is on the decline. They will in no wise, nor on any
account, embrace any other religion, although they do not strictly adhere to any
of the rules of their own. There is only
one Catholic priest in all these upper districts, half Indian, but a very zealous
preacher, and, they say, a good Christian.

The lands in California are mostly used
for grazing, and are varied, in large tracts,
from three leagues square to fifty leagues.
Some men own 20,000 head of cattle, but
the mountains and hills are not fit for agriculture on account of the want of rain—
we have scarcely any from April to December—but the valleys and low grounds, particularly where they can be irrigated, produce abundantly. (John A. Sutter of New
Helvetia),[23] on the river Sacramento, raises
annually twelve to twenty thousand bushels
of wheat, which he gets entirely reaped by

---

[23] The original copy reads "Mr. Luther van Helvetia;"
Apparently this meaningless phrase represents the com-
positor's effort to decipher what the author really
wrote.

the Indians. General Vallyo[24] and his
brother in Sonoma own most all the good
lands northward from here, and we expect,
as soon as this country is under American
law, that taxation will cause them to sell
their lands in farms or quantities to suit
emigrants, which will be the first step
towards improving this country. Almost
all the luxuries of nature, as respects the
vegetable kingdom, thrive here. Potatoes
are raised only by a few; as yet they sell
for six rials the arobe of 25 lbs.; nor can
they boast of much fruit as yet in Lower
California. At the mission they raise
apples, pears, &c.—they cost us here a
dollar the hundred. Beef is the only or
principal sustenance of man; it is sold at
$2\frac{1}{2}$ to 3 cents per lb., but it is cheaper to

[24] Mariano Guadalupe Vallejo, prominent mid-nine-
teenth century citizen of California, was born at Monterey, July 7, 1806. A soldier almost from boyhood, he
figured actively in the political life and military activities of Spanish California from about 1829 onward.
He welcomed the early American immigrants to California and exerted his influence to secure its submission
to the United States. He served in the Constitutional
Convention of 1849 and subsequently endeavored, un-
successfully, to have the State Capital located at Vallejo.
The remainder of his long life was chiefly devoted to the
affairs of his extensive estate, and to filling the role of a
princely country gentleman. He died, comparatively
poor, in January, 1890.

purchase the creature. The hide will sell for one and a half dollars, and then the meat will cost no more than one cent per lb.; it is seldom better. Flour is sold at $12 per barrel, but it will be on the decline.

We have got a first outline of American law here. Each district has an Alcalde or chief magistrate, or two together, with a town council—but like every new colony, for want of better, we are obliged to have some men whose first object is self-protection. We have two weekly newspapers here, who print the conduct of public officers in their true colors, but without much effect. One paper, edited by Mr. Bucklew, is called the *Californian*; the other is under Mormon influence, called the *Star*, but it is not supposed to sparkle very brightly, particularly in summer weather.[25] We have, as yet, no higher court for the trial of crimi-

[25] On July 28, 1846 Commodore Stockton appointed Rev. Walter Colton, chaplain of the U.S. Ship *Congress*, Alcalde of Monterey. Finding there an old press and some type which had belonged to the Mexican government, Colton, in partnership with Robert Semple, undertook to publish a newspaper. On August 15 the first number of the weekly *Californian* appeared, scarcely a month after the raising of the American flag. For lack of other paper stock, the newspaper was printed on sheets of letter paper used for writing official communications. One-half was printed in Spanish and the other

nal offences than the court martial; and this, like every new colony, populated by people of a roving headstrong disposition, renders murders frequent. Mostly all carry pistols and dirk knives. Horse stealing is quite common, also, on the mountains.

The Indians are not very hostile here. A few of them are located on each ranch or farm, living in huts, and work for their food and a little clothing. The wild Indians frequent the mountains, go almost naked, use bows and arrows, and sometimes are brought in by their governor to work for the season and return in the winter. They are not over fastidious in respect to dress, a small patch of skin in front only, and sometimes a little patch between the

half in English; since the Spanish alphabet font contained no w, in the English half of the paper this letter was represented by a vv.

In May, 1847 the *Californian* was moved from Monterey to San Francisco. There, meanwhile, enterprising Sam Brannan, who had led a colony of 238 Mormons from New York by sea to San Francisco in the summer of 1846, had established the weekly *California Star*, its first issue appearing on January 9, 1847. Although Brannan, who had been a printer in New York, was a Mormon, he declared that his paper should be free from sectarian influences, and seems to have made this promise good. In November, 1848 the two papers were consolidated under the name of the *California Star and Californian*.

shoulders. The Digger tribe being next us here, are the most abject, loathsome creatures in the world. They are revengeful and lazy, and are kept in a kind of slavery and bondage by the rancheros, and often flogged and punished. Their performing all the drudgery and heavy labor leaves but little demand for laborers of white complexion; and, besides, there are numbers of Conyackers or Sandwich Islanders here who work reasonably.

Mechanics here, however, get good wages; three dollars per day. Board here is pretty dear; $16 per month in the taverns, and four times that much in the hotels. Young women are very scarce here—very few Americans. There are a few Mormons.[26] Some of our countrymen, however, get married to Californians or Mexicans. Having given you a hasty outline of the army, the geography, &c., of California, I overlooked a few facts which may be somewhat interesting to you, viz: respecting the im-

[26] The party of 238 Mormons led by Sam Brannan arrived at San Francisco July 31, 1846. The Mormon Battalion, over 500 strong, which had been recruited for the war, had arrived in southern California in January, 1847, too late to take part in it, and was then mustered out. Apparently most of its members joined the Saints in Utah; it seems probable, however, that a considerable number remained in California.

ports and exports of this country, together with the mineral kingdom and shipping. Several mines have lately been discovered in this country; one at Santa Clara, on this bay, belonging to Messrs. Forbes, with the labor of fifteen hands in three weeks yielded 11,200 lbs. of quicksilver, worth in Mexico two dollars per pound. Two silver mines have lately been discovered also, one about three miles from Sonoma, on the lands of Mr. Illig, and another on the lands of J. F. Reed, Esq. about four miles from the Puebla de San José, which is supposed to be very rich, and the enterprising proprietor has already commenced operations.

I am credibly informed that a quantity of gold worth in value $30 was picked up lately in the bed of a stream of the Sacramento. There are also numerous mines of coal and some of copper discovered in this neighborhood, to the Southward and Northward. Two immense caves are known to exist in the vicinity of Clear Lake, north of this bay, and about 112 miles from Sonoma; one containing inexhaustible quantities of saltpeter, the other abounding in sulphur, and both said to be of purest quality. There are immense beds of copper ore, lately discovered, in the vicinity of said lake. Little, however, is known in relation to mineral coal in California as yet; however, there are different reports of its having been discovered in various places— Santa Cruz mountains, San Luis Obispo, San Diego, and Todos los Santos.

There is another discovery, of a copious fountain of semi-fluid asphaltum, near Santa Barbara, running into the sea and impregnating the atmosphere for several miles. This substance becomes hard, so as to break like rosin when exposed to the cold air, and is highly combustible. It has been already exported, to be used in the arts, in Peru, and has been used as fuel in steamboats in Chili. Near the lower Puebla los Angeles there are extensive fields where it is continually boiling up from the earth. This is believed to be the asphaltum petroleum, or mineral tar of commerce. At present it is used in covering the flat earthen roofs of California houses, to render them impervious to rain. Perhaps this may be the asphaltum of the ancients, so much spoken of by Josephus in his "Wars of the Jews." Limestone has been found in abundance, and already all the lime necessary to be mixed with the quicksilver ore in the extensive mine near Santa Clara can be procured in the vicinity. Several soda springs are interspersed in all parts of this country, particularly in the mountains. There is one near Sonoma and another near the above described quicksilver mines, which are considered by judges to be equal to Saratoga or Balston waters, and similar to the Congress water. We have received information lately that a large emigration from China may be soon expected. We have already two or three "Celestials" among us, who have found ready employment.[27] We were yesterday shown a specimen of salt taken from a large bowl spring twelve miles west of the Sacramento, which is of fine quality.

The gold mine discovered in December last on the south branch of the American Fork, in a range of low hills forming the base of the Sierra Nevada, distant thirty

---

[27] Strange as it seems in the light of subsequent developments the immigration of Chinese to California was welcomed for many years as affording a convenient supply of labor. As late as 1868 the Burlingame Treaty between the two nations established free immigration between them. Completion of the first transcontinental railroad following the Civil War brought more white laborers into the West and before long their resentment over the competition of Chinese labor found expression in bloody riots. An act restricting Chinese immigration was passed by Congress in 1877, but was vetoed by President Hayes as constituting a violation of the treaty of 1868. The issue of Chinese exclusion continued to vex the country for a generation.

miles from New Helvetia, is only three feet below the surface, in a strata of soft sand rock. From explorations south twelve miles and north five miles the continuance of this strata is reported, and the mineral said to be equally abundant, and from twelve to eighteen feet in thickness; so that, without allowing any golden hopes to puzzle my prophetic vision of the future, I would predict for California a Peruvian harvest of the precious metals as soon as a sufficiency of miners, &c., can be obtained.

Number of Vessels arrived at this Port from April 1st, 1847 to April 1st, 1848— From New York, 2; Sandwich Islands, 14; Oregon, 8; San Pedro, 4; Monterey, 16; Bodega, 3; Santa Cruz, 5; San Pedro, 4; Chili, 3; North-West Coast, 4; Southern Coast, 2; New Bedford, 6; New London, 3; San Diego, 2; Sitka, 1; Callao, 2; Canton, 1; Boston, 1; United States, 2; Men-of-War—U. S. ships *Preble, Congress, Columbus*, and sloop *Dale*.

Of the above, sixteen were whalers; so that you will perceive this is destined to be a place of great trade before long.

I will give you an abridged sketch of the imports and exports, obtained through the politeness of Capt. Folsom, U.S. Army, and collector of this port, for the three months

ending December 31st, 1847:-Total value
of exports for the quarter, $49,597.53. Of
this amount $30,353.85 were of the pro-
duce of California, and shipped as follows:
$320 to the Sandwich Islands, $21,448.35
to Peru, $560 to Mazatlan, (Mexico),
$7,285.50 to Russian America, (Sitka),
$700 to Tahiti; $19,343.68 were of the produce of foreign countries, and shipped as
follows:—$2,060 to the United States,
$12,442.18 to the Sandwich Islands, (of
which $11,340 were coined gold and silver)
and $4,840.50 to Mazatlan, Mexico.

The total value of imports for the same
period was $53,589.73. Of this amount
$6,790.54 came from the United States,
$7,701.59 from Oregon, $3,676.44 from
Chili, $31,740.73 from the Sandwich Is-
lands, $2,471.59 from Sitka, Russian Ameri-
ca, $492.57 from Bremen, and $550.54 and
$160 from Mexico. This shows a large
balance against us as yet, and has occasioned a heavy drain of cash to meet
the balance. The principal exports, as yet,
are hides and tallow; but when our mines
and forests come into operation, we expect
to turn the scale. At present the duty on
American merchandise is 20 percent, which
must be borne by the inhabitants. This
is shameful.

The climate is delightful and healthy. In San Francisco the wind blows mostly from the west. We expect to be disbanded next fall, many of the regiment not relishing the country. I have not space to give you the market prices, but hope ere long to be able to forward them.

Chapter 5*

A BETTER idea of San Francisco in the beginning of September, 1849 cannot be given than by the description of a single day. Supposing the visitor to have been long enough in the place to sleep on a hard plank and in spite of the attacks of innumerable fleas, he will be awakened at daylight by the noises of building, with which the hills are all alive. The air is temperate, and the invariable morning fog is just beginning to gather. By sunrise, which gleams hazily over the Coast Mountains across the Bay, the whole populace is up and at work. The wooden buildings unlock their doors, the canvas houses and tents throw back their front curtains; the lighters on the water are warped out from ship to ship; carts and porters are busy along the beach; and only the gaming-tables, thronged all night by the votaries of chance, are idle and deserted. The temperature is so fresh as to inspire an active habit of body, and even without the stimulus of trade and

*For the editor's introductory note to this chapter, see Appendix, pages 356–57.

speculation there would be few sluggards at this season.

As early as half-past six the bells begin to sound to breakfast, and for an hour thenceforth, their incessant clang and the braying of immense gongs drown all the hammers that are busy on a hundred roofs. The hotels, restaurants and refectories of all kinds are already as numerous as gaming-tables, and equally various in kind. The tables d'hôte of the first class, (which charge $2 and upwards the meal,) are abundantly supplied. There are others, with more simple and solid fare, frequented by the large class who have their fortunes yet to make. At the United States and California restaurants, on the plaza, you may get an excellent beefsteak, scantily garnished with potatoes, and a cup of good coffee or chocolate for $1. Fresh beef, bread, potatoes, and all provisions which will bear importation, are plenty; but milk, fruit and vegetables are classed as luxuries, and fresh butter is rarely heard of. On Montgomery Street, and the vacant space fronting the water, venders of coffee, cakes and sweetmeats have erected their stands, in order to tempt the appetite of sailors just arrived in port, or miners coming down from the mountains.

By nine o'clock the town is in the full flow of business. The streets running down to the water, and Montgomery Street which fronts the Bay, are crowded with people, all in hurried motion. The variety of characters and costumes is remarkable. Our own countrymen seem to lose their local peculiarities in such a crowd, and it is by chance epithets rather than by manner that the New Yorker is distinguished from the Kentuckian, the Carolinian from the Down-Easter, the Virginian from the Texan. The German and Frenchman are more easily recognized. Peruvians and Chilians go by in their brown ponchos, and the sober Chinese, cool and impassive in the midst of excitement, look out of the oblique corners of their long eyes at the bustle, but are never tempted to venture from their own line of business. The eastern side of the plaza, in front of the Parker House and a canvas hell called the Eldorado are the general rendezvous of business and amusement —combining 'change, park, club-room and promenade all in one. There, everybody not constantly employed in one spot may be seen at some time of the day. The character of the groups scattered along the plaza is oftentimes very interesting. In one place are three or four speculators bargaining for lots, buying and selling "fifty varas square" in towns, some of which are canvas and some only paper; in another, a company of miners, brown as leather and rugged in features as in dress; in a third, perhaps, three or four naval officers speculating on the next cruise, or a knot of genteel gamblers, talking over the last night's operations.

The day advances. The mist which after sunrise hung low and heavy for an hour or two has risen above the hills and there will be two hours of pleasant sunshine before the wind sets in from the sea. The crowd in the streets is now wholly alive. Men dart hither and thither as if possessed with a never-resting spirit. You speak to an acquaintance—a merchant, perhaps. He utters a few hurried words of greeting, while his eyes send keen glances on all sides of you; suddenly he catches sight of somebody in the crowd; he is off, and in the next five minutes has bought up half a cargo, sold a town lot at treble the sum he gave, and taken a share in some new and imposing speculation. It is impossible to witness this excess and dissipation of business without feeling something of its influence. The very air is pregnant with the magnetism of bold, spirited, unwearied action, and he who but ventures into the outer circle of the whirlpool, is spinning, ere he has time for thought, in its dizzy vortex.

But see! the groups in the plaza suddenly scatter; the city surveyor jerks his pole out of the ground and leaps on a pile of boards; the venders of cakes and sweetmeats follow his example, and the place is cleared, just as a wild bull which has been racing down Kearney Street makes his appearance. Two vaqueros, shouting and swinging their lariats, follow at a hot gallop; the dust flies as they dash across the plaza. One of them, in mid-career, hurls his lariat in the air. Mark how deftly the coil unwinds in its flying curve, and with what precision the noose falls over the bull's horns! The horse wheels as if on a pivot and shoots off in an opposite line. He knows the length of the lariat to a hair, and the instant it is drawn taught plants his feet firmly for the shock and throws his body forward. The bull is brought up with such force as to throw him off his legs. He lies stunned a moment, and then, rising heavily, makes another charge. But by this time the second vaquero has thrown a lariat around one of his hind legs, and thus checked on both sides, he is dragged off to slaughter.

The plaza is refilled as quickly as it was emptied, and the course of business is resumed. About twelve o'clock a wind begins to blow from the northwest, sweeping with most violence through a gap between the hills opening towards the Golden Gate. The bells and gongs begin to sound for dinner, and these two causes tend to lessen the crowd in the streets for an hour or two. Two o'clock is the usual dinner-time for business men, but some of the old and successful merchants have adopted the fashionable hour of five. Where shall we dine today? the restaurants display their signs invitingly on all sides; we have choice of the United States, Tortoni's, the Alhambra, and many other equally classic resorts, but Delmonico's, like its distinguished original in New York, has the highest prices and the greatest variety of dishes. We go down Kearney Street to a two-story wooden house on the corner of Jackson. The lower story is a market; the walls are garnished with quarters of beef and mutton; a huge pile of Sandwich Island squashes fills one corner, and several cabbage-heads, valued at $2 each, show themselves in the window. We enter a little door at the end of the building, ascend a dark, narrow flight of steps and find ourselves in a long, low room, with ceiling and walls of white muslin and a floor covered with oil-cloth.

There are about twenty tables disposed
in two rows, all of them so well filled that
we have some difficulty in finding places.
Taking up the written bill of fare, we find
such items as the following:

SOUPS.

Mock Turtle............................$0.75
St. Julien............................. 1.00

FISH.

Boiled Salmon Trout, Anchovy sauce...... 1.75

BOILED.

Leg Mutton, caper sauce............... 1.00
Corned Beef, Cabbage..... .... 1.00
Ham and Tongues.................... 0.75

ENTREES.

Fillet of Beef, mushroom sauce.......... 1.75
Veal Cutlets, breaded................. 1.00
Mutton Chop....................... 1.00
Lobster Salad....................... 2.00
Sirloin of Venison.................... 1.50
Baked Maccaroni..................... 0.75
Beef Tongue, sauce piquante........... 1.00

So that, with but a moderate appetite, the
dinner will cost us $5, if we are at all epi-
curean in our tastes. There are cries of
"steward!" from all parts of the room—
the word "waiter" is not considered sufficiently respectful, seeing that the waiter
may have been a lawyer or merchant's

clerk a few months before. The dishes look very small as they are placed on the table, but they are skilfully cooked and very palatable to men that have ridden in from the diggings. The appetite one acquires in California is something remarkable. For two months after my arrival, my sensations were like those of a famished wolf.

In the matter of dining, the tastes of all nations can be gratified here. There are French restaurants on the plaza and on Dupont Street; an extensive German establishment on Pacific Street; the *Fonda Peruana:* the Italian Confectionary; and three Chinese houses, denoted by their long three-cornered flags of yellow silk. The latter are much frequented by Americans on account of their excellent cookery, and the fact that meals are $1 each, without regard to quantity. Kong-Sung's house is near the water; Whang-Tong's in Sacramento Street, and Tong-Ling's in Jackson Street. There the grave Celestials serve up their chow-chow and curry, besides many genuine English dishes; their tea and coffee cannot be surpassed.

The afternoon is less noisy and active than the forenoon. Merchants keep within-doors, and the gambling-rooms are crowded with persons who step in to escape the

wind and dust. The sky takes a cold gray
cast, and the hills over the bay are barely
visible in the dense, dusty air. Now and
then a watcher who has been stationed on
the hill above Fort Montgomery comes
down and reports an inward-bound vessel,
which occasions a little excitement among
the boatmen and the merchants who are
awaiting consignments. Towards sunset
the plaza is nearly deserted; the wind is
merciless in its force, and a heavy overcoat
is not found unpleasantly warm. As it
grows dark there is a lull, though occasional gusts blow down the hill and carry
the dust of the city out among the shipping.

The appearance of San Francisco at
night, from the water, is unlike anything
I ever beheld. The houses are mostly of
canvas, which is made transparent by the
lamps within, and transforms them, in the
darkness, to dwellings of solid light. Seated
on the slopes of its three hills, the tents
pitched among the chaparral to the very
summits, it gleams like an amphitheater
of fire. Here and there shine out brilliant
points, from the decoy-lamps of the gam-
ing-houses; and through the indistinct murmur of the streets comes by fits the sound
of music from their hot and crowded pre-
cincts. The picture has in it something un-

real and fantastic, it impresses one like the cities of the magic lantern, which a motion of the hand can build or annihilate.

The only objects left for us to visit are the gaming-tables, whose day has just fairly dawned. We need not wander far in search of one. Denison's Exchange, the Parker House, and Eldorado stand side by side; across the way are the Veranda and Aguila de Oro; higher up the plaza the St. Charles and Bella Union; while dozens of second-rate establishments are scattered through the less frequented streets. The greatest crowd is about the Eldorado; we find it difficult to effect an entrance. There are about eight tables in the room, all of which are thronged; copper-hued Kanakas, Mexicans rolled in their sarapes and Peruvians thrust through their ponchos, stand shoulder to shoulder with the brown and bearded American miners. The stakes are generally small, though when the bettor gets into a streak of luck, as it is called, they are allowed to double until all is lost or the bank breaks. Along the end of the room is a spacious bar supplied with all kinds of bad liquors, and in a sort of gallery, suspended under the ceiling, a female violinist tasks her talent and strength of muscle to minister to the excitement of play.

139

The Veranda, opposite, is smaller, but boasts an equal attraction in a musician who has a set of Pandean pipes fastened at his chin, a drum on his back, which he beats with sticks at his elbows, and cymbals in his hands. The piles of coin on the monte tables clink merrily to his playing, and the throng of spectators, jammed together in a sweltering mass, walk up to the bar between the tunes and drink out of sympathy with his dry and breathless throat. At the Aguila de Oro there is a full band of Ethiopian serenaders, and at the other hells, violins, guitars or wheezy accordions, as the case may be. The atmosphere of these places is rank with tobacco smoke and filled with a feverish, stifling heat, which communicates an unhealthy glow to the faces of the players.

We shall not be deterred from entering by the heat and smoke or the motley characters into whose company we shall be thrown. There are rare chances here for seeing human nature in one of its most dark and exciting phases. Note the variety of expression in the faces gathered around this table! They are playing monte, the favorite game in California, since the chances are considered more equal and the opportunity of false play very slight. The dealer throws out his cards with a cool, nonchalant air; indeed, the gradual increase of the hollow square of dollars at his left hand is not calculated to disturb his equanimity. The two Mexicans in front, muffled in their dirty sarapes, put down their half-dollars and dollars and see them lost without changing a muscle. Gambling is a born habit with them and they would lose thousands with the same indifference. Very different is the demeanor of the Americans who are playing; their good or ill luck is betrayed at once by involuntary exclamations and changes of countenance, unless the stake should be very large and absorbing, when their anxiety, though silent, may be read with no less certainty. They have no power to resist the fascination of the game. Now counting their winnings by thousands, now dependent on the kindness of a friend for a few dollars to commence anew, they pass hour after hour in those hot, unwholesome dens. There is no appearance of arms, but let one of the players, impatient with his losses and maddened by the poisonous fluids he has drank, threaten one of the profession, and there will be no scarcity of knives and revolvers.

There are other places, where gaming is carried on privately and to a more ruinous

extent—rooms in the rear of the Parker
House, in the City Hotel and other places,
frequented only by the initiated. Here the
stakes are almost unlimited, the players
being men of wealth and apparent respecta-
bility. Frequently, in the absorbing interest of some desperate game the night
goes by unheeded and morning breaks upon
haggard faces and reckless hearts. Here
are lost, in a few turns of a card or rolls
of a ball, the product of fortunate ventures
by sea or months of racking labor on land.

During my absence in Monterey more
than four thousand emigrants by sea had
landed in San Francisco. The excitement
relative to gold-digging had been kept up
by new discoveries on the various rivers;
the rage for land speculation had increased,
and to all this was added the gathering
heat of political conflict. San Francisco
was something of a whirlpool before, but
now it had widened its sweeps and seemed
to be drawing everything into its vortex.

The morning after I arrived I went about
the town to note the changes and improvements. I could scarcely believe my eyes.
The northern point, where the Bay pours
its waters into the Golden Gate, was

covered with houses nearly to the summit—many of them large three-story warehouses. The central and highest hill on which the town is built was shorn of its chaparral and studded with tents and dwellings; while to the eastward the streets had passed over the last of the three hills and were beginning to encroach on the Happy Valley. The beautiful crescent of the harbor, stretching from the Rincon to Fort Montgomery, a distance of more than a mile, was lined with boats, tents, and warehouses, and near the latter point, several piers jutted into the water. Montgomery Street, fronting the Bay, had undergone a marvellous change. All the open spaces were built up, the canvas houses replaced by ample three-story buildings, an Exchange with lofty sky-light fronted the water, and for the space of half a mile the throng of men of all classes, characters and nations, with carts and animals, equaled Wall Street before three o'clock.

In other parts of the town the change was equally great. Tents and canvas houses had given place to large and handsome edifices, blanks had been filled up, new hotels opened, market houses in operation, and all the characteristics of a great commercial city fairly established. Portsmouth Square was filled with lumber and house frames, and nearly every street in the lower part of the city was blocked up with goods. The change which had been wrought in all parts of the town during the past six weeks seemed little short of magic. At first I had difficulty in believing that what I looked upon was real, so utterly inadequate seemed the visible means for the accomplishment of such wonderful ends.

On my way to call upon Col. Frémont, whom I found located with his family in the Happy Valley, I saw a company of Chinese carpenters putting up the frame of a Canton-made house. In Pacific Street another Celestial restaurant had been opened, and every vessel from the Chinese ports brought a fresh importation. An Olympic circus on a very handsome scale had been established, and a company of Ethiopian serenaders nightly amused the public. Delmonico's was the fashionable eating-house, where you had boiled eggs at seventy-five cents each and dinner at $1.50 to $5, according to your appetite. A little muslin shed rejoiced in the title of Irving House. A number of fine billiard rooms and bowling alleys had been opened, and all other devices for spending money brought into successful operation. The gamblers complained no longer of dull prospects; there were hundreds of monte, roulette, and faro tables, which were crowded nightly until a late hour, and where the most inveterate excesses of gaming might be witnessed. The rents of houses had increased rather than fallen. I might give hundreds of instances, but it would be only a repetition of the stories I have already told. Money brought fourteen per cent monthly, on loan. A gentleman of Baltimore who came out in the *Panama*, sold for $15,000 a steam engine which cost him $2,000. Some drawing paper which cost about $10 in New York brought $164. I found little change in the prices of provisions and merchandise, though the sum paid for labor had diminished. Town lots were continually on the rise; fifty-vara lots in the Happy Valley half a mile from town brought $3,500. I met with a number of my fellow passengers, nearly all of whom had done well, some of them having already realized $20,000 and $30,000.

The population of San Francisco at that time, was estimated at fifteen thousand; a year before it was about five hundred. The increase since that time had been made in the face of the greatest disadvantages under which a city ever labored; an uncultivated country, an ungenial climate, exorbitant rates of labor, want of building materials, imperfect civil organization—lacking everything, in short, but gold dust and enterprise. The same expense on the Atlantic Coast would have established a city of a hundred thousand inhabitants. The price of lumber was still $300 to $400 per thousand feet. In addition to the five saw-mills at Santa Cruz, all the mills of Oregon were kept going, lumber, even there, bringing $100 per thousand. There was no end to the springs of labor and traffic which that vast emigration to California had set in motion, not only on the Pacific Coast, but throughout all Polynesia and Australia.

The activity throughout the mining region during the fall season gave rise to a thousand reports of golden discoveries, the effect of which was instantly seen on the new-comers. Their highest anticipations of the country seemed realized at once, and their only embarrassment was the choice of so many places of promise. The stories told were marvellous even to Californians, what wonder, then, that the green emigrants, who devoutly swallowed them whole, should be disappointed and disgusted with the reality? The actual yield on most of the rivers was, nevertheless, sufficiently encouraging. The diggers on the forks of the American, Feather, and Yuba Rivers met with a steady return for their labors. On the branches of the San Joaquin, as far as the Tuolumne, the big lumps were still found. Capt. Walker, who had a company on the Pitiuna—a stream that flows into the Tularè Lakes—was in Monterey buying supplies at the time I left. His company was alone in that desolate region, and working to advantage, if one might judge from the secrecy which attended their movements. The placers on Trinity River had not turned out so well as was expected, and many of the miners were returning disappointed to the Sacramento. Several companies had been absent among the higher ridges of the Sierra Nevada for a month or more, and it was suspected that they had discovered diggings somewhere on the eastern side.

The sickly season on the Sacramento and its tributaries was nearly over, but numbers of pale, emaciated frames, broken down by agues and diarrhœas, were daily arriving in the launches and steamers. At least one-third of the miners suffered more or less from these diseases, and numbers of men who had landed only a few months before in the fulness of hale and lusty manhood were walking about nearly as shrunken and bloodless as the corpses they would soon become. One of the most pitiable sights I ever beheld was one of these men, who had just been set ashore from a launch. He was sitting alone on a stone beside the water, with his bare feet purple with cold, on the cold, wet sand. He was wrapped from head to foot in a coarse blanket which shook with the violence of his chill as if his limbs were about to drop in pieces. He seemed unconscious of all that was passing; his long, matted hair hung over his wasted face; his eyes glared steadily forward, with an expression of suffering so utterly hopeless and wild that I shuddered at seeing it. This was but one out of a number of cases equally sad and distressing. The exposure and privations of a miner's life soon sap a frame that has not previously been hardened by the elements, and the maladies incident to a new country assail with double force the constitutions thus prepared to receive them.

I found the climate of San Francisco vastly improved during my absence. The temperature was more genial and equable, and the daily hurricanes of the summer had almost entirely ceased. As a consequence of this the streets had a more active and pleasant aspect, and the continual whirl of business was enlivened by something like cheerfulness. Politics had taken root in this appropriate hot-bed of excitement, and was flourishing with a rapidity and vigor of growth which showed that, though an exotic plant, it would soon be native in the soil. Meetings were held nearly every night at Denison's Exchange, where the rival parties—for the different personal interests were not slow in arraying themselves against each other—had their speeches, their huzzas, and their drinks. The Congressional candidates bore the brunt of the struggle, since three or four of them were residents; but the Senatorship gave rise to the most deep-laid and complicated machinations. The principal candidates, T. Butler King, Col. Frémont and Dr. Gwin, had each his party of devoted adherents, who occupied the two weeks intervening between the nomination and election in sounding and endeavoring to procure the votes of the candidates for the State Legislature, on whom the choice of Senators depended.

Col. Frémont was residing at the time in the Happy Valley, in a Chinese house which he had erected on one of his lots. Mr. King

was at Sonoma, where he had gone to re-
cruit, after an illness which was near prov-
ing fatal. His friends, however, called a
meeting in his favor, which was held in
Portsmouth Square—an injudicious movement as the consequence proved. Dr. Gwin
was making an electioneering tour through
the mining districts for the purpose of secur-
ing the election of the proper Delegates to
the State Senate and Assembly. It was curious how soon the American passion for
politics, forgotten during the first stages of
the State organization, revived and emulated
the excitement of an election in the older
States.

A day or two after my arrival the Steamer
Unicorn came into the harbor, being the
third which had arrived without bringing a
mail. These repeated failures were too
much for even a patient people to bear; an
indignation meeting in Portsmouth Square
was called, but a shower, heralding the rainy
season, came on in time to prevent it.
Finally, on the last day of October, on the
eve of the departure of another steamer down
the coast, the *Panama* came in, bringing the
mails for July, August, and September all
at once! Thirty-seven mail-bags were hauled
up to the little Post Office that night, and
the eight clerks were astounded by the

receipt of forty-five thousand letters, besides uncounted bushels of newspapers. I was at the time domiciled in Mr. Moore's garret and enjoying the hospitalities of his plank table; I therefore offered my services as clerk-extraordinary, and was at once vested with full powers and initiated into all the mysteries of counting, classifying and distributing letters.

The Post Office was a small frame building, of one story, and not more than forty feet in length. The entire front, which was graced with a narrow portico, was appropriated to the windows for delivery, while the rear was divided into three small compartments—a newspaper room, a private office, and kitchen. There were two windows for the general delivery, one for French and Spanish letters, and a narrow entry at one end of the building, on which faced the private boxes to the number of five hundred, leased to merchants and others at the rate of $1.50 per month. In this small space all the operations of the Office were carried on. The rent of the building was $7,000 a year, and the salaries of the clerks from $100 to $300 monthly, which, as no special provision had been made by Government to meet the expense, effectually confined Mr. Moore to these narrow limits. For his strict and conscientious adherence to the law he received the violent censure of a party of the San Franciscans, who would have had him make free use of the Government funds.

The *Panama's* mail-bags reached the Office about nine o'clock. The doors were instantly closed, the windows darkened, and every preparation made for a long siege. The attack from without commenced about the same time. There were knocks on the doors, taps on the windows, and beseeching calls at all corners of the house. The interior was well lighted; the bags were emptied on the floor, and ten pairs of hands engaged in the assortment and distribution of their contents. The work went on rapidly and noiselessly as the night passed away, but with the first streak of daylight the attack commenced again. Every avenue of entrance was barricaded; the crowd was told through the keyhole that the Office would be opened that day to no one: but it all availed nothing. Mr. Moore's Irish servant could not go for a bucket of water without being surrounded and in danger of being held captive. Men dogged his heels in the hope of being able to slip in behind him before he could lock the door.

We labored steadily all day, and had the satisfaction of seeing the huge pile of letters considerably diminished. Towards evening

POST OFFICE, SAN FRANCISCO, CALIFORNIA
From Chicago Historical Society Collections

the impatience of the crowd increased to a
most annoying pitch. They knocked; they
tried shouts and then whispers and then
shouts again; they implored and threatened
by turns; and not seldom offered large
bribes for the delivery of their letters. "Curse
such a Post-Office and such a Post-Master!"
said one; "I'll write to the Department by
the next steamer. *We'll* see whether things
go on in this way much longer." Then comes a
messenger slyly to the back-door: "Mr. ⸺
sends his compliments, and says you would
oblige him very much by letting me have
his letters; he won't say anything about it to
anybody." A clergyman, or perhaps a naval
officer, follows, relying on a white cravat or
gilt buttons for the favor which no one else
can obtain. Mr. Moore politely but firmly
refuses; and so we work on, unmoved by
the noises of the besiegers. The excitement
and anxiety of the public can scarcely be
told in words. Where the source that governs business, satisfies affection, and supplies
intelligence had been shut off from a whole
community for three months, the rush from
all sides to supply the void was irresistible.

In the afternoon a partial delivery was
made to the owners of private boxes. It
was effected in a skillful way, though with
some danger to the clerk who undertook the

opening of the door. On account of the crush and destruction of windows on former occasions, he ordered them to form into line and enter in regular order. They at first refused, but on his counter-refusal to unlock the door, complied with some difficulty. The moment the key was turned, the rush into the little entry was terrific; the glass faces of the boxes were stove in, and the wooden partition seemed about to give way. In the space of an hour the clerk took in postage to the amount of $600; the principal firms frequently paid from $50 to $100 for their correspondence.

We toiled on till after midnight of the second night, when the work was so far advanced that we could spare an hour or two for rest and still complete the distribution in time for the opening of the windows at noon the next day. So we crept up to our blankets in the garret, worn out by forty-four hours of steady labor. We had scarcely begun to taste the needful rest, when our sleep, deep as it was, was broken by a new sound. Some of the besiegers, learning that the windows were to be opened at noon, came on the ground in the middle of the night in order to have the first chance for letters. As the nights were fresh and cool they soon felt chilly, and began a stamping

march along the portico which jarred the
whole building and kept us all painfully
awake. This game was practised for a week
after the distribution commenced, and was a
greater hardship to those employed in the
Office than their daily labors. One morning
about a week after this a single individual
came about midnight, bringing a chair with
him, and some refreshments. He planted
himself directly opposite the door and sat
there quietly all night. It was the day for
dispatching the Monterey mail, and one of
the clerks got up about four o'clock to have
it in readiness for the carrier. On opening the
door in the darkness he was confronted by
this man, who, seated solemnly in his chair,
immediately gave his name in a loud voice:
"John Jenkins!"

When, finally, the windows were opened,
the scenes around the office were still more
remarkable. In order to prevent a general
riot among the applicants, they were recom-
mended to form in ranks. This plan once
established, those inside could work with
more speed and safety. The lines extended
in front all the way down the hill into Portsmouth Square, and on the south side across
Sacramento Street to the tents among the
chaparral; while that from the newspaper
window in the rear stretched for some dis-

tance up the hill. The man at the tail of the longest line might count on spending six hours in it before he reached the window. Those who were near the goal frequently sold out their places to impatient candidates, for ten, and even twenty-five dollars; indeed, several persons in want of money practised this game daily as a means of living! Venders of pies, cakes, and newspapers established themselves in front of the office to supply the crowd, while others did a profitable business by carrying cans of coffee up and down the lines.

The labors of the Post Office were greatly increased by the necessity of forwarding thousands of letters to the branch offices or to agents among the mountains, according to the orders of the miners. This part of the business, which was entirely without remuneration, furnished constant employment for three or four clerks. Several persons made large sums by acting as agents, supplying the miners with their letters at $1 each, which included the postage from the Atlantic side. The arrangements for the transportation of the inland mail were very imperfect, and these private establishments were generally preferred.

The necessity of an immediate provision for the support of all branches of Government service, was (and still remains, at the time I write) most imminent. Unless something be speedily done, the administration of many offices in California must become impossible. The plan of relief is simple and can readily be accomplished—in the Civil Department by a direct increase of emolument, in the Military and Naval, by an advance in the price of rations during service on the Pacific Coast. Our legislators appear hardly to understand the enormous standard of prices, and the fact that many years must elapse before it can be materially lessened. Men in these days will not labor for pure patriotism when the country is so well able to pay them.

Chapter 6*

THE NEWS COMES TO MONTEREY

MONDAY, *May 29.* Our town was startled out of its quiet dreams to-day by the announcement that gold had been discovered on the American Fork. The men wondered and talked, and the women too; but neither believed. The sibyls were less skeptical; they said the moon had, for several nights, appeared not more than a cable's length from the earth; that a white raven had been seen playing with an infant; and that an owl had rung the church bells.

Saturday, June 3. The most faithful and reliable guard that I have ever had over the prisoners is himself a prisoner. He had been a lieutenant in the Mexican army and was sentenced, for a flagrant breach of the peace, to the public works for the term of one year. Being hard up for funds, I determined to make an experiment with this lieutenant; had him brought before me; ordered the ball and chain to be taken from his leg, and placed a double-barrelled gun, loaded and primed, in his hands. "Take

*For the editor's introductory note to this chapter, see Appendix, pages 357-59.

that musket and proceed with the prisoners to the stone quarry; return them to their cells before sunset and report to me." "Your order, Señor Alcalde, shall be faithfully obeyed," was the reply. I then ordered one of the constables, well mounted and armed, to reconnoiter the quarry and, unseen by the prisoners or guard, ascertain how things went on. He returned, and reported well of their regularity. At sunset the lieutenant entered the office and reported the prisoners in their cells, and all safe. "Very well, José; now make yourself safe, and that will do." He accordingly returned to his prison and from that day to this has been my most faithful and reliable guard.

Monday, June 5. Another report reached us this morning from the American Fork. The rumor ran that several workmen, while excavating for a millrace, had thrown up little shining scales of a yellow ore that proved to be gold; that an old Sonoranian who had spent his life in gold mines pronounced it the genuine thing. Still the public incredulity remained, save here and there a glimmer of faith, like the flash of a fire-fly at night. One good old lady, however, declared that she had been dreaming of gold every night for several weeks, and that it had so frustrated her simple household economy that she had relieved her conscience by confessing to her priest—

"Absolve me, father, of that sinful dream."

Tuesday, June 6. Being troubled with the golden dream almost as much as the good lady, I determined to put an end to the suspense and dispatched a messenger this morning to the American Fork. He will have to ride, going and returning, some four hundred miles, but his report will be reliable. We shall then know whether this gold is a fact or a fiction—a tangible reality on the earth or a fanciful treasure at the base of some rainbow, retreating over hill and waterfall, to lure pursuit and disappoint hope.[28]

Monday, June 12. A straggler came in today from the American Fork bringing a piece of yellow ore weighing an ounce. The young dashed the dirt from their eyes, and the old from their spectacles. One brought a spyglass, another an iron ladle; some wanted to melt it, others to hammer it, and a few were satisfied with smelling it. All were full of tests; and many, who could not be gratified in making their experiments, declared it a humbug. One lady sent me a huge gold ring, in the hope of reaching the

[28] Note that four and one-half months had already passed since the discovery on January 24.

truth by comparison; while a gentleman placed the specimen on the top of his gold-headed cane and held it up, challenging the sharpest eyes to detect a difference. But doubts still hovered in the minds of the great mass. They could not conceive that such a treasure could have lain there so long undiscovered. The idea seemed to convict them of stupidity. There is nothing of which a man is more tenacious than his claims to sagacity. He sticks to them like an old bachelor to the idea of his personal attractions, or a toper to the strength of his temperance ability, whenever he shall wish to call it into play.

Thursday, June 15. Found an Indian to-day perfectly sober, who is generally drunk, and questioned him of the cause of his sobriety. He stated that he wished to marry an Indian girl, and she would not have him unless he would keep sober a month; that this was but his third day, and he should never be able to stand it unless I would put him beyond the reach of liquor. So I sentenced him to the public works for a month; this will pay off old scores and help him to a wife, who may perhaps keep him sober, though I fear there is little hope of that.

Tuesday, June 20. My messenger sent to the mines has returned with specimens of

Pictures of Gold Rush California

the gold; he dismounted in a sea of upturned
faces. As he drew forth the yellow lumps
from his pockets and passed them around
among the eager crowd the doubts, which
had lingered till now, fled. All admitted
they were gold, except one old man, who
still persisted they were some Yankee in-
vention got up to reconcile the people to the
change of flag. The excitement produced
was intense; and many were soon busy in
their hasty preparations for a departure to
the mines. The family who had kept house
for me caught the moving infection. Husband and wife were both packing up; the
blacksmith dropped his hammer, the carpenter his plane, the mason his trowel, the
farmer his sickle, the baker his loaf, and the
tapster his bottle. All were off for the
mines, some on horses, some on carts, and
some on crutches, and one went in a litter.
An American woman who had recently established a boarding-house here pulled up
stakes and was off before her lodgers had
even time to pay their bills. Debtors ran,
of course. I have only a community of wom-
en left, and a gang of prisoners; with here and
there a soldier, who will give his captain the
slip at the first chance. I don't blame the
fellow a whit; seven dollars a month, while
others are making two or three hundred a

day! that is too much for human nature to stand.

Saturday, July 15. The gold fever has reached every servant in Monterey; none are to be trusted in their engagement beyond a week, and as for compulsion, it is like attempting to drive fish into a net with the ocean before them. Gen Mason, Lieut. Lanman, and myself form a mess; we have a house and all the table furniture and culinary apparatus requisite; but our servants have run, one after another, till we are almost in despair: even Sambo, who we thought would stick by from laziness if no other cause, ran last night; and this morning, for the fortieth time, we had to take to the kitchen, and cook our own breakfast. A general of the United States Army, the commander of a man-of-war, and the Alcalde of Monterey in a smoking kitchen, grinding coffee, toasting a herring, and peeling onions! These gold mines are going to upset all the domestic arrangements of society, turning the head to the tail and the tail to the head. Well, it is an ill wind that blows nobody any good: the nabobs have had their time and now comes that of the niggers. We shall all live just as long and be quite as fit to die.

Tuesday, July 18. Another bag of gold from the mines, and another spasm in the community. It was brought down by a sailor from Yuba River and contains a hundred and thirty-six ounces. It is the most beautiful gold that has appeared in the market; it looks like the yellow scales of the dolphin passing through his rainbow hues at death. My carpenters, at work on the school-house, on seeing it, threw down their saws and planes, shouldered their picks, and are off for the Yuba. Three seamen ran from the *Warren*, forfeiting their four years' pay; and a whole platoon of soldiers from the fort left only their colors behind. One old woman declared she would never again break an egg or kill a chicken without examining yolk and gizzard.

Saturday, July 22. The laws by which an alcalde here is governed, in the administration of justice, are the Mexican code as compiled in Frebrero and Alverez—works of remarkable comprehensiveness, clearness, and facility of application. They embody all the leading principles of the civil law, derived from the Institutes of Justinian. The common law of England is hardly known here, though its rules and maxims have more or less influenced local legislation. But with all these legal provisions a vast many questions arise which have to be determined *ex cathedra*. In minor matters the alcalde is often himself the law; and the records of his court might reveal some very exquisite specimens of judicial prerogative; such as shaving a rogue's head—*lex talionis*—who had shaved the tail of his neighbor's horse; or making a busybody, who had slandered a worthy citizen, promenade the streets with a gag in his mouth; or obliging a man who had recklessly caused a premature birth to compensate the bereaved father for the loss of that happiness which he might have derived from his embryo hope, had it budded into life. This last has rather too many contingencies about it; but the principle, which reaches it and meets the offender does very well out here in California, and would not be misapplied in some of those pill-shops which slope the path to crime in the United States.

Thursday, July 27. I never knew mosquitoes turned to any good account save in California; and here it seems they are sometimes ministers of justice. A rogue had stolen a bag of gold from a digger in the mines and hid it. Neither threats nor persuasions could induce him to reveal the place of its concealment. He was at last sentenced to a hundred lashes, and then informed that he would be let off with thirty provided he would tell what he had done with the gold; but he refused. The thirty lashes were inflicted, but he was still stubborn as a mule.

He was then stripped naked and tied to a tree. The mosquitoes with their long bills went at him, and in less than three hours he was covered with blood. Writhing and trembling from head to foot with exquisite torture, he exclaimed, "Untie me, untie me, and I will tell where it is." "Tell first," was the reply. So he told where it might be found. Some of the party then, with wisps, kept off the still hungry mosquitoes, while others went where the culprit had directed and recovered the bag of gold. He was then untied, washed with cold water, and helped to his clothes, while he muttered, as if talking to himself, "I couldn't stand that anyhow."

Saturday, Aug. 12. My man Bob, who is of Irish extraction, and who had been in the mines about two months, returned to Monterey four weeks since, bringing with him over two thousand dollars as the proceeds of his labor. Bob, while in my employ required me to pay him every Saturday night in gold, which he put into a little leather bag and sewed into the lining of his coat, after taking out just twelve and a half cents, his weekly allowance for tobacco. But now he took rooms and began

to branch out; he had the best horses, the
richest viands, and the choicest wines in
the place. He never drank himself, but it
filled him with delight to brim the spark-
ling goblet for others. I met Bob today and
asked him how he got on. "Oh, very well,"
he replied, "but I am off again for the
mines." "How is that, Bob? you brought
down with you over two thousand dollars;
I hope you have not spent all that: you
used to be very saving; twelve and a half
cents a week for tobacco, and the rest you
sewed into the lining of your coat." "Oh,
yes," replied Bob, "and I have got *that*
money yet; I worked hard for it; and the
diel can't get it away; but the two thousand
dollars came asily by good luck, and has
gone as asily as it came." Now Bob's
story is only one of a thousand like it in
California, and has a deeper philosophy in
it than meets the eye. Multitudes here
are none the richer for the mines. He who
can shake chestnuts from an exhaustless tree
won't stickle about the quantity he roasts.

Thursday, Aug. 16. Four citizens of
Monterey are just in from the gold mines
on Feather River, where they worked in
company with three others. They employed about thirty wild Indians, who are
attached to the rancho owned by one of

the party. They worked precisely seven weeks and three days, and have divided seventy-six thousand eight hundred and forty-four dollars,—nearly eleven thousand dollars to each. Make a dot there, and let me introduce a man, well known to me, who has worked on the Yuba river sixty-four days and brought back, as the result of his individual labor, five thousand three hundred and fifty-six dollars. Make a dot there, and let me introduce another townsman who has worked on the North Fork fifty-seven days and brought back four thousand five hundred and thirty-four dollars. Make a dot there, and let me introduce a boy, fourteen years of age, who has worked on the Mokelumne fifty-four days and brought back three thousand four hundred and sixty-seven dollars. Make another dot there, and let me introduce a woman of Sonoranian birth[29] who has worked in the dry diggings forty-six days and brought back two thousand one

[29] Sonora, a state of northwestern Mexico, is a mountainous country rich in deposits of silver, copper, and gold. Because of proximity and their knowledge of mining methods, the Sonorans were among the first to flock to Upper California following the news of the discovery of gold. Their presence and success soon provoked the jealousy of the Yankee gold-seekers, who frequently employed violence to drive them away.

hundred and twenty-five dollars. Is not this enough to make a man throw down his ledger and shoulder a pick? But the deposits which yielded these harvests were now opened for the first time; they were the accumulation of ages; only the footprints of the elk and wild savage had passed over them. Their slumber was broken for the first time by the sturdy arms of the American emigrant.

Tuesday, Aug. 28. The gold mines have upset all social and domestic arrangements in Monterey; the master has become his own servant, and the servant his own lord. The millionaire is obliged to groom his own horse and roll his wheelbarrow; and the hidalgo—in whose veins flows the blood of all the Cortes—to clean his own boots! Here is Lady L——, who has lived here seventeen years, the pride and ornament of the place, with a broomstick in her jewelled hand! And here is Lady B—— with her daughter—all the way from "old Virginia," where they graced society with their varied accomplishments—now floating between the parlor and kitchen, and as much at home in the one as the other! And here is Lady S——, whose cattle are on a thousand hills, lifting, like Rachel of old, her bucket of water from the deep well! And here is Lady M. L——, whose honeymoon is still full of soft seraphic light, unhouseling a potato and hunting the hen that laid the last egg. And here am I, who have been a man of some note in my day, loafing on the hospitality of the good citizens and grateful for a meal, though in an Indian's wigwam. Why, is not this enough to make one wish the gold mines were in the earth's flaming center, from which they sprung? Out on this yellow dust! it is worse than the cinders which buried Pompeii, for there high and low shared the same fate!

Saturday, Sept. 9. I met a Scotchman this morning bent half double, and evidently in pain. On inquiring the cause, he informed me that he had just seen a lump of gold from the Mokelumne as big as his double fist, and it had given him the colic. The diagnosis of the complaint struck me as a new feature in human maladies, and one for which it would be difficult to find a suitable medicament in the therapeutics known to the profession; especially in the allopathic practice, which has stood still for three thousand years, except in the discovery of quinine for ague and sulphur for itch. The gentlemen of this embalmed school must wake up; their antediluvian owl may do on an Egyptian obelisk, but

we must have a more wide-awake bird in
these days of progress. Here is a man bent
double with a new and strange disease,
taken from looking at gold: your bleeding,
blistering, and purging won't free him of
it. What is to be done? Shall he be left
to die, or be delivered over to the homœo-
pathics? They have a medicament that
acts as a specific, on the principle that the
hair of the dog is good for the bite. If you
burn your hand, what do you do—clasp a
piece of ice?—no, seize a warm poker; if
you freeze your foot, do you put it to the
fire?—no, dash it into the snow; and so if
you take the gold-colic, the remedy is,
aurum—similia similibus curantur.

Saturday, Sept. 16. The gold mines are
producing one good result; every creditor
who has gone there is paying his debts.
Claims not deemed worth a farthing are
now cashed on presentation at nature's
great bank. This has rendered the credit
of every man here good for almost any
amount. Orders for merchandise are
honored which six months ago would have
been thrown into the fire. There is none
so poor, who has two stout arms and a
pickaxe left, but he can empty any store
in Monterey. Nor has the first instance
yet occurred in which the creditor has suffered. All distinctions indicative of means

have vanished; the only capital required is muscle and an honest purpose. I met a man today from the mines in patched buckskins, rough as a badger from his hole, who had fifteen thousand dollars in yellow dust swung at his back. Talk to him of brooches, gold-headed canes, and carpenter's coats! Why he can unpack a lump of gold that would throw all Chesnut Street into spasms. And there is more where this came from. *His* rights in the great domain are equal to yours, and his prospects of getting it out vastly better. With these advantages, he bends the knee to no man, but strides along in his buckskins, a lord of earth by a higher prescriptive privilege than what emanates from the partiality of kings. His patent is medallioned with rivers which roll over golden sands, and embossed with mountains which have lifted for ages their golden coronets to heaven. Clear out of the way with your crests, and crowns and pedigree trees and let this democrat pass. Every drop of blood in his veins tells that it flows from a great heart, which God has made and which man shall never enslave. Such are the genuine sons of California; such may they live and die.

"They will not be the tyrant's slaves,
   While heaven has light, or earth has graves."

Chapter 7*

From our Log Cabin, Indian Bar, August 4, 1852.

WE have lived through so much of excitement for the last three weeks, dear M., that I almost shrink from relating the gloomy events which have marked their flight. But if I leave out the darker shades of our mountain life, the picture will be very incomplete. In the short space of twenty-four days we have had murders, fearful accidents, bloody deaths, a mob, whippings, a hanging, an attempt at suicide, and a fatal duel. But to begin at the beginning, as according to rule one ought to do.

I think that even among these beautiful hills I never saw a more perfect "bridal of the earth and sky" than that of Sunday, the eleventh of July. On that morning, I went with a party of friends to the head of the "Ditch," a walk of about three miles in length. I do not believe that Nature herself ever made anything so lovely as this artificial brooklet. It glides like a liv-

*For the editor's introductory note to this chapter, see Appendix, pages 359–63.

ing thing through the very heart of the forest; sometimes creeping softly on, as though with muffled feet, through a wilderness of aquatic plants; sometimes dancing gaily over a white pebbled bottom; now making a "sunshine in a shady place," across the mossy roots of the majestic old trees—and anon leaping with a grand anthem adown the great, solemn rocks which lie along its beautiful pathway. A sunny opening at the head of the ditch is a garden of perfumed shrubbery and many-tinted flowers—all garlanded with the prettiest vines imaginable, and peopled with an infinite variety of magnificent butterflies. These last were of every possible color— pink, blue, and yellow, shining black splashed with orange, purple fleshed with gold, white, and even green. We returned about three in the evening loaded with fragrant bundles, which, arranged in jars, tumblers, pitcher, bottles, and pails (we are not particular as to the quality of our vases in the mountains, and love our flowers as well in their humble chalices as if their beautiful heads lay against a background of marble or porcelain) made the dark old cabin, a bower of beauty for us.

Shortly after our arrival a perfectly deafening volley of shouts and yells elicited from my companion the careless remark, "that the customary Sabbath-day's fight was apparently more serious than usual." Almost as he spoke there succeeded a death-like silence, broken in a minute after by a deep groan at the corner of the cabin, followed by the words, "Why Tom, poor fellow, are you really wounded?" Before we could reach the door it was burst violently open by a person who inquired hurriedly for the Doctor—who, luckily, happened at that very moment to be approaching. The man who called him then gave us the following excited account of what had happened. He said that in a melee between the Americans and the foreigners, Domingo—a tall, majestic-looking Spaniard, a perfect type of the novelistic bandit of Old Spain—had stabbed Tom Somers, a young Irishman, but a naturalized citizen of the United States—and that at the very moment said Domingo, with a *Mexicana* hanging upon his arm, and brandishing threateningly the long, bloody knife with which he had inflicted the wound upon his victim, was parading up and down the street unmolested. It seems that when Tom Somers fell, the Americans, being unarmed, were seized with a sudden panic and fled. There was a rumor (unfounded, as it afterwards proved) to the effect that the Spaniards had on this day conspired to kill all the Americans on the river. In a few moments, however, the latter rallied and made a rush at the murderer, who immediately plunged into the river and swam across to Missouri Bar; eight or ten shots were fired at him while in the water, not one of which hit him. He ran like an antelope across the flat, swam thence to Smith's Bar, and escaped by the road leading out of the mountains from the Junction. Several men went in pursuit of him, but he was not taken, and without doubt is now safe in Mexico.

In the meanwhile the consternation was terrific. The Spaniards, who, with the exception of six or eight, knew no more of the affair than I did, thought that the Americans had arisen against them; and our own countrymen, equally ignorant, fancied the same of the foreigners. About twenty of the latter, who were either sleeping or reading in their cabins at the time of the emeute, aroused by the cry of "Down with the Spaniards!" barricaded themselves in a drinking-saloon, determined to defend themselves as long as possible against the massacre which was fully expected would follow this appalling shout. In the bakeshop, which stands next door to our cabin, young Tom Somers lay straitened for the grave (he lived but fifteen minutes after he was wounded) while over his dead body a Spanish woman was weeping and moaning in the most piteous and heart-rending manner. The Rich Barians, who had heard a most exaggerated account of the rising of the Spaniards against the Americans, armed with rifles, pistols, clubs, dirks, etc., were rushing down the hill by hundreds. Each one added fuel to his rage by crowding into the little bakery to gaze upon the blood-bathed bosom of the victim, yet warm with the life which but an hour before it had so triumphantly worn. Then arose the most fearful shouts of "Down with the Spaniards!" "Drive every foreigner off the river!" "Don't let one of the murderous devils remain." "Oh, if you have a drop of American blood in your veins, it must cry out for vengeance upon the cowardly assassins of poor Tom." All this, mingled with the most horrible oaths and execrations, yelled up as if in mockery into that smiling heaven which in its fair Sabbath calm bent unmoved over the hell which was raging below.

After a time the more sensible and sober part of the community succeeded in quieting, in a partial degree, the enraged and excited multitude. During the whole affair I had remained perfectly calm, in truth, much more so than I am now when re-calling it. The entire catastrophe had been so unexpected, and so sudden in its con-summation, that I fancy I was stupefied into the most exemplary good behavior. F. and several of his friends, taking ad-vantage of the lull in the storm, came into the cabin and entreated me to join the two women who were living on the hill. At this time it seemed to be the general opinion that there would be a serious fight, and they said I might be wounded accidentally if I remained on the Bar. As I had no fear of anything of the kind, I plead hard to be allowed to stop, but when told that my presence would increase the anxiety of our friends, of course, like a dutiful wife, I went on to the hill.

We three women, left entirely alone, seated ourselves upon a log overlooking the strange scene below. The Bar was a sea of heads, bristling with guns, rifles, and clubs. We could see nothing, but fan-cied, from the apparent quiet of the crowd, that the miners were taking measures to investigate the sad event of the day. All at once we were startled by the firing of a

178

gun, and the next moment, the crowd dispersing, we saw a man led into the log cabin, while another was carried, apparently lifeless, into a Spanish drinking-saloon, from one end of which were burst off instantly several boards, evidently to give air to the wounded person. Of course we were utterly unable to imagine what had happened; and to all our perplexity and anxiety one of the ladies insisted upon believing that it was her own husband who had been shot, and as she is a very nervous woman you can fancy our distress. It was in vain to tell her—which we did over and over again—that that worthy individual wore a *blue* shirt, and the wounded person a *red* one; she doggedly insisted that her dear M. had been shot, and having informed us confidentially and rather inconsistently that "she should never see him again, never, never," plumped herself down upon the log in an attitude of calm and ladylike despair which would have been infinitely amusing had not the occasion been so truly a fearful one. Luckily for our nerves a benevolent individual, taking pity upon our loneliness, came and told us what had happened.

It seems that an Englishman, the owner of a house of the vilest description, a person who is said to have been the primary cause of all the troubles of the day, attempted to force his way through the line of armed men which had been formed at each side of the street. The guard very properly refused to let him pass. In his drunken fury he tried to wrest a gun from one of them, which being accidentally discharged in the struggle inflicted a severe wound upon a Mr. Oxley, and shattered in the most dreadful manner the thigh of Señor Pizarro, a man of high birth and breeding, a *porteño* of Buenos Ayres. This frightful accident recalled the people to their senses and they began to act a little less like madmen than they had previously done. They elected a Vigilance Committee and authorized persons to go to the Junction and arrest the suspected Spaniards.

The first act of the Committee was to try a *Mexicana*, who had been foremost in the fray. She has always worn male attire, and on this occasion, armed with a pair of pistols, she fought like a very fury. Luckily, inexperienced in the use of fire-arms, she wounded no one. She was sentenced to leave the Bar by day-light, a perfectly just decision, for there is no doubt that she is a regular little demon. Some went so far as to say she ought to be hung, for

she was the *indirect* cause of the fight.
You see, always, it is the old, cowardly
excuse of Adam in Paradise: "The *woman*
tempted me, and I did eat." As if the
poor, frail head, once so pure and beautiful, had not sin enough of its own, dragging
it forever downward, without being made
to answer for the wrong-doing of a whole
community of men.

The next day the Committee tried five
or six Spaniards, who were proven to have
been the ringleaders in the Sabbath-day
riot. Two of them were sentenced to be
whipped, the remainder to leave the Bar
that evening; the property of all to be con-
fiscated to the use of the wounded persons.
Oh Mary! imagine my anguish when I
heard the first blow fall upon those
wretched men. I had never thought that
I should be compelled to hear such fearful
sounds, and although I immediately buried
my head in a shawl nothing can efface from
memory the disgust and horror of that moment. I had heard of such things, but heretofore had not realized that in the nineteenth century men could be beaten like
dogs, much less that other men not only
could sentence such barbarism, but could
actually stand by and see their own manhood degraded in such disgraceful manner.

One of these unhappy persons was a very gentlemanly young Spaniard who implored for death in the most moving terms. He appealed to his judges in the most eloquent manner—as gentlemen, as men of honor; representing to them that to be deprived of life was nothing in comparison with the never-to-be-effaced stain of the vilest convict's punishment to which they had sentenced him. Finding all his entreaties disregarded, he swore a most solemn oath that he would murder every American that he should chance to meet alone, and as he is a man of the most dauntless courage, and rendered desperate by a burning sense of disgrace which will cease only with his life, he will doubtless keep his word.

Although in my very humble opinion, and in that of others more competent to judge of such matters than myself, these sentences were unnecessarily severe, yet so great was the rage and excitement of the crowd that the Vigilance Committee could do no less. The mass of the mob demanded fiercely the death of the prisoners, and it was evident that many of the Committee took side with the people. I shall never forget how horror-struck I was (bombastic as it now sounds) at hearing no less a personage than the Whig candidate for representative say, "that the condemned had better fly for their lives, for the Avenger of Blood was on their tracks!" I am happy to say that said very worthy, but sanguinary individual, "The Avenger of Blood!" represented in this case by some half dozen gambling rowdies, either changed his mind or lost scent of his prey; for the intended victims slept about two miles up the hill, quite peacefully until morning.

The following facts, elicited upon the trial, throw light upon this unhappy affair: Seven miners from Old Spain, enraged at the cruel treatment which their countrymen had received on the "Fourth," and at the illiberal cry of "Down with the Spaniard," had united for the purpose of taking revenge on seven Americans whom they believed to be the originators of their insults. All well armed, they came from the Junction, where they were residing at the time, intending to challenge each one his man, and in fair fight compel their insolent aggressors to answer for the arrogance which they had exhibited more than once towards the Spanish race. Their first move on arriving at Indian Bar was to go and dine at the Humboldt, where they drank a most enormous quantity of champagne and claret. Afterwards, they proceeded to the house of the Englishman whose brutal carelessness caused the accident which wounded Pizarro and Oxley, when one of them commenced a playful conversation with one of his countrywomen. This enraged the Englishman, who instantly struck the Spaniard a violent blow and ejected him from the shanty. Thereupon ensued a spirited fight, which, through the exertion of a gentleman from Chili, a favorite with both nations, ended without bloodshed. This person knew nothing of the intended duel or he might have prevented, by his wise counsels, what followed. Not suspecting for a moment anything of the kind, he went to Rich Bar. Soon after he left, Tom Somers, who is said always to have been a dangerous person when in liquor, without any apparent provocation struck Domingo (one of the original seven), a violent blow, which nearly felled him to the earth. The latter, a man of "dark antecedents" and the most reckless character, mad with wine, rage, and revenge, without an instant's pause drew his knife and inflicted a fatal wound upon his insulter. Thereupon followed the chapter of accidents which I have related.

On Tuesday following the fatal Sabbath, a man brought the news of the murder of a Mr. Bacon, a person well known on the river,

who kept a ranch about twelve miles from
Rich Bar. He was killed for his money by
his servant, a negro, who not three months
ago was our own cook. He was the last one
anybody would have suspected capable of
such an act.

A party of men appointed by the Vigilance
Committee left the Bar immediately in
search of him. The miserable wretch was
apprehended in Sacramento and part of the
gold found upon his person. On the following Sunday he was brought in chains to
Rich Bar. After a trial by the miners he
was sentenced to be hung at four o'clock in
the evening. All efforts to make him con-
fess proved futile. He said, very truly, that
whether innocent or guilty they would hang
him; and so he "died and made no sign,"
with a calm indifference, as the novelists
say, worthy of a better cause. The dreadful
crime and death of Josh, who, having been
an excellent cook and very neat and respectful,
was a favorite servant with us, added to the
unhappiness which you can easily imagine
that I was suffering under all these horrors.

On Saturday evening about eight o'clock,
as we sat quietly conversing with the two
ladies from the hill—who, by the way, we
found very agreeable additions to our society, hitherto composed entirely of gentle-

men—we were startled by the loud shouting, and rushing close by the door of the
cabin, which stood open, of three or four
hundred men. Of course, we feminines, with
nerves somewhat shattered from the events
of the past week, were greatly alarmed.

We were soon informed that Henry
Cook, *vice* "Josh" had, in a fit of delirium
tremens, cut his throat from ear to ear. The
poor wretch was alone when he committed
the desperate deed, and in his madness,
throwing the bloody razor upon the ground,
he ran part of the way up the hill. Here he
was found almost senseless and brought
back to the Humboldt, where he was very
nearly the cause of hanging poor "Paganini
Ned"—who returned a few weeks since
from the valley—for his first act on recovering himself was to accuse that culinary individual of having attempted to murder
him. The mob were for hanging one poor
"Vattel" without judge or jury, and it was
only through the most strenuous exertions
of his friends that the life of this illustrious
person was saved. Poor Ned! it was forty-
eight hours before his cork-screws returned
to their original graceful curl; he threatens
to leave us to our barbarism and no longer
to waste his culinary talents upon an ungrateful and unappreciative people. He has

sworn war to the knife against Henry, who was formerly his most intimate friend, as nothing can persuade him that the accusation did not proceed from the purest malice on the part of the suicide.

Their majesties the mob, with that beautiful consistency which usually distinguishes those august individuals, insisted upon shooting poor Harry—for said they, and the reasoning is remarkably conclusive and clear, "a man so hardened as to raise his hand against his *own* life will never hesitate to murder another!" They almost mobbed F. for binding up the wounds of the unfortunate wretch and for saying that it was possible he might live. At last, however, they compromised the matter by determining that if Henry should recover, he should leave the Bar immediately. Neither contingency will probably take place, as it will be almost a miracle if he survives.

On the day following the attempted suicide, which was Sunday, nothing more exciting happened than a fight and the half-drowning of a drunken individual in the river, just in front of the Humboldt.

On Sunday last, the thigh of Señor Pizarro was amputated; but alas, without success. He had been sick for many months with chronic dysentery, which after the operation returned with great violence, and he died at two o'clock on Monday morning with the same calm and lofty resignation which had distinguished him during his illness. When first wounded, believing his case hopeless, he had decidedly refused to submit to amputation, but as time wore on he was persuaded to take this one chance for his life for the sake of his daughter, a young girl of fifteen, at present at school in a convent in Chili, whom his death leaves without any near relation. I saw him several times during his illness, and it was melancholy indeed to hear him talk of his motherless girl who, I have been told, is extremely beautiful, talented and accomplished.

The state of society here has never been so bad as since the appointment of a Committee of Vigilance. The rowdies have formed themselves into a company called the Moguls, and they parade the streets all night, howling, shouting, breaking into houses, taking wearied miners out of their beds and throwing them into the river, and in short, murdering sleep in the most remorseless manner. Nearly every night they build bonfires fearfully near some rag shanty, thus endangering the lives (or I should rather say the property—for as it is impossible to sleep, lives are emphatically safe)

188

of the whole community. They retire about five o'clock in the morning; previously to this blessed event posting notices to that effect, and that they will throw any one who may disturb them into the river. I am nearly worn out for want of rest, for truly they make night hideous with their fearful uproar. Mr. O——, who still lies dangerously ill from the wound received on what we call the "fatal Sunday," complains bitterly of the disturbance; and when poor Pizarro was dying, and one of his friends gently requested that they would be quiet for half an hour and permit the soul of the sufferer to pass in peace, they only laughed and yelled and hooted louder than ever, in the presence of the departing spirit, for the tenement in which he lay, being composed of green boughs only, could of course shut out no sounds. Without doubt if the Moguls had been sober, they would never have been guilty of such horrible barbarity as to compel the thoughts of a dying man to mingle with curses and blasphemies; but alas! they were intoxicated, and may God forgive them, unhappy ones, for they knew not what they did. The poor, exhausted miners, for even well people cannot sleep in such a pandemonium, grumble and complain, but they —although far outnumbering the rioters—

are too timid to resist. All say "It is shameful; something ought to be done; something *must* be done," etc. and in the meantime the rioters triumph. You will wonder that the Committee of Vigilance does not interfere; it is said that some of that very Committee are the ringleaders among the Moguls.

I believe I have related to you everything but the duel—and I will make the recital of this as short as possible, for I am sick of these sad subjects, and doubt not but you are the same. It took place on Tuesday morning at eight o'clock, on Missouri Bar, when and where that same Englishman who has figured so largely in my letter, shot his best friend. The duelists were surrounded by a large crowd, I have been told, foremost among which stood the Committee of Vigilance! The man who received his dear friend's fatal shot was one of the most quiet and peaceable citizens on the Bar. He lived about ten minutes after he was wounded. He was from Ipswich, England, and only twenty-five years of age when his own high passions snatched him from life. In justice to his opponent, it must be said that he would willingly have retired after the first shots had been exchanged, but poor Billy Leggett, as he was familiarly called, insisted upon having the distance between them shortened, and continuing the duel until one of them had fallen.

There, my dear M., have I not fulfilled my promise of giving you a dish of horrors? And only think of such a shrinking, timid, frail thing, as I used to be "long time ago," not only living right in the midst of them, but almost compelled to hear, if not see, the whole. I think that I may without vanity affirm, that I have "seen the elephant." "Did you see his tail?" asks innocent Ada J., in her mother's letter. Yes, sweet Ada, the "entire Animal" has been exhibited to my view.[30] "But you must remember that this is California," as the newcomers are so fond of informing *us!* who consider ourselves "one of the oldest inhabitants" of the Golden State.

And now dear M., *A Dios*. Be thankful that you are living in the beautiful quiet of beautiful A.,[31] and give up "hankering arter" (as you know what dear creature says—) California, for believe me, this coarse, barbarous life would suit you even less than it does your sister.

[30] To "see the elephant" was a popular expression of the period signifying to be satiated, or in present-day slang parlance, to be "fed up."

[31] Amherst, Massachusetts, the former home of the writer, and the home of the sister to whom the letter is presumed to have been addressed.

Chapter 8*

HOW THE GOLD WAS MINED

OF the thousands who note the semi-monthly arrivals of treasure, and who, from habit, have at last come to consider California a sort of gold-producing Croton, whence the supply is expected as a matter of course, comparatively few are acquainted with the methods by which these riches are drawn from the bowels of the earth. I have even found men who supposed that the primitive rocker or cradle of 1849 is still in general use in 1860. I believe that it will be a service to our friends in the Atlantic States to set them right on various points connected with the miners of California.

The old localities, such as the beds of well-known rivers and the adjacent "bars," being partially exhausted, it has been believed that mining could not now be followed so successfully as formerly, and that only gleanings remained for the future adventurer. But for ten years the great gold fountain of the Pacific coast has never

*For the editor's introductory note to this chapter, see Appendix, pages 363–64.

failed; and instead of a decreased supply, each year's returns have shown that, with the improvements in machinery and contrivances for saving the gold, the yield is steadily augmenting; and this without a material increase in the number of workmen engaged. If the shipments are sometimes smaller, it is no evidence that the gold region is becoming exhausted, but rather proves that our resources have been so developed that many articles formerly imported, such as flour, beef, pork, hay, lumber, potatoes, bricks, grain, and coal, are now produced in the State, and consequently have not to be paid for abroad. Business being dull or brisk in San Francisco is not always a criterion of the prosperity of the extensive gold-producing regions, where the stalwart sons of toil pursue their labors, almost forgetting the existence of the distant emporium, which thousands of them who came across the plains never saw or desired to see. It is to the multitudes who labor in the mines and on farms that we must turn, to estimate the prosperity or decline of the State. The various methods of gold mining and the important improvements which have been introduced since 1850 must prove of interest to all whose attention has been seriously directed toward the rapid development of the Pacific States since the conquest.

It was with the view of personally examining these improvements, as well as to renew old mining associations, that the writer of this joined a party who recently made the tour of the gold region. We laid out our course and left San Francisco early in May, when the great plains and rolling lands extending down from the spurs of the sierras were carpeted with flowers and clover, the sky cloudless, and the air clear as crystal. As the limits of this article will not permit the narration of every strange scene and adventure we met, I shall waive descriptions of towns and villages and confine myself to illustrating, as nearly as possible, the various methods of mining in which some of the party had once been engaged, or which were explained to us during our journey.

When, in 1848 the news of the gold discovery by J. W. Marshall at Sutter's mill became generally known, all the little world of California hastened into the mountains to hunt for gold. Those were indeed the primitive days of mining. Machinery had not then been invented, and the materials for constructing the rudest implements

were with difficulty obtained. In many
instances baskets or basins of willow twigs
were used. The sand or earth supposed
to contain gold was agitated in these, and
so rich in many instances was the earth
that even with these imperfect appliances
a very short term of labor was certain to
reward the adventurer. At that time gold
was found in the crevices of the rocks, pro-
truding from the banks of the streams, and
dazzled the eye here and there in bright
nuggets on the surface of the earth as it
reflected the sun's rays. Many gold-seekers
used no other instrument than a common
sheath-knife, with which to pry out these
chispas, and thus, as they averred, saved
time and the expense of machinery.
Thousands of dollars' worth were thus collected long before the cradle was introduced.

As the wonderful news became more
widely diffused the common washing-pan
was brought into use. This was doubtless
suggested by the Spanish-American *batea*,
or bowl, as the method of using both is
similar. The pan is filled with auriferous
earth. The operator, sitting or squatting
upon the edge of the stream in which he
submerges the load, holds the pan by the
rims, and by an alternate gyratory and

oscillating motion, with an occasional stirring and kneading of the mass with one hand, the earth is completely moistened. The largest stones are thrown out and a flow of water is made to pass constantly around the inner circumference of the pan, by which the load is gradually reduced to a few pebbles and specks of black, metallic sand, among which the particles of gold, if there be any, will be found. The rotary movement by which the heavier pebbles or bits of gold are kept in the center, and the lighter earth thrown rapidly over the edges, is acquired only by long practice; and very few Americans can rival the dexterity of the Sonorians in this art, which many of them have practiced from childhood in the gold regions of northern Mexico. The fine gold can not be separated from the black sand, which has nearly an equal specific gravity, until the whole has been dried in the sun or by a fire, when the sand is blown away with the breath.

Before going farther it will be as well to premise that the known fact of the superior specific gravity of gold over all known metals and minerals (except platinum) underlies the principle of nearly all gold-saving inventions. This will appear more prominently as we proceed.

Pictures of Gold Rush California

At the middle bar of the Mokelumne River we found a few Sonorians engaged in this panning, a method now confined to them, and which, among Americans, is only used as an adjunct to more extended operations. Nevertheless, one of our party, who had a pan scraped some "good-looking dirt" from the bottom of a deserted hole, and squatting beside Don Antonio the two had a trial of dexterity, in which our friend, though no novice, was "nowhere." He had, however, the pleasure of finding nearly half a dollar's worth of gold in his pan. Six years before, two of our party had been among the company who inaugurated gold-digging at this place; but, with the exception of the immovable mountains and huge rocks on the opposite banks, all had been changed under the tireless hand of the miners. Whole acres of land had been upturned and the earth and sand passed through a second and third washing, and apparently every particle of gold extracted; yet the less ambitious Chinese and Mexicans find enough in these deserted places to reward them for their tedious labors.

A volume would be required to perpetuate the fabulous tales still circulated of the former richness of the *placeres* along the banks of this river, and to which two of us could, in part, bear witness from personal experience. How the price of a common Irish potato in 1849 was one dollar; a pinch of gold dust paid for a drink of bad whisky; the same for a "chaw" of tobacco; and a doctor did not look at you under twenty dollars. The Indians, when pressed with hunger, would occasionally hunt for gold, and often with astonishing success, though it was alleged that until the arrival of the whites they knew naught of the rich placers they were daily treading over. A Yankee had set up a small tent among the miners' cabins, whence he dispensed whisky, tobacco, physic, raisins, and other groceries. It is related that an Indian came to the tent with a handful of gold wrapped in a rag. This he placed in one of the scales, which the shop-keeper weighed down with raisins in the other, much to the satisfaction of the customer. He was so careful, however, to evince no imprudent haste in the transaction that the Indian, fearing the other might repent of his bargain, suddenly seized the paper of raisins, and disappeared into the woods with the speed of a deer. Of course our Yankee did not pursue him, the raisins costing him about five cents and the gold amounting to more than thirty dollars.

Pictures of Gold Rush California

The success of mining in California, as well as in all other gold districts, depends mainly upon a constant supply of water, without which the gold can not be separated from the earth. For this reason the earliest efforts of the miner were directed along the banks of the rivers. There were, however, many *placeres* discovered on ground too elevated for any running stream to reach; and here the gold had to be packed on the shoulders of miners or the backs of donkeys to the nearest water, often a distance of miles. Of course the earth must be unusually rich to warrant such an outlay of labor and time. Chinese Diggings in Tuolumne County was an instance of this. Here were seen troops of sturdy Chinamen groaning along under the weight of huge sacks of earth brought to the surface from a depth of eighteen feet and deposited in heaps after a weary tramp along the banks of a muddy pool. These were washed by other parties stationed there for the purpose, and the day's proceeds equally divided. At Shaw's Flat, at the time of its discovery, similar means were used. A curious method was the dry washing, or winnowing process, which was confined to places where water could not be obtained. Two Mexicans, partners of course, would collect a heap of earth from some spot where the ground contained grain-gold, and rejecting all the pebbles, the remainder, pounded to the consistency of sand was placed upon a sheet or coarse cotton cloth, the corners of which were held in the hands of the operators, and the earth tossed to a height of three or four feet, somewhat in the style of Sancho Panza's treatment by the citizens of Segovia. The strong breeze carried away the light dust and particles of earth, while the superior gravity of the gold, if ever so fine, caused it to drop again into the cloth. Bellows were sometimes used by solitary adventurers, and where these could not be obtained Mexicans could be seen here and there tossing little clouds of dust into the air from their wooden *bateas*.

These primitive methods soon gave way to the more practical rocker, or cradle. The peculiar form of this useful machine is, doubtless, familiar to most readers. Rude and simple as it is, the California rocker has been the means of enriching thousands. It is not known who was the inventor, but its enlivening rattle began to be heard in the mines as early as 1848. At that time its form was, indeed, rough and awkward. Before saw-mills or lumber were within reach, the cradle was hewn out of logs and the trunks of trees; but it is safe to believe that in those early days these ungainly machines yielded a richer harvest than the neatly-finished ones of the present time.

Our journey from the Mokelumne River led us to Sonora, the principal mining town of Tuolumne County, and situated about two hundred miles from San Francisco. Here, again, we found all changed; the town had been entirely destroyed by fire since our last visit and was now rebuilt, with the addition of many fine brick stores. Not far from here, to the northward, is a bar or bend in the Stanislaus River, where in the "days of '49," two of our party had rocked our cradles and lined our buckskin purses to some purpose. Here we resolved to locate on the old spot. The river tumbled and foamed along its rocky bed and the loud voice of the rapids echoed far and near among the surrounding mountains. The bank was shelving and smooth like an ocean beach and a tiny surf, caused by the swift torrent, combed in miniature breakers upon an expanse of speckled sand, glittering with mica and smooth as a planed board. We placed our "bed pieces," set the rocker with the requisite pitch, and then attacked the long-deserted *placer*. After throwing aside a few tons of stones, and uprooting a dense undergrowth of shrubbery which nearly hid our old treasure-house, we came upon the place where our last efforts had been directed. This we had deserted some years before, after collecting from it several thousand dollars in coarse gold, and the hole, now nearly filled with stones, had not since been appropriated. But times had somewhat changed since, in the plentitude of fortune, we had quit this for better diggings, and we now resumed the work with all the ardor of new miners. A large boulder which had formerly discouraged us was first pried out, revealing a long deep crevice filled with a tough clay, the lower part of which we found stuffed with the shining nuggets. A pan was soon filled with this, and when washed by G— in the cold waters of the river resulted in about eighty dollars of beautifully-rounded gold. Thus encouraged we commenced with the cradle.

This little machine consists of a box about three and a half feet long by about twenty inches wide and eighteen inches deep. The top and one end are open: upon the back half of the top is fitted a closely-jointed box, with a sheet-iron bottom pierced with holes of a size sufficient to allow small pebbles to drop through into the machine. Into this box is thrown the earth designed to be washed, which is disintegrated and made to pass through by a rocking motion given to the machine, and for which it is provided with rockers like a child's cradle. The water is bailed by hand from the stream, near which the cradle must be placed. The gold thus separated from the earth is arrested in its passage through the machine by wooden cleats nailed along the bottom, while the lighter materials, such as earth and pebbles, are carried out of the open or lower end by the stream of water.

Rocking the cradle, digging, carrying earth, and bailing water were equally divided among the party. By night we had exhausted the lead, and returned to Sonora the next day four hundred and thirty dollars the richer for our adventure.

For the labors of one man the cradle is probably the most economical method of gold mining, as the several operations may be conducted without aid. It is now, however, mainly confined to Chinese and Mexicans, whose ambition seldom aspires to the later improvements.

A short distance north of Sonora is the town or diggings of Murphy's, once the most celebrated gold mine in California, and still employing hundreds of workmen to advantage. The discoverer, a Missourian, after whom the place was named, is said to have enjoyed his good fortune alone for some time, trading with the Indians, afterward known as the Murphy tribe, and supplying them with cheap articles of finery in return for their labor in the mines. With his two sons he thus amassed an immense sum in a few months.

Here we saw the first improvement made upon the cradle. This came out in 1850, and at that time was regarded as the *ne plus ultra* of mining machinery. It is called the long tom and consists of a shallow trough from ten to twenty feet long and generally about sixteen inches wide; one end, which slightly turns up like a shovel, is shod with iron and perforated like the sieve of a cradle. This trough is placed on slightly inclined ground, the sieve being at the lower end. A stream of water is then turned on at the upper end, and several hands supply the tom with water, which finds its way to the sieve, carrying with it the earth, which it washes and disintegrates in its passage. A man is stationed at the end to clear away the "tailings," or earth discharged from the machine, and also to stir up the earth accumulated in the tom. Directly beneath the sieve is placed a box, which is furnished with riffles

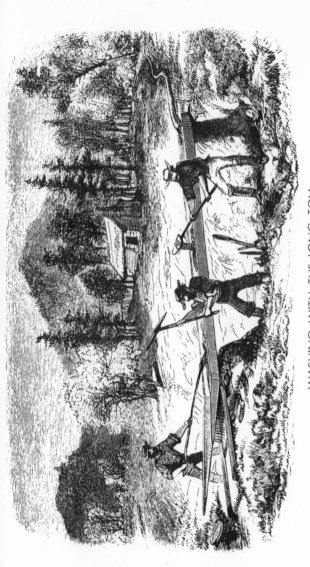

WASHING WITH THE LONG TOM

or cleats to catch the gold as it falls through the tom-iron. The machine differs little in principle from the cradle. Sometimes, where the gold is very fine and liable to be carried away by the force of the water, a box containing a quantity of quicksilver is attached to the end of the riffle, where the finer particles are saved by amalgamation. The long tom is calculated to wash ten times more earth than cradles employing an equal number of hands. The work is not performed in a more thorough manner, but there is a great saving of time and labor. When its value became generally appreciated the cradle began to disappear from many localities, and the long tom is now almost exclusively used by small companies.

Within a few miles of Auburn, a considerable mining town of Placer County, we visited a well known bend in the middle fork of the American River called Murderer's Bar, where one of the earliest attempts were made to turn the course of a large river with the view of exploring the bottom for gold. Every bend or shallow place in the numerous mountain streams of the gold region has been thus attacked, the waters diverted from their course and made to pass through artificial channels, leaving the old course dry for mining op-

erations. Works such as that shown in
the illustration of Murderer's Bar, in El
Dorado County, are carried on by large
companies, who have among them carpenters, surveyors, engineers, and stout
hands. Sometimes the water is taken into
a strongly-built flume from above and conducted in a long box through the old bed
of the river, by this avoiding the necessity
of a canal. The bed of the river thus laid
dry, the company enter it and search in
every crevice and pocket for the golden
deposits which should naturally have accumulated by the action of the river against
the bases of the adjacent hills. These
enterprises often yield immense riches,
every depression in the bed-rock holding
its quota of brightly-burnished gold. The
operations are frequently so extensive as
to occupy several successive seasons before
the whole can be explored. At others,
the premature approach of the rainy season, and the consequent freshets, carry
away the whole works in a night; but on
renewing them the following year, the
crevices and holes are often found to have
collected an amount of gold almost equal
to the original deposits brought down by
the floods from the numerous diggings
above. Frequently the place has been

RIVER OPERATIONS AT MURDERER'S BAR

Reproduced from Harper's New Monthly Magazine, Vol. XX, p. 603

injudiciously chosen and after months of hard labor the river proves entirely bare of gold. No amount of judgment can select with any certainty a favorable location for "jamming" or turning a river. The long space of still water below a series of rapids will sometimes contain pounds of gold; but the same rule followed, in another instance, will perhaps result in a total failure, and the company who have located above the rapids be the fortunate adventurers. The river operations at Murderer's Bar are the property of a company of some seventy-five men, one of whom informed us that they employed nearly two hundred more during the dry season. As fresh deposits of gold are made each year, the place may be considered a perpetual investment. It is estimated that only one in three of these river enterprises proves remunerative.

One of the richest *placeres* of California was an extensive sloping flat near the center of Calaveras County, at the foot of a range of quartz mountains separating it from the valley of the Stanislaus, and known as Carson's Flat. The gold deposits were first struck at this place in 1851. The discoverers sank a small hole in the shallowest part of the flat where the bed-rock lay about ten feet below the surface. Here they panned out several thousand dollars during the first week; but though their labors were continued with great secrecy, they were speedily tracked and multitudes flocked to the place. A small town was built where Carson's Creek discharged into the Stanislaus, goods came pouring in, Jew clothiers, rum-dealers, and gamblers followed the crowds of working men, and in a month every foot of ground, supposed to be auriferous was appropriated.

At a certain distance beneath the surface, throughout the gold region of California, a layer of rock is found down to which the gold, by its superior specific gravity, has gradually worked itself, and here it has become wedged into the inequalities of this hard pan. Long experience has taught the miner to discard the upper earth, which is generally valueless, and to seek for gold either in these cracks and pockets, or in the earth or layer of clay covering the bed-rock. The discovery of this fact gave rise to the method of "coyoting" or drifting, which has since been superseded by the improvement of tunneling. The first received its name from its fancied resemblance to the subterranean burrowing of a little animal resembling the fox, and known in California as the coyote. As the ledge, or bed-rock, at Carson's and other diggings of this kind is often found thirty or forty feet beneath the surface, and no gold can be got except within a few feet of it, the expense of shoveling away the upper earth is avoided by burrowing, and following the leads, or crevices of the rock in and around which the gold is deposited.

About six months sufficed to completely honeycomb the flat—an area of twenty acres—so that the workmen could pass through each other's claims for a distance of half a mile. These passages are made through a firm but sticky clay, and are only of a sufficient height for the workmen to sit upright in. Following the windings of the various leads they are as irregular as the intricacies of any labyrinth of mythology. A tallow candle stuck into a niche hewn into the damp wall serves to light the burrow. Descending into one of these holes we stood on a square space of rock at a depth of twenty feet from the surface. On the sides of this square were four arched entrances leading off into subterranean passages. We crawled into one and followed our conductor, hitching along in a sitting posture with an unhappy feeling of insecurity at hearing flakes of the moist clay fall from the low roof and partly impeding our progress. Here and there wooden stanchions had been placed to support the roof, but the immense weight had warped and bent these, while the superincumbent mass bulged on each side as if about to close down upon us forever. The muffled blows of other subterranean laborers were heard around us (for these diggings were still worked) and as we progressed we could discern the lights of dimly-burning candles shedding a ghastly glare upon cadaverous faces.

Our conductor led the way into a small chamber about six feet by eight and four feet in height, and, having lighted several other candles, we obtained a full view of our tomb-like apartment. On each side of this damp cave, as well as in the passages we had just crawled through, the stones and other refuse were piled up with the most scrupulous regard to economy of room. They had been carefully scraped to save any fine gold that might be contained in the clay adhering to them. On the floor of the cavern were two small picks and as many short crow-bars of tempered steel, which had been made of miniature size for the express purpose of "coyoting."

The owner of the claim now directed our attention to a side of the cavern where we heard the blows of an adjacent miner, and a moment after, the point of a pick came through the clay partition. A few more blows and the boundary between the two claims was broken away; a rough, bearded face looked through with the exclamation,

"Hello, strangers! How's diggins?"

We soon became on intimate terms with our underground acquaintance, and, when he had picked away the wall sufficiently to give us passage, we crept on hands and knees into his possessions, which rivaled in size and richness that of our *cicerone*. He had just found the end of a crevice, and had a pan filled with clay, earth, and pebbles, in which dozens of minute specks of gold glittered in the light of the candles. As the day was nearly spent we crawled out to the nearest shaft, whence we accompanied him to the creek and saw him wash out his day's work. There were nearly four ounces of coarse gold in his pan, valued at about sixty dollars.

Sometimes these coyote diggings cave in without warning, despite the subterranean supports placed by the miners for security. The earth thus undermined settles upon the bed-rock, and so slowly and silently that the victims are buried in a living tomb unknown to the outside world.

Shortly after our arrival at Carson's a twelve-pound lump of gold, slightly mixed with quartz, was found in the deepest part of the flat. This was valued at about two thousand dollars. The fortunate possessor walked leisurely along toward the store, bearing his glittering treasure in his hands and followed by a crowd of admiring companions. He had been prying out of his lead a nest of smooth stones, which he scraped clean before throwing them into the heap. One of these struck him as being rather heavy, but the thought of its being gold did not occur to him until, in scraping the supposed stone, the yellow metal reflected the rays of his candle. With that exception his claim had not yielded remarkably well. The earth taken from these diggings is either carted or carried in panniers, by mules or donkeys, to Carson's Creek, near by, and panned out in the usual manner. It is asserted that, counting the celebrated deposit found on the quartz mountain near by, more than four million dollars have been taken from Carson's.

One of the principal tributaries of the Stanislaus is the stream passing through Mormon Gulch and running within a stone's throw of Tuttletown. The diggings in this vicinity have been celebrated for their richness, especially toward the head of the cañon known as Mormon Creek. Desirous of ascertaining if our old diggings had been worked out during our four years of absence, we purchased an old quicksilver machine at this place, which we stationed in a certain bend, half-way between Tuttletown and the river. The gold in the bed of this stream is so fine as to escape from the riffles of a long tom, and can only be worked to advantage by the use of quicksilver. Minute particles in the shape of flakes are found adhering to the blades of grass in the shallow parts of the stream. Our machine, which resembled the "bumper," or Virginia rocker, consisted of a wooden trough furnished with quicksilver riffles, placed in a frame-work and so hung as to be rocked to and fro by hand. This motion was made by one man, and the machine was supplied with earth by the others, who shoveled it in from the bed of the creek. The water was led through canvas hose from a series of rapids above us; and the operation of shoveling and rocking was continued for a week without interruption. At the end of that time the amalgam was taken from the machine and retorted, when we found nearly three hundred dollars as the reward of our labor. Most of this gold was fine as snuff, and could only have been

saved by coming in contact with the quicksilver, with which it instantly amalgamates.
There were, however, many pieces from the
size of shot to that of a pea.

The elevation of many rich mines has
given rise to a variety of ingenious inventions for raising and supplying them with
water. Among these is the flutter-wheel,
which the traveler will find erected in every
conceivable manner and place; carried, in
all cases, by the force of the river currents.
It consists of a wheel, sometimes thirty feet
in diameter, the paddles of which are furnished with large buckets made to catch
themselves full of water at each revolution,
and to discharge into a trough, through
which it flows to the tom, or sluice where the
mining operations are being conducted.
This contrivance differs little from the common undershot wheel. They may be seen
by the dozens along the Tuolumne and
Stanislaus rivers, and supply countless
miners with the indispensable water. We
saw many of them in the vicinity of Jacksonville, a mining town of considerable importance, standing at the junction of the
Tuolumne River and Wood's Creek. Seven
years of steady working have not exhausted
the mines in this vicinity, and new *placeres*
are constantly discovered.

Near here we witnessed an instance of the habitual gallantry of the California miner. A party among whom were two ladies was traveling through the mines, and visited a well-known claim near Jacksonville to see how gold was dug. One of the ladies, a celebrated beauty, went by invitation into a formidable-looking tunnel, where she evinced so much *sang froid* that one of the proprietors, filling a pan with earth, promised her all the gold it might contain if she dared soil her hands by washing it out. She gayly consented, and went through the operation amidst the laughter of her companions. As the earth was gradually reduced so that the bottom of the pan could be seen, the rattling of gold could plainly be heard on the tin, and when thoroughly washed there remained nearly fifty dollars' worth of gold. This is the special prerogative of ladies, who are always at liberty to wash out a pan of earth at any claim they may honor with their presence, and the miners take special care that the labor shall be well rewarded.

Our tour of the mines carried us into the famous gold country of Mariposa—the far-famed region claimed by the pioneer Frémont. One of the largest mining counties in the State is that bearing this name, which is mellifluous Spanish for our word butterfly. In the center of its richest portion stands the picturesque town of Mariposa. This county ranks Number Four in the quartz-crushing interest, which has grown into an immense and lucrative business, despite the disaster and ruin attending it in 1850-'51. It employs millions of capital and thousands of miners, and has grown into the most important occupation in the State.

In every part of the mining region there are found veins of quartz rock, outcropping in many places, and often traceable through leagues of country. These generally contain gold: sometimes so fine as to be invisible to the naked eye; at others the quartz, when broken, is completely studded with the glittering particles. In some instances the proportion of gold is so small that the most economical methods of pulverizing it to extract the gold will not pay the necessary expenses; again the yield has been so large that costly mills carried by steam and water power have been erected, and with such astonishing results that savants have at last been compelled to admit that quartz is the mother of gold; and it is now generally believed that gold has been originally formed in, or together with,

quartz, and that it is by the gradual dis-
integration of the latter by the action of
water and atmospheric influences that the
gold has been distributed over the country.

The mill situated at the Frémont vein
in Mariposa County was among those visited during our journey. Like most of the
principal ones this mill is carried by steam
power; and some description of this, and
another in Nevada County, will give the
reader some idea of the great interest of
quartz crushing. The quartz is conveyed
to the works by carts or mule panniers
from the vein, near which they are generally erected. The machinery is under the
cover of a large shed; the apparatus consisting of a series of iron stampers, placed
in a line and made to fit into iron boxes
which receive the quartz, previously broken
into egg size. The stampers are moved by
cogs or cams connected with a revolving
wheel which alternately lifts and lets them
fall into the boxes containing the quartz.
By this means from ten to fifty tons per
day are crushed, according to the power of
the mills—yielding, at Mariposa, from $30
to $80 per ton.

The quartz operations at Grass Valley
in Nevada County have probably made the
largest returns. Some of the richest veins

in the State have been discovered in this
vicinity, some of them yielding occasionally two hundred dollars to the ton, but
by no means averaging as much. The Helvetia quartz mill at this place is one of the
principal, working thirty-four stampers and
crushing on an average thirty tons a day.
The stamping-box, already described, is
supplied with water by a hose or pipe.
Through a hole made for the purpose the
quartz, as it is crushed, passes out in the
form of a thick, milky water, carrying with
it much of the fine gold, which is thus discharged upon a frame-work across which
are placed several quicksilver riffles, where
the gold amalgamates in its passage. Any
fine particles escaping the quicksilver are
arrested below as they pass over a hide or
blanket stretched tightly across a frame.
But even these careful preparations for saving the gold are not always successful; for
the tailings, or refuse from the mill, is
found to pay nearly as well under a second
process as by the original crushing. The
question how to avoid this waste of gold
has long been agitated among miners, and
is apparently now as far from practical
solution as ever.

Besides the quartz mill proper there is
the primitive Spanish-American *rastra*, or

drag, which we saw in operation at Bear Valley in Mariposa County and other places. This consists of two heavy stones attached by a strap to a horizontal bar. These are dragged by mule-power slowly around a circular trough, paved at the bottom, and through which a small stream of water is constantly flowing. The gold-bearing quartz, previously broken into small pieces, is ground to paste in the trough, and flows away in the usual milky form, to which it is reduced by friction or crushing; and the gold amalgamates with quick-silver, which at short intervals is sprinkled into the trough during the grinding. After a certain time the water is turned off, the entire pavement of the trough taken up, and the amalgam carefully collected and retorted. A single ton of quartz often affords a day's work for one of these slow-jogging machines; but they do their work more effectually than the crushing-mills, as the quartz is more thoroughly pulverized by this constant friction and rubbing than by stamping; and in proportion as the stone can be thoroughly reduced to a paste, so much the more completely can the gold be extracted. Hence the *rastra* is used with success at veins which had been abandoned as profitless for the modern quartz mill.

These machines are usually put up, worked, and owned by Mexicans, who take the grinding of quartz, by the job or ton, from mining companies who lack capital to erect steam mills.

In the more retired parts of California, where the distance and difficulties of access have hitherto prevented the rush of population, there are extensive gold regions which have as yet only begun to be known. Years must elapse before the mineral wealth of Siskiyou, Klamath, and Shasta counties can be fully developed, though mining enterprises of great importance have been successfully attempted in all. Not many miles north of the California line on the Pacific is an extent of sea-coast, called Gold Bluff from the extraordinary gold discoveries made there in 1851. An American officer in pursuit of hostile Indians with a detachment of troops discovered on the ocean beach small shining particles in the sand, which extended many miles along the coast. These on examination proved to be gold. In a few months the report reached San Francisco in an exaggerated form and crowds flocked to Gold Bluff. The result was ruin and death to many, and fortune to a few. This style of mining has since been pursued with great success. Whether this gold is thrown up by the surf from the bed of the ocean or washed down from the inland bluffs remains unexplained. It is found by throwing off the upper or white sand, which discovers a layer of smooth, round stones embedded in a bank of black sand, in which the gold dust literally sparkles in the sunlight. The stones are thrown aside and the auriferous sand shoveled into a long trough, on the bottom of which is tacked a coarse blanket or hide. A stream of water is let on which carries away the sand while the gold is caught in the furze of the blanket. If any escapes, it is secured below in a short series of quicksilver riffles at the end of the trough or sluice. Instances are known at Gold Bluff and at Cape Blanco in Oregon where parties of four men have made from five to ten thousand dollars by gold-beach washing in a single season.

A very popular method of mining is that called ground-sluicing. This we saw in operation in hundreds of instances. I have already described the manner of getting at the pay dirt underneath a heavy layer of barren earth, by "coyoting." Ground-sluicing accomplishes the same result with half the labor, and with the chance of obtaining from the upper earth some gold which, did any exist, would be lost by the first plan. At Gold Hill in Placer County this operation was in very general use, and one of our party, during our short stay there, bought an interest in a company of ground-sluicers by which he cleared three ounces of gold dust, and on our departure, sold out his share at an advance.

It has been found that the principal deposits of gold are on the great rocky ridge already referred to as the bed-rock, and extending throughout the mining region, sometimes outcropping at the surface, and at others sinking to a depth of above a hundred feet. Where the bed-rock is not at too great a depth, the miners, instead of sinking a shaft to reach the deposits of gold, turn a heavy stream of water upon the bank which is to be removed, and with the aid of picks and spades reduce it so as to leave the lower or gold-bearing earth accessible to be worked. The force of the water is such as to carry away the debris, while any gold it may contain remains by its own gravity and is saved with the earth intended to be washed by the ordinary methods. Ground-sluicing is thus, to a certain extent, used as a substitute for shoveling, to remove heavy layers of earth from places where gold is supposed to be deposited, rather than to separate the gold, which is done by a style of sluicing hereafter to be considered.

Passing through Tuolumne County is a remarkable plateau about twelve hundred feet above the surrounding country, which from its flat surface and peculiar form has been named Table Mountain. A few years since, a miner (Mr. T. A. Ayres) while prospecting here was led to believe that it had anciently been the course of a river—a conclusion which has since proved correct, by the alluvial deposit and fossils found there by the miners. Here had accumulated, in distant ages, vast amounts of gold, which, however, could only be reached by shafts or tunnels. One of these had been commenced by the discoverer, and was abandoned; but others carried it through and struck the interior basin or bed of an ancient river, in which were found deposits of gold of fabulous richness. The news spread, and the adjacent country was quickly staked off into claims, according to the local mining rules of that neighborhood.

One of the largest tunnels which have been driven into the mountain is on its western slope, about six miles from the town of Sonora, and has been worked en-

tirely through a bed of talcose slate and
vitreous volcanic matter. It has more than
paid its way by the richness of the mass
through which it passes, though the object was to reach as quickly as possible
the interior deposits. The proprietor invited us to enter the tunnel, which was
made with no small pretensions to skill in
such work. It enters horizontally and follows the uneven surface of the bed-rock.
On each side of us as we entered the damp
walls reflected the light of our candles,
while the roof, which was of sufficient
height to allow us to walk upright, was
strongly timbered at regular distances, and
down the sides the water dripped from
numerous subterranean springs, doubtless
far above our heads. Passing along the
middle is a railroad upon which cars loaded
with earth are run out by mule-power. Beneath this is a drain, carrying off, in a large
stream, the accumulations of water from
the works, and which affords enough for
all mining purposes. As the work progresses
the quantity of gold increases. While we
were exploring a lateral chamber leading
off from the main tunnel one of the workmen came upon a pocket, or nest of gold,
which had accumulated in a hollow place
in the bed-rock. We held the candles and

watched with curious interest the process of gathering the gold. The hole, which was about the size of a common wash-bowl, was filled with a collection of black mud, clay, disintegrated slate, and some black vitreous matter which occurs in alternate layers with sand and pebbles in the body of the mountain. This substance yielded like clay to a few blows of the pick; and as the slices were turned carefully up, they resembled chunks of plum-cake, the clay being stuffed in every part with the golden lumps. Upon breaking these pieces in the hand like bread, the interior was still found plugged with pellets of gold, and the whole mass was heavy with it.

When we had reached the end of the tunnel we were fifteen hundred feet into the solid heart of the mountain. The proprietor had invested the earnings of three years in this enterprise, and had been eighteen months patiently working toward the treasures which were certainly to reward his enterprise. This description, with slight variations, would answer for hundreds of such tunnels in the golden State—such as those at Michigan Bluff, Placerville, and Iowa Hill.

The very general mode of mining known as "sluicing" (which is quite distinct from ground sluicing, already described) employs not far from one-half of the entire mining population of California; and with the hydraulic process of which it forms a necessary part, is undoubtedly the chief method to which is due the enormous sums still obtained from the soil. With them are inseparably connected the great system of flumes or aqueducts, cobwebbing and interlacing the gold region, and leading to extensive and ingenious mining operations. The allusion to these I have reserved for the close of the article, not only because they constitute the latest improvements in gold mining, but because all improvements hereafter to be made, it would seem, must necessarily be based upon them.

As the rivers and creeks were gradually worked over there remained to the miner only those localities which, though gold-bearing, had not become such depositories of the precious metal as the vicinity of rivers which had gradually collected the gold in their beds as they passed through the country. It was at first believed that the only available places for gold-washing were the river beds, bars, flats, and cañons which were so generally attacked in 1849 and '50. As these were exhausted, the hue and cry was raised abroad that the mines

were worked out. California was then, as
since, pronounced played out. "She had
gone up," it was said, "like a rocket, and
come down like a stick." The bubble had
burst—it had long been anticipated—and
sagacious newspaper editors remembered
that they had often warned their readers,
and predicted all this long before. True, the
monthly millions continued to pour in upon
New York as before, and that staggered
the doubts of some; but this, it was said,
was only the natural draining of the great
amounts still floating about the country;
and California, after giving a new impulse
to the world's commerce and prosperity,
was about to be laid quietly on the shelf as
a used-up concern.

It was now that intelligent miners began
to realize that their operations must be extended to the districts which had thus far
been neglected for the more immediate results to be obtained from the rivers. The
gold region of California embraces a country
equal in area to the whole of New England,
and throughout this great space there is no
part which does not contain gold; but in
most places the amount is so small that at
the present rates of living it will not pay
for the working, except by some improved
process by which a much greater amount

of earth could be washed than by the cradle. I have shown how this necessity was in part supplied by the long tom. The great inventions of hydraulic mining and the sluice-box formed the next step; and as it is merely executing in miniature a process which has been performed since the creation by the mountain streams, no very material improvements can be made upon the principle, though alterations in the manner of its application may be suggested.

At French Corral we visited every place of interest with the gentlemanly proprietors of the Shady Creek Canal, who have become identified with that section of the country. Here may be seen the various works of sluicing, canaling, fluming, and hydraulic mining.

A hill of moderate size which is found to contain gold throughout its formation, but too thinly scattered for cradle-washing, is generally selected for the operation of hydraulic mining. A series of boxes fourteen inches in length by about three feet wide called sluice-boxes, are fitted together at the ends so as to form a continuous, strongly built trough as long as may be desired, sometimes extending several thousand feet. This is made of the stoutest boards, and of sufficient strength to allow the passage

of any amount of earth and stones forced
through by a flood of water. It is lined on
the bottom with wooden blocks, like the
octagonal street pavement, for the double
purpose of resisting the friction of the debris intended to pass through it, and to
make place in the interstices for quicksilver
which secures the fine gold. Sometimes the
bottom is furnished with small transverse
gutters or riffles charged with quicksilver for
the same purpose. The sluice, thus prepared,
is firmly placed in a slanting position near
the foot of the hill intended to be attacked.

To shovel a mass of several million tons
of earth into this sluice for washing would,
of course, prove a profitless job. It is now
that the art of hydraulic mining is called
into play, by which the labor of many men
is cheaply performed, and the hill torn down
to its base. The operation is simply throwing an immense stream of water upon the
side of the hill with hose and pipe, precisely as a fire-engine plays upon a burning
building, and few who have not witnessed
it can imagine the effect. The water is led
through gutta percha or oftener double canvas hose, and generally from a great height
above the scene of operations. It is consequently thrown with such force as to eat
into the hill-side as if it were made of sugar

or salt. Neither man nor beast can stand for a moment against the projectile power of the hydraulic hose; they become a weapon of defense, and a miner with a hose-pipe in his hand need not fear the advance of half a dozen adversaries. Several of these streams directed upon a hill-side bring down more earth than a hundred men with shovels and picks could throw. But the art of the miner does not rest here. It is his constant aim to undermine as well as to break down; he consequently works, in a single day, huge caverns into the hill-side with his water-batteries, until by certain indications he knows that a cave-in is about to take place. Then every body flies from the spot. The earth far above their heads begins to quake and crinkle, and slowly the face of the precipice topples over and falls to the earth with the noise of an avalanche. Thus the miner makes one of the simplest laws of nature subservient to his will, and hundreds of tons of earth are leveled down for washing.

Now they return and commence throwing into the sluice. Here again the water becomes their giant servant; for it not only carries the earth through the sluice, completely disintegrating it, and allowing the gold it may contain to lodge in the interstices of the octagonal pavement, but it acts the part of many shovels and rushes the earth into the sluice with tremendous force. By these means a few men find it profitable to work earth which, with the discarded, snail-paced rocker, could never have been advantageously washed.

When it is considered that in California there are at least one hundred million superficial acres of gold-bearing territory, from ten to two hundred feet deep, most of which may be profitably submitted to this hydraulic process, the folly of predicting the failure of the mines will be apparent. Vast as have been the sums already extracted from the soil, the mines are said to have been but scratched over as yet; and with all the quick-succeeding improvements, gold-mining is yet in its infancy.

But experience has shown that most of this earth will pay for a second process; and numberless are the tailing companies, whose labors are confined to washing by a more careful method the tailings or refuse discharged from the end of the sluices, often with a success which leads one to doubt the efficacy of the original process.

So perceptible already have been the effects of this sluicing process that the entire face of the country is being changed by the removing of hills and filling up of flats and cañons, while some of the larger mountain affluents of the Sacramento and San Joaquin rivers are becoming filled with the deposits constantly poured into them from innumerable sluices, each discharging its daily tons of earth. The muddy current extends the entire length of the Yuba into the Feather River, and thence into the Sacramento far below Marysville. The country papers have more than once sounded the alarm at this threatened invasion of their inland stream navigation, which the political theorists regard as the first spur of necessity toward forcing railroads into general use. Such is a brief outline of the arts of hydraulic mining and sluicing—twin sisters—the natural offspring of gold.

The one great mining interest which remains to be explained is that of the water-companies. It has already been shown that water is the grand desideratum, without which the richest mines are not available. Many of the most famous *placeres* have been discovered at elevations above the level of the adjacent water-courses, and the attention of enterprising companies was at once turned to obtaining an artificial supply by diverting the mountain streams from their channels through ditches and canals, following the sinuosities of the hills at a proper grade by means of flumes supported by stout pine trestle-work. To obtain the requisite level it is often necessary to go back into the Sierra Nevada and tap some river near its head waters. Some of these aqueducts extend across valleys, through tunnels, and along the brows of mountains over leagues of country, and more resemble great public works than private enterprises. The water is supplied to the various mining companies by lateral branches, tapping the main trunk along its entire course, which in many instances exceeds fifty miles, and in a few is more than one hundred. Water is sold by the inch; that is, a price is charged for all the water that will flow by the day with a certain pressure through an aperture a given number of inches high and wide. Nearly all the hill diggings and hydraulic mining claims are thus supplied with their heavy batteries of water. The Shady Creek Canal, owned by Messrs. Pollard and Eddy, which receives its waters from a stream of that name in Nevada County, has proved one of the most successful, though not among the largest of these enterprises.

It is thus that gold mining is conducted in California. From a hap-hazard scrambling of uninitiated adventurers, scraping here and there among the rocks, it has grown into a well-organized and wonderful system, employing millions of capital and tens of thousands of stout hearts and strong hands, and bringing into action an amount of energy and inventive genius which must result in building up a great Pacific empire. With her boundless expanse of arable lands, her matchless climate, and the inexhaustible gold mines, California invites the world to share with her the blessings of Providence.

Reader, when next you notice in your morning paper, among other "distinguished arrivals" from California, the little item of "$1,500,000 IN GOLD DUST!" think not of the youngest sister of the Republic as a creature of premature and unhealthy growth, but as a child blooming in her freshest charms, and smiling in the confidence of a glorious future. And above all, when some pompous wiseacre tells you that California is played out, ask him if he ever heard of hydraulic mining.

Chapter 9[*]

CHINESE, MEXICANS, AND INDIANS

I: *The Chinese*[32]

WHILE at this camp I went down the river two or three miles to see a place called Mississippi Bar, where a company of Chinamen were at work. After an hour's climbing along the rocky banks, and having crossed and recrossed the river some half-dozen times on pine logs, I at last got down among the Celestials.

There were about a hundred and fifty of them here, living in a perfect village of small tents, all clustered together on the rocks. They had a claim in the bed of the river, which they were working by means of a wing dam. A wing dam, I may here mention, is one which first runs half-way across the river, then down the river, and back again to the same side, thus damming off a portion of its bed without the necessity of the more expensive operation of lifting up the whole river bodily in a flume.

[*]For the editor's introductory note to this chapter, see Appendix, pages 364–66.
[32] From Chapter XVII of J. D. Borthwick, *Three Years in California*.

The Chinamen's dam was two or three hundred yards in length, and was built of large pine trees laid one on the top of the other. They must have had great difficulty in handling such immense logs in such a place; but they are exceedingly ingenious in applying mechanical power, particularly in concentrating the force of a large number of men upon one point.

There were Chinamen of the better class among them, who no doubt directed the work and paid the common men very poor wages—poor at least for California. A Chinaman could be hired for two, or at most three dollars a day by any one who thought their labor worth so much; but those at work here were most likely paid at a still lower rate, for it was well known that whole shiploads of Chinamen came to the country under a species of bondage to some of their wealthy countrymen in San Francisco, who, immediately on their arrival, shipped them off to the mines under charge of an agent, keeping them completely under control by some mysterious celestial influence, quite independent of the laws of the country.

They sent up to the mines for their use supplies of Chinese provisions and clothing, and thus all the gold taken out by them remained in Chinese hands and benefited the rest of the community but little by passing through the ordinary channels of trade.

In fact, the Chinese formed a distinct class which enriched itself at the expense of the country, abstracting a large portion of its latent wealth without contributing in a degree commensurate with their numbers to the prosperity of the community of which they formed a part.

The individuals of any community must exist by supplying the wants of others; and when a man neither does this nor has any wants of his own but those which he provides for himself, he is of no use to his neighbors; but when, in addition to this, he also diminishes the productiveness of the country, he is a positive disadvantage in proportion to the amount of public wealth which he engrosses, and becomes a public nuisance.

What is true of an individual is true also of a class; and the Chinese, though they were no doubt, as far as China was concerned, both productive and consumptive, were considered by a very large party in California to be merely destructive as far as that country was interested.

They were, of course, not altogether so, for such a numerous body as they were could

not possibly be so isolated as to be entirely
independent of others; but any advantage
which the country derived from their presence was too dearly paid for by the quantity
of gold which they took from it; and the
propriety of expelling all the Chinese from
the State was long discussed, both by the
press and in the Legislature; but the principles of the American constitution prevailed;
the country was open to all the world, and
the Chinese enjoyed equal rights with the
most favored nation. In some parts of the
mines, however, the miners had their own
ideas on the subject, and would not allow
the Chinamen to come among them; but
generally they were not interfered with, for
they contented themselves with working
such poor diggings as it was not thought
worth while to take from them.

This claim on the Yuba was the greatest
undertaking I ever saw attempted by them.

They expended a vast deal of unnecessary
labor in their method of working, and their
individual labor, in effect, was as nothing
compared with that of other miners. A
company of fifteen or twenty white men
would have wing-dammed this claim and
worked it out in two or three months, while
here were about a hundred and fifty Chinamen humbugging round it all the season,

and still had not worked one-half the ground.

Their mechanical contrivances were not in the usual rough straightforward style of the mines; they were curious, and very elaborately got up, but extremely wasteful of labor, and, moreover, very ineffective.

The pumps which they had at work here were an instance of this. They were on the principle of a chain-pump, the chain being formed of pieces of wood about six inches long, hinging on each other, with cross-pieces in the middle for buckets, having about six square inches of surface. The hinges fitted exactly to the spokes of a small wheel, which was turned by a Chinaman at each side of it working a miniature tread-mill of four spokes on the same axle. As specimens of joiner work they were very pretty, but as pumps they were ridiculous; they threw a mere driblet of water: the chain was not even encased in a box—it merely lay in a slanting trough, so that more than one-half the capacity of the buckets was lost. An American miner, at the expenditure of one-tenth part of the labor of making such toys, would have set a water-wheel in the river to work an elevating pump, which would have thrown more water in half an hour than four-and-twenty China-

men could throw in a day with a dozen of
these gimcrack contrivances. Their camp
was wonderfully clean: when I passed
through it I found a great many of them at
their toilet, getting their heads shaved or
plaiting each other's pigtails; but most of
them were at dinner, squatted on the rocks
in groups of eight or ten round a number of
curious little black pots and dishes from
which they helped themselves with their
chopsticks. In the center was a large bowl
of rice. This is their staple article, and they
devour it most voraciously. Throwing back
their heads, they hold a large cupful to their
wide-open mouths, and with a quick motion of the chopsticks in the other hand they
cause the rice to flow down their throats in
a continuous stream.

I received several invitations to dinner,
but declined the pleasure, preferring to be a
spectator. The rice looked well enough, and
the rest of their dishes were no doubt very
clean, but they had a very dubious appearance and were far from suggesting the idea of
being good to eat. In the store I found the
storekeeper lying asleep on a mat. He was a
sleek dirty-looking object, like a fat pig with
the hair scalded off, his head being all close-
shaved excepting the pigtail. His opium
pipe lay in his hand, and the lamp still

burned beside him, so I supposed he was already in the seventh heaven. The store was like other stores in the mines, inasmuch as it contained a higgledy-piggledy collection of provisions and clothing, but everything was Chinese excepting the boots. These are the only articles of barbarian costume which the Chinaman adopts, and he always wears them of an enormous size, on a scale commensurate with the ample capacity of his other garments.

II: *The Mexicans* [33]

From Angel's Camp I went on a few miles to Carson's Creek, on which there was a small camp lying at the foot of a hill, which was named after the same man. On its summit a quartz vein cropped out in large masses to the height of thirty or forty feet, looking at a distance like the remains of a solid wall of fortification. It had only been worked a few feet from the surface, but already an incredible amount of gold had been taken out of it.

Every place in the mines had its traditions of wonderful events which had occurred in the olden times; that is to say, as far back as "'49"—for three years in such a fast

[33] From Chapter XXII of J. D. Borthwick, *Three Years in California.*

country were equal to a century; and at this place the tradition was that when the quartz vein was first worked, the method adopted was to put in a blast, and after the explosion to go round with handbaskets and pick up the pieces. I believe this was only a slight exaggeration of the truth, for at this particular part of the vein there had been found what is there called a pocket, a spot not more than a few feet in extent, where lumps of gold in unusual quantities lie imbedded in the rock. No systematic plan had been followed in opening the mine with a view to the proper working of it; but several irregular excavations had been made in the rock wherever the miners had found the gold most plentiful. For nearly a year it had not been worked at all, in consequence of several disputes as to the ownership of the claims; and in the meantime the lawyers were the only parties who were making anything out of it.

On the other side of the hill, however, was a claim on the same vein which was in undisputed possession of a company of Americans, who employed a number of Mexicans to work it, under the direction of an experienced old Mexican miner. They had three shafts sunk in the solid rock, in a line with each other, to the depth of two

hundred feet, from which galleries extended
at different points, where the gold-bearing
quartz was found in the greatest abundance.
No ropes or windlasses were used for descending the shafts; but at every thirty feet
or so there was a sort of step or platform,
resting on which was a pole with a number
of notches cut all down one side of it; and
the rock excavated in the various parts of
the mine was brought up in leathern sacks
on men's shoulders, who had to make the
ascent by climbing a succession of these
poles. The quartz was then conveyed on
pack mules down to the river by a circuitous
trail which had been cut on the steep side of
the mountain, and was there ground in the
primitive Mexican style in "rasters." The
whole operation seemed to be conducted at
a most unnecessary expenditure of labor;
but the mine was rich and, even worked in
this way, it yielded largely to the owners.

Numerous small wooden crosses were
placed throughout the mine, in niches cut
in the rock for their reception, and each
separate part of the mine was named after
a saint who was supposed to take those
working in it under his immediate protection. The day before I visited the place had
been some saint's day, and the Mexicans,
who of course had made a holiday of it, had

employed themselves in erecting on the side of the hill over the mine a large cross, about ten feet high, and had completely clothed it with the beautiful wildflowers which grew around in the greatest profusion. In fact, it was a gigantic cruciform nosegay, the various colors of which were arranged with a great deal of taste.

This mine is on the great quartz vein which traverses the whole State of California. It has a direction northeast and southwest, perfectly true by compass; and from many points where an extensive view of the country is obtained, it can be distinctly traced for a great distance as it crops out here and there, running up a hillside like a colossal stonewall and then disappearing for many miles, till, true to its course, it again shows itself crowning the summit of some conical-shaped mountain, and appearing in the distant view like so many short white strokes, all forming parts of the same straight line.

The general belief was that at one time all the gold in the country had been imbedded in quartz, which, being decomposed by the action of the elements, had set the gold at liberty, to be washed away with other debris and to find a resting-place for itself. Rich diggings were frequently found in the neighborhood of quartz veins, but not invariably so, for different local causes must have operated to assist the gold in travelling from its original starting-point.

As a general rule, the richest diggings seemed to be in the rivers at those points where the eddies gave the gold an opportunity of settling down instead of being borne farther along by the current, or in those places on the highlands where, owing to the flatness of the surface or the want of egress, the debris had been retained while the water ran off; for the first idea one formed from the appearance of the mountains was that they had been very severely washed down, but that there had been sufficient earth and debris to cover their nakedness, and to modify the sharp angularity of their formation.

I crossed the Stanislaus—a large river, which does not at any part of its course afford very rich diggings—by a ferry which was the property of two or three Englishmen who had lived for many years in the Sandwich Islands. The force of the current was here very strong, and by an ingenious contrivance was made available for working the ferry. A stout cable was stretched across the river, and traversing on this were two blocks, to which were made fast the head and stern of a large scow. By lengthening the stern line the scow assumed a diagonal position, and, under the influence of the current and of the opposing force of the cable she travelled rapidly across the river, very much on the same principle on which a ship holds her course with the wind a-beam.

Ferries or bridges on much-travelled roads were very valuable property. They were erected at those points on the rivers where the mountain on each side offered a tolerably easy ascent, and where, in consequence, a line of travel had commenced. But very frequently more easy routes were found than the one first adopted; opposition ferries were then started and the public got the full benefit of the competition between the rival proprietors, who sought to secure the travelling custom by improving the roads which led to their respective ferries.

In opposition to this ferry on the Stanislaus, another had been started a few miles down the river; so the Englishmen, in order to keep up the value of their property and maintain the superiority of their route, had made a good wagon-road, more than a mile in length, from the river to the summit of the mountain.

After ascending by this road and travelling five or six miles over a rolling country cov-

ered with magnificent oak trees, and in
many places fenced in and under cultiva-
tion, I arrived at Sonora, the largest town
of the southern mines. It consisted of a
single street, extending for upwards of a
mile along a sort of hollow between gently
sloping hills. Most of the houses were of
wood, a few were of canvas, and one or two
were solid buildings of sun-dried bricks.
The lower end of the town was very peculiar
in appearance as compared with the prevailing style of California architecture.
Ornament seemed to have been as much consulted as utility, and the different tastes of
the French and Mexican builders were very
plainly seen in the high-peaked overhanging roofs, the staircases outside the houses,
the corridors round each story, and other
peculiarities; giving the houses—which were
painted, moreover, buff and pale blue—
quite an old-fashioned air alongside of the
staring white rectangular fronts of the
American houses. There was less pretence
and more honesty about them than about
the American houses, for many of the latter
were all front, and gave the idea of a much
better house than the small rickety clap-
board or canvas concern which was concealed behind it. But these façades were
useful as well as ornamental, and were

intended to support the large signs, which conveyed an immense deal of useful information. Some small stores, in fact, seemed bursting with intelligence, and were broken out all over with short spasmodic sentences in English, French, Spanish, and German, covering all the available space save the door, and presenting to the passer-by a large amount of desultory reading as to the nature of the property within and the price at which it could be bought. This, however, was not by any means peculiar to Sonora— it was the general style of things throughout the country.

The Mexicans and the French also were very numerous, and there was an extensive assortment of other Europeans from all quarters, all of whom, save French, English, and "Eyetalians," are in California classed under the general denomination of Dutchmen, or more frequently "d—d Dutchmen," merely for the sake of euphony.

Sonora is situated in the center of an extremely rich mining country, more densely populated than any other part of the mines. In the neighborhood are a number of large villages, one of which, Columbia, only two or three miles distant, was not much inferior in size to Sonora itself. The place took its name from the men who first struck the diggings and camped on the spot —a party of miners from the state of Sonora in Mexico. The Mexicans discovered many of the richest diggings in the country—not altogether, perhaps, through good luck, for they had been gold-hunters all their lives and may be supposed to have derived some benefit from their experience. They seldom, however, remained long in possession of rich diggings; never working with any vigor, they spent most of their time in the passive enjoyment of their cigaritas or in playing monte, and were consequently very soon run over and driven off the field by the rush of more industrious and resolute men.

There were a considerable number of Mexicans to be seen at work round Sonora, but the most of those living in the town seemed to do nothing but bask in the sun and loaf about the gambling-rooms. How they managed to live was not very apparent, but they can live where another man would starve. I have no doubt they could subsist on cigaritas alone for several days at a time.

I got very comfortable quarters in one of the French hotels, of which there were several in the town, besides a number of good American houses, German restaurants, where lager beer was drunk by the gallon; Mexican fondas, which had an exceedingly greasy look about them; and also a Chinese house, where everything was most scrupulously clean. In this latter place a Chinese woman, dressed in European style, sat behind the bar and served out drinkables to thirsty outside barbarians, while three Chinamen entertained them with celestial music from a drum something like the top of a skull covered with parchment and stuck upon three sticks, a guitar like a long stick with a knob at the end of it, and a sort of fiddle with two strings. I asked the Chinese landlord, who spoke a little English, if the woman was his wife. "Oh, no," he said, very indignantly, "only hired woman—China woman; hired her for show—that's all." Some of these Chinamen are pretty smart fellows and this was one of them. The novelty of the "show," however, wore off in a few days, and the Chinawoman disappeared—probably went to show herself in other diggings.

One could live here in a way which seemed perfectly luxurious after cruising about the mountains among the small out-of-the-way camps; for, besides having a choice of good hotels, one could enjoy most of the comforts and conveniences of ordi-

nary life; even ice-creams and sherry-cob-
blers were to be had, for snow was packed
in on mules thirty or forty miles from the
Sierra Nevada, and no one took even a
cocktail without its being iced. But what
struck me most as a sign of civilization was
seeing a drunken man who was kicking
up a row in the street deliberately collared
and walked off to the lock-up by a police-
man. I never saw such a thing before in
the mines, where the spectacle of drunken
men rolling about the streets unmolested
had become so familiar to me that I was
almost inclined to think it an infringement
of the individual liberty of the subject—or
of the citizen, I should say—not to allow
this hog of a fellow to sober himself in the
gutter, or to drink himself into a state of
quiescence if he felt so inclined. This po-
liceman represented the whole police force
in his own proper person, and truly he had
no sinecure. He was not exactly like one
of our own blue-bottles; he was not such a
stoical observer of passing events, nor so
shut out from all social intercourse with
his fellow-men. There was nothing to distinguish him from other citizens, except
perhaps the unusual size of his revolver
and bowie knife; and his official dignity
did not prevent him from mixing with the

crowd and taking part in whatever amusement was going on.

The people here dressed better than was usual in other parts of the mines. On Sundays especially, when the town was thronged with miners, it was quite gay with the bright colors of the various costumes. There were numerous specimens of the genuine old miner to be met with— the miner of '49, whose pride it was to be clothed in rags and patches; but the prevailing fashion was to dress well; indeed there was a degree of foppery about many of the swells, who were got up in a most gorgeous manner. The weather was much too hot for any one to think of wearing a coat, but the usual style of dress was such as to appear quite complete without it; in fact, a coat would have concealed the most showy article of dress, which was a rich silk handkerchief, scarlet, crimson, orange, or some bright hue, tied loosely across the breast, and hanging over one shoulder like a shoulder-belt. Some men wore flowers, feathers, or squirrel's tails in their hats; occasionally the beard was worn plaited and coiled up like a twist of tobacco, or was divided into three tails hanging down to the waist. One man, of original ideas, who had very long hair, brought it

down on each side of the face and tied it
in a large bow-knot under his chin; and
many other eccentricities of this sort were
indulged in. The numbers of Mexican
women with their white dresses and spark-
ling black eyes were by no means an un-
pleasing addition to the crowd, of which
the Mexicans themselves formed a con-
spicuous part in their variegated blankets
and broad-brimmed hats. There were men
in *bonnets rouges* and *bonnets bleus*, the cut
of whose mustache and beard was of itself
sufficient to distinguish them as Frenchmen; while here and there some forlorn individual exhibited himself in a black coat and
a stove-pipe hat, looking like a bird of evil
omen among a flock of such gay plumage.

III: *The Indians*[34]

It can hardly be expected that in three
months I could gain a perfect knowledge

[34] From Alonzo Delano, *Life on the Plains and at the
Diggings*, Chapters XX and XXI, Delano had engaged
in the speculation of laying out a townsite on Feather
River, twenty miles above Marysville, hopefully antici-
pating a golden harvest through the sale of town lots.
But no purchasers appeared, and the speculation proved
a failure. Near the townsite was an Indian village, whose
inhabitants he treated fairly, winning their friendship
and respect. This acquaintance afforded the basis for
his description of them which is here reprinted.

of the Indian customs and superstitions, without understanding their language; but it was my chief amusement to study their character and language while I remained, and I thus learned more of them than I could have done by simply passing through their country. It was my first business to cultivate their good will. An occasion was not long wanting to turn a little circumstance to my advantage. Owing to their extreme filth and dirt, they are very subject to an eruption of the skin, which commences first by painful swellings, and then suppuration ensues, which, on its discharge, irritates whatever portion of the body it touches, producing large and disgusting sores, so that not unfrequently their body and limbs are covered with scabs and running sores. This has been sometimes mistaken by the common observer for venereal disease, but justice obliges me to declare that this assertion is wholly unfounded, for I never in my life saw an Indian afflicted with this vile disease where they had no intercourse with debased whites. I found that the most simple remedy soon restored them to perfect health.

Soon after I had got my house erected, mercantile and housekeeping arrangements completed, I strolled one evening into the village and saw the chief sitting by the fire in front of his house, apparently suffering from pain. I inquired by signs if he was sick. He put his hand just back of his ear and signified that he had been in such pain that he had not slept for two nights. Feeling the spot indicated, I found a tumor gathering, when, returning to my house, I got some strong volatile liniment, with which I rubbed the affected part well, and giving him a pretty good pill of opium, I directed him to go to bed, assuring him that he would sleep. When morning came the swelling had nearly subsided, and he felt much better. I then washed the place with Castile soap and water and made a second application of liniment, and by the second morning the poor savage was completely restored to health. This was wonderful; and my credit as a medicine man was established at once. I continued my practice on others with complete success, and very soon my reputation became so high that every sore toe and scabbed skin was submitted to my inspection; and if it had been a matter of dollars and cents, my fortune had been surely made; but, unfortunately for me, they neither had nor understood the value of money. I was soon looked upon as a friend, and for aught I know recognized as of the tribe of Oleepa. When I first arrived, the men manifested no interest in me; and on drawing near the houses, the women and children almost always retired, as if in fear; but my uniform kindness soon dispelled this feeling, and when I went among them I was surrounded by numbers, with the utmost cordiality, and always invited to share their meals or to partake of their luxuries, and they never seemed weary in showing me little attentions.

It has been supposed that they are taciturn in their dispositions. This may be so in their intercourse with whites and others with whom they are not acquainted; but among themselves, and with those in whom they confide, a more jolly, laughter-loving, careless, and good-natured people do not exist. The air resounded with their merry shouts as we sat around their fires at night, when some practical joke was perpetrated, or funny allusion made. And they were always ready to dance or sing at the slightest intimation, and nothing seemed to give them more pleasure than to have me join in their recreations. To each other they were uniformly kind, and during the whole of my residence with them I never saw a quarrel or serious disagreement.

I soon began to get hold of their words, and to aid my memory, wrote them down. They were very fond of instructing me— repeating each word slowly and distinctly until I caught the sound. It was not long before I comprehended enough to make myself understood on common occasions. Whenever I was at a loss for the word I referred to my glossary, and it was a matter of wonder to them that the paper could tell me how to speak. They frequently took it in their hands and looked at it every way, turned it upside down and around, but they could make nothing of it. Sometimes they would take my pencil, examine it closely, and then try to write, but in their hands it would not go off, and with a long drawn *waugh!* of wonder, they returned it to me.

For intelligence, they are far behind the Indians east of the Rocky Mountains, but although they are affectionate and kind to each other, as is the custom among all civilized tribes, their women are held to be inferior to the males and are reduced to unmitigated slavery. The men are idle vagabonds, and spend most of their time in lounging; occasionally shooting birds and small game or spearing fish, and, as it seemed to me, more for amusement than

257

from any desire to be useful to their families. While thus engaged, the women were almost constantly occupied, either in gathering nuts, seeds or wood; cooking, pounding acorns, weaving blankets, or in some way providing for the comfort of their lords. I have often seen a woman staggering under a heavy load, attended by her husband, who never offered to relieve her. Yet this is not always the case, for on a long march, and when human endurance is not sufficient to stand longer under the burden, an Indian will take the load on his own back and relieve his squaw for awhile. And yet these very men can be employed by whites and will carry, frequently, over an hundred pounds on their backs, with the package fastened by a strap which passes across their foreheads, and in this way will climb long and steep mountains with apparent ease, when a white man would tire at once.

Their chief aim seemed to be to get enough to eat. Usually, about nine o'clock in the morning half the squaws in the village, attended by the young girls who were old enough to work, and one or two men, to act as a kind of body-guard, start out with their baskets hanging on their heads by a strap from their foreheads to gather seeds, nuts, or anything to support their miserable existence. They are usually thus employed till three or four o'clock in the afternoon, when they return to cook and prepare acorn flour. Weaving baskets occupies the rest of their time till nearly sundown, when there is a general suspension of labor, the evening being generally spent in sitting around fires in groups, talking and laughing, or on moonlight nights in dancing. Sometimes they procured enough to last two or three days, and then a large number of the women have but little to do and are at liberty to be idle; but this does not very often occur. The men and women never eat together, and each congregate by themselves. Even around their fires at night it rarely happens that the males sit in the same circle with the females. Sometimes men will be standing around, and now and then condescend to laugh and joke a little, but it is not common, and as a general thing they seem to prefer the society of their kind, rather than mix in social chat as we do. Even little boys and girls do not play together, and the latter are brought up to yield obedience to the former from childhood. Frequently a bevy of little girls would come to my store, and though timid and shy, liked the *kiethta* and *loopa* (bread and sugar) of the *Americano*, when, if the boys came, they would all retire at once; and I have seen a dozen women retire in the same way at the approach of a single man of their tribe. Yet there seemed nothing like jealousy in the men, for I often sat down in the circle with the women while they were standing around, and such little familiarity seemed to give pleasure rather than annoy them. I recollect sitting thus one beautiful evening, when they were endeavoring to teach me to pronounce their words and laughing immoderately at my uncouth mistakes, when a young man approached, and looking at me, said something good-naturedly, and then gazing around, he saw one of the best looking squaws, full of frolic, at the farther side of the circle. He approached, seized her, and dragging her along, placed her in my lap, saying that she was my sweetheart. There were several Indians standing near, and among them the husband of the squaw. The men and women set up a joyous shout of laughter and passed several jokes which seemed to mortify the poor squaw, and she soon returned to her former seat. All seemed affectionate and kind to each other, and readily shared a tid-bit. When laying out my plot, I employed a young Indian to carry stakes. At dinner I gave him an ample plateful, when two other Indians came along and sat down without ceremony and shared his meal as readily as if it had been their own. For the purpose of trying two boys who came into my store, I would give one of them a single cracker, when he would invariably break it in two and give half to his companion.[35]

I could never learn much about their ideas of a Supreme Being. That they have some ideas of a Spirit superior to themselves is certain; for at times they have peculiar dances in honor of the moon, and a superstitious reverence for their dead. At intervals, as often as once a year, they have large bonfires, and spend the night in wailings, and sometimes in peculiar dances and ceremonies, not only to lament for their departed friends, but to propitiate a good Being in their behalf. Different tribes have peculiar customs, but this seems to be universal, both among the mountain and valley Indians. The valley Indians usually bury, while those of the mountains burn their

[35] This conduct had a significance which seems to have escaped our author. The primitive North American Indian was pretty much of a communist with respect to material goods. As a consequence, there was practically no inducement for the individual warrior to labor, since those who did not would join in consuming the fruit of his toil. With such a social concept, but little in the way of progress could ever be achieved.

dead. I was one day talking with the war chief who belonged to the upper village, (who, by the way, was a frank, open-hearted, generous fellow, and intelligent beyond his people) when near my own village I observed a small rail enclosure, like that around graves in some of our pioneer settlements. I asked him what it was. We had been talking together gaily, but the moment I propounded the question his whole manner changed to sadness, and sinking his voice to a whisper, he said it was bad, very bad. I told him I would go and see what it was—that I did not think it could be bad. "No, no," he continued, "do not go; it is bad," and stooping down, he scraped a little hole in the ground, putting a chip in it, carefully covered it with dirt, and pointing expressively to the enclosure, made me understand that one was buried there. Of course I respected his feelings, and did not visit it.

I attended the burial of a young man who died at the upper village. The body was bent into a sitting posture and closely wound with cord, so as to form a kind of ball, after which some squaws dug a pit about four feet deep and ten feet in front of the father's door. The corpse was then put therein in a sitting posture; two squaws got in, and while the dirt was being thrown in they trod it down hard around the body till the hole was nearly filled to the surface, when they retired. Up to this time not a tear was shed nor a lamentation uttered; but when the ceremony was completed, the old man took a little broom and commenced sweeping the ground over the grave and in front of his house till a large space was cleaned, accompanying his labor by a long and loud wail, which at regular intervals was responded to by the women and children in the house, while the tears streamed down his face as if his heart was nearly broken. Their lamentation was continued nearly all night long, and at intervals for several days, until they gradually ceased, and the burial rites were concluded.

Captain Yates[36] told me an affecting anecdote of a mountain Indian which strongly illustrates their affection and never-dying love for the memory of their friends. A few years since Mr. Johnson, late proprietor of the ranch which bears his name, at the foot of the hills on Bear River, brought up an Indian boy and girl from childhood. They were educated as well as the circumstances of the country would permit, and while the

[36] Captain Yates was a retired English sea-captain who had laid out a townsite a short distance above the one Delano was developing. Near his town was another Indian village, with whose occupants the Captain maintained friendly relations.

girl was instructed in the domestic arts the boy was taught the science of agriculture. Both were trusty and faithful, and Mr. Johnson became much attached to them. In process of time they grew up, and the boy wanted a wife. Mr. Johnson proposed to him to marry the girl, which being perfectly in unison with their feelings, their marriage was celebrated with the usual rejoicing, and they lived together in the utmost harmony. In a year or two the boy was taken sick and died. Mr. Johnson, to testify his regard for his adopted children, desired to have a somewhat expensive funeral. Numerous guests were invited, and he gave his Indian relatives new clothes and purchased a new hat for each, for which he paid eighteen dollars apiece, in order that they might make a decent appearance at the ceremony. Mr. Johnson intended to bury the body in a beautiful spot on his farm. But the poor girl begged him to let her lay her beloved husband beside the bones of her fathers in the hills. Of course he at once consented, and when all was ready he set out, accompanied by his guests and retainers, to escort the body to the mountains. They were met by the rude mountaineers with every demonstration of sorrow, who placed the body on a pile and set fire to it. As it was consuming, the Indians began to dance around it with a slow and measured tread, accompanied with songs of lamentation, each casting into the flames some precious offering, while the widow stripped herself completely of her civilized garments and threw them into the fire, and Mr. Johnson's domestics each pulled off his hat and cast it into the burning pile of his deceased fellow and friend. When all was consumed, the Indians gathered up the ashes in their hands and scattered them to the winds.

After the ceremony was concluded Mr. Johnson told the young widow that her mule was ready, and they would return, but she refused to go. "My husband, my heart, is dead; I will stay in the mountains with him; I will watch his ashes on the hills, and his spirit shall be with me. I am an Indian now. I love you, my father, but I will go no more to the valley. I will be an Indian till I die."

It was in vain that she was promised new clothes, a life of ease and comfort, and the wants and miseries of a savage life exhibited to her. She would not go. "Her heart was here now. His bones were with her father's. Hers should be with his;" and no entreaty could prevail on her to change her determination. She assumed the usual grass apron worn by the squaws, and remains with them now.

Their language does not consist of as great variety of words as our own; they are comparatively few and simple, yet sufficiently expressive, and, like those of Indian tribes in general, they use some metaphor in a lengthened address. Of course, they have no terms of their own for things to which they are not accustomed; for instance, in articles of dress—they use the Spanish words for hat, coat, shirt, shoes, &c. I append a few of their common words, giving the sound by letters as near as possible:

ENGLISH.	INDIAN.
Bread,	Ki-eth-ta.
Acorn bread,	Mah-tee.
Acorn or wh't flour,	Hi-de-e-nah.
Wood,	Charp.
Fish,	Mocco.
Salmon,	Mi-eemh.
Hair,	Oleem.
Ground,	Cowepe.
Work,	Tow-wal-te.
House,	Koom-ballum.
Man,	Wah-nah-mah.
Woman,	Maam.
Boy,	Yah-mush-tim.
Girl,	Cola.
Captain,	Hoko'm.
Come here,	Upeah.
Go away,	Wanok.
Good,	To-pe.

Although there seems to be a general language by which many of the valley tribes can communicate with each other, and even with the mountain Indians; yet the provincial dialects are so different that those separated only fifteen or twenty miles seem to speak almost an entirely different language, and the examples which I have quoted above might not be understood by tribes twenty miles distant.

The Indians of California are more swarthy in complexion and of smaller stature than those east of the Rocky Mountains; and although they may be placed in situations where they will fight bravely, they are less bold, and more cowardly in the main, than those on the great plains west of the Missouri; while they are more gentle in their natures, and become willing slaves to those who will feed and clothe them, if they are not overworked. They have more of the Asiatic cast of countenance than the eastern tribes, and are easily controlled if properly managed. Strict justice and a uniform but firm and gentle behavior will conciliate them, and gain their good will and respect. The mountain and valley tribes are in perpetual warfare, and rarely venture into each other's possessions, unless in considerable force, or by stealth.

Their staple article of food is acorns. These they gather in the proper season in large quantities, which constitute their principal supply of winter provisions. Before each house cribs are built, which will hold from thirty to fifty bushels each, and these are filled by the industrious squaws. None are thrown away from being worm eaten or mouldy, but good and bad are pounded up together in holes worked in rocks, having a long, round stone for a pestle. The flour, if it may be so called, is put into a place scooped out of the sand and wet with water and formed into a kind of paste, frequently mixed with the pulp of clover or with wild berries and then dried in the sun or baked in hot ashes.

Were it not for their abominable filth in preparing it, this kind of bread would be very palatable. In addition to their acorn bread, they gather several kinds of grass seeds, one of which resembles mustard seed in its outward appearance, but on being pounded is converted into a coarse, white flour, agreeable to the taste. Fish, birds, and insects are also used, being baked on hot stones covered with earth; and their fastidiousness does not prompt them to take the entrails out. Everything which can be eaten is saved. I have frequently seen them eat handfuls of fresh clover. I was one day sauntering along through the village when

I discovered a new dish, which appeared to be some kind of nut nicely browned. I took one in my fingers and was about conveying it to my mouth, when I recognized it as the chrysalis of a caterpillar. I dropped it with some signs of disgust, when an Indian exclaimed, "*To-pe, to-pe;*" and to convince me that it was good, he ate a handful before my face. I replied that it might be good for an Indian, but it was not for an "Americano."

Their habits are filthy—frequently in the extreme. I have seen them eating the vermin which they picked from each other's heads, and from their blankets. Although they bathe frequently, they lie for hours in the dirt, basking in the sun, covered with dust. They generally wear their hair short, and their mode of cutting it is somewhat primitive. They either burn it off with ignited sticks, or turn it over a piece of wood and saw it off with a clam shell!

They manufacture but few articles, and in these they exhibit considerable ingenuity. Their baskets, made of willows, are perfectly water-tight, and are of the different sizes that may be required. Their bows are of cedar, about thirty inches long, covered on the outer side with deer sinew, and will throw an arrow with amazing force. The arrows are a species of reed, pointed with flint or volcanic glass, and are made in two parts. When it enters the body, the short piece, containing the point, is left in the wound, from which it is impossible to extract it, thus leaving it to fester and rankle till it produces death. Their spears are pointed with bone, with which they are very expert in striking salmon. A line is attached to the spear, and after striking the fish they gradually draw him in as he becomes exhausted by his struggles. Their houses in form resemble pits made for burning charcoal. An excavation is made in the ground, a frame work is set up, tied together with raw hide; this is covered with small pieces of wood and brush, and then covered with earth a foot or more deep. A hole is left at the top by which smoke escapes. The door is simply a hole, about two feet square, into which they crawl on their hands and knees. A net work of small poles and willows is made overhead, which serves them for beds. Some of these houses are quite capacious—and are cool in summer and warm in winter, but dark, dingy with smoke, and abounding with vermin.

The form of marriage among the Oleepas resembles, in some respects, that of the Tartars. When a young man has fixed his affections on a girl, he makes a proposal to the parents, and with their consent, which is easily obtained, she goes out and hides. The lover then sets out in search, and if he finds her twice out of three times, she is his without further ceremony. But if he fails he is on probation for about three weeks, when he is allowed to make another trial, when, if he does not succeed, the matter is final. The simple result is, that if the girl likes him she hides where she is easily found, but if she disapproves of the match a dozen Indians cannot find her.

Their government is patriarchal. There is a civil chief who has control of the affairs in the village in time of peace, and a war chief who takes command of war parties. To these the Indians yield obedience, as a son to his father, and the authority exercised is more that of love than of terror. I never saw their commands disputed, nor their authority unduly exercised; and it was more like one large family of dutiful sons and daughters, having but one general interest in common, than that of many families with conflicting tastes and interests.

Unless they have been brought into contact with the whites, where articles of dress can be procured, the Indians of California wear no clothes. The men go entirely naked;

but the women, with intuitive modesty, wear a small, narrow, grass apron, which extends from the waist to the knees, leaving their bodies and limbs partially exposed. Still they adopt the American dress when they can get it, and in or near the settlements it is a common thing to see the men and women with simply a shirt on. Some, who have had better luck, are arrayed in pantaloons, with or without the shirt; and sometimes a coat or vest without either shirt, pants, or hat—making a more grotesque appearance than in their native nakedness.

They are most inveterate gamblers and frequently play away every article of value they possess; but beads are their staple gambling currency. They have two or three games; one of which is with small sticks held in the hand, which being suddenly opened, some roll on the fingers, when the opposite player guesses at a glance their number. If he guesses right, he wins, if wrong, pays the forfeit. Another is with two small pieces of bone, one of which is hollow. These they roll in a handful of grass, and tossing them in the air several times, accompanied with a monotonous chant, they suddenly pull the ball of grass in two with the hands, and the antagonist guesses which hand the hollow bone is in. They have small sticks for counters, and as they win, or lose, a stick is passed from one to the other, till the close of the game, when he who has the most sticks is the winner. They will sometimes play all day long, stopping only to eat. I gave the chief a shirt and pantaloons, with which he was delighted. About an hour after, I saw him strutting about entirely naked, and asking him where his clothes were, he replied, with perfect coolness—"Oh, another man got 'em. I lost 'em gambling;" and my shirt and pants were actually worn by three different Indians the same day!

The Indians of California are regarded as being treacherous, revengeful, and dishonest. This may be so to a certain extent, when judged by the customs and laws of civilization; but it should be qualified by the fact that they are governed by their own sense of propriety and justice, and are probably less likely to break the laws which they recognize as right than are the whites to break theirs. Living in a state of nature, surrounded continually by enemies, emphatically the children of Esau—"their hand against every man, and every man's hand against them"—they are taught from necessity to be watchful and wary and to look upon all men as enemies whom they do not know to be friends. Being in a state of perpetual warfare, they hold it to be a virtue to steal from those with whom they are not in alliance, and to avenge an insult upon those whom they do not regard as friends. They do not steal from their own people, and during my residence with the Oleepas I never saw a quarrel; and I firmly believe that nine-tenths of the troubles between the whites and Indians can be traced to imprudence in the former in the first instance. Thus revengeful feelings are instigated, and being unable to distinguish between the innocent and the guilty, it being their custom to visit the insult of an individual upon his tribe, they take vengeance on the first white man they meet, as they do on the first Indian of a hostile tribe. Looking, too, on the whites as encroachers upon their territory, and as doubtful friends—their cupidity tempted by an unusual display of articles useful to them —they look upon it as a merit to steal; and they are sometimes forced to take cattle, mules, and provisions to eat when a poor season limits their own supplies.

Renegade whites and Mexicans in whom they have confidence are not wanting to stir them up to acts of hostility: and this has been one fruitful source of their wars with the whites. It cannot be denied that there are evil-disposed Indians as well as white men; for human propensities are alike in all ages and climes; but the dogma of visiting vengeance upon the innocent as well as the guilty widens instead of heals the breach. In their wild state they are, from the force of circumstances and education, suspicious, and like wild beasts they must be tamed and enlightened before they can fully understand our laws and our notions of right and wrong.

I was completely in their power and might have been killed or robbed at any moment; but while I was with them I am not aware that I lost the worth of a dollar, although I had five thousand dollars' worth of goods with me at one time. Yet they would steal from passers-by. I sometimes had occasion to be gone all day from home, but leaving my house and goods in the care of the chief or some of the old men I invariably found everything safe on my return. My confidence was never abused. I never abused theirs. I was uniform in my conduct with them, never but once making a promise I did not perform. In that instance it was unavoidable, and was explained to their satisfaction. If I was leaving my store, although a hundred Indians were in, every one followed me out unless I told some one to stay, when all would remain.

The indiscretion of some of the whites was strongly exemplified in the spring of 1850 on the middle fork of Feather River. It had become common to charge every theft of cattle on the Indians. A party of miners missed several head of oxen, and a cry was raised that the Indians had stolen them. Fifteen men were started out, well armed, swearing vengeance. Proceeding to a rancheria about twelve miles higher in the mountains, they found a few bones, which they considered proof positive of the guilt of the inhabitants. They immediately surrounded the huts, when the Indians came out, and seeing their hostile attitude, without understanding the cause, and impelled by the instinct of self-preservation, attempted to fly. A deadly discharge of firearms was made and fourteen Indians fell dead. After demolishing the houses the brave whites set out on their return, with the glory of having taken signal and successful vengeance on the mountain robbers. When they had nearly reached home, their sense of justice was a little shaken by seeing every ox which they had supposed stolen quietly feeding in a somewhat isolated gorge, whither they had strayed in search of grass. Had the Indians, under similar circumstances, killed fourteen whites, an exterminating warfare would have ensued.

Captain Yates related an anecdote which is a further illustration of the want of discretion often shown by the Americans. An Indian visited a miner's camp and begged for something to eat. The miners told him to chop some wood and they would give him some bread. He accordingly took their axe and commenced work near the brink of a creek. The axe being loose, worked off the helve and flew into a deep hole, which, owing to high water, could not then be gotten out. Fearing that the miners would charge him with theft, he ran away. On discovering their loss the men swore vengeance against the Indian, and having armed themselves they were proceeding towards the rancheria, when, being met by Yates, it was with much difficulty that they were persuaded by him to desist, assuring them that if the Indian had stolen it, he could recover it. He sent for the chief, and a true statement of the case was elicited. When the water had subsided the captain took the Indian to the spot, and making him dive into the hole, the axe was brought up. Thus by a little forbearance and common sense a cruel wrong was avoided. They are impulsive because they have not been taught reflection.

At the first settlement of Grass Valley, in Nevada County, a general war was at one time apprehended, from a difficulty which resulted in the murder by the Indians of an innocent and good man. Two brothers named Holt had erected a sawmill four or five miles from where the town now stands. Their uniform kindness and justice had secured the Indians' friendship, and they all lived on amicable terms. Not far off lived a heedless and dissolute miner who one day took a squaw into his cabin, where he kept her two or three days, to gratify his lustful passion. This incensed the Indians so much that they determined to take revenge, and not being able to find the perpetrator of the outrage, with characteristic sense of right they determined to take vengeance on any of the white man's tribe they could find. The elder Holt was one morning busily at work in his mill, while his brother was out a short distance, when a number of Indians advanced with their usual friendly demeanor. They suddenly commenced an assault on poor Holt, who fell under their murderous weapons. He could barely cry out to his brother before he fell, to save himself. His brother, seeing the attack, fled, receiving two arrows, but succeeded in making his escape to the cabin of Judge Walsh at Grass Valley and gave the alarm. Walsh had one man with him, and at night was joined by three miners who had been out prospecting. This little band prepared themselves in the best manner they could, resolving to sell their lives as dearly as possible. They watched all night, momentarily expecting an attack; but Indian vengeance was appeased, and they did not appear. The miners in the neighborhood were aroused, and stood upon the defensive; but a talk was held, and the affair happily compromised. Thus the indiscretion of one man had nearly caused the death of many. Reversing the picture: Had the outrage been perpetrated by an Indian on a white woman, her kindred would quite as likely have taken revenge on the whole tribe, by killing or driving them off.

Soon after I got my plat surveyed a gentleman named Gray became my neighbor and built a house adjoining mine. He was of a pleasant, jovial disposition, but at times, when depressed, could not maintain his equanimity of temper; and though he frolicked and laughed occasionally with the

Indians, and they, on the whole, liked him,
yet when he was vexed, he did not hesitate
to repulse them with some rudeness. Of
course, although some Indians liked him,
others did not. One day I had gone to
Marysville, leaving my store in his care. He
had imprudently given some of the Indians
liquor, and when they became excited they
wanted more, which he refused and drove
them off. I did not return till the second
day after nightfall. On my way up I met
Captain Yates, who told me there was
trouble in my village and that the Indians
were much incensed at Gray, and he feared
it would not end well. It was nine o'clock
in the evening when I rode up to my store,
and had scarcely got off my horse when a
large number turned out as usual to welcome
me; and while one took the bridle another
took off the saddle and a third led my horse
to grass and a fourth brought me fresh
water. But Gray was not to be seen, and on
inquiry the Indians could not tell me where
he was. Striking a light, I stepped into
his store, and as I went in I saw an Indian
dodging out of the back door in a rather
equivocal manner. Soon I heard the gur-
gling sound of running liquor, and on looking
about I discovered that the plug was pulled
out of his brandy cask and a pail was stand-

ing under, which was nearly half full. Comprehending the matter at once, I poured the liquor back, put in the tap, and broke it off—telling the chief that he had a bad Indian and that he must be accountable if anything was lost, after which I quietly went to bed and slept soundly till morning.

About nine o'clock Gray came in, and after expressing surprise that I should have the hardihood to sleep there, told me about his difficulties: When the Indians found that he would give them no more liquor three of them laid a plot to murder him that night. Soon after dark, while he was unconscious of his danger, a squaw rushed into his tent from the back way, and, much excited, told him to go into the woods to sleep, for the Indians intended to kill him; saying which, she hurried out in a roundabout way and gained the village unperceived. Her husband was to be one of the murderers. Gray went up to Captain Yates', and spent the night; and the Indians, not finding him, meant to make sure of the liquor before I came; but fortunately I arrived in time to prevent it. Why they did not steal mine, or my goods, at the time, I do not know, for they had every opportunity.

Polygamy is practised among them. But it sometimes happens that there are more males than females in a village, when they content themselves with one wife. Indiscriminate cohabitation is never practiced.

I was one day talking with the civil chief, and he asked me how many wives I had. I told him but one. He only inquired if women were scarce in my village.

"No, they are as numerous as the leaves on the trees."

"Wah!" he exclaimed with surprise, and holding up his fingers and pointing to his koomballum, he signified that he had four.

"Well, you old Solomon, (I said this in English,) what do you do with so many?"

"I make them gather acorns, make bread, pick up wood, and work for me."

"And I work for myself," said I.

"Humph!" said he, contemptuously. "Good for nothing. Does your wife dress like you?"

I could have added that she did not exactly wear the breeches, but I told him that she wore a long shirt, shoes and stockings, and a kind of hat.

He thought I must have "much clothes, or I was a very great fool to spend so much on one woman."

They can be taught to plow, to herd cattle, and perform manual labor very well. But I was once somewhat amused at the awkwardness of an Indian in a (to him) new branch of business. A sack of sugar had been landed for me about half a mile below, on the opposite bank of the river, and taking two Indians, I went after it. I found it too heavy for them to carry, so I borrowed a wheelbarrow and set them to wheeling it to the landing. As I expected, they made awkward work of it, but by dint of perseverance one of them made out to keep the one-wheeled wagon in the track and we managed to get it to the landing. Thinking the other Indian would find no difficulty in wheeling back the empty barrow, I directed him to return it. He stood a moment, looking irresolutely at it, when, calling for the aid of his companion, he hoisted it on his head and deliberately marched off with it.

At the close of my residence with them, when making arrangements to return to the mines, I had saved from my stock, which had been sold out, a summer's supply of provisions, and it being necessary for me to visit Marysville, I packed all securely up, and going into the village, told the chief and some of the old men that I was going to Yuba, that I should be gone some days, and that I wanted them to take care of my house and goods until I came back, to which they gave their usual assent. It so happened that I was obliged to go to Sacramento City, and I was unwell a day or two, so that I did not return until the thirteenth day. I came back on the opposite side of the river, and calling to the Indians, they came over on their log canoes and conveyed me across. On ascending the bank, the men of the village came out as usual to see me, but I observed this time that they kept a little back instead of coming around me as they generally did. In a moment an old man advanced and slowly, and with much dignity, addressed me with,

"Wah-ne-mah, when you left us you said you would be gone so many sleeps," and holding out a string he showed me seven knots tied in it. "You have been gone so many," and slipping his hand along he showed me thirteen. "How is this?"

"I explained to him that I was seven days at Yuba, two days I was sick, two days I had to go to Sacramento, and it took me two days to come home.

"It is good," said he, "it is all right."

When this important matter was explained the others came up and greeted me cordially and I stood upon my usual footing.

"Come," said I, "let us go to my house," and I led the way, when on reaching it I saw that they had piled the door full of limbs and brush, which according to their custom, signifies that the owner is absent, and no one enters. Pulling these away, we entered, when I discovered that all my provisions were gone; not a single article was left. At first I was a little startled, but I exhibited no surprise. In a short time I observed, "Come, let us go to the village, I want to see the women and children." I was followed by the crowd, and going into the town, I found the chief, sitting on a beef's hide, and he invited me to sit beside him. After a due pause, and explaining the cause of my long absence, I observed, "Well, you have taken good care of my house, did you take care of my goods?"

"Yes."

"Are they all safe?"

"Yes—all safe."

"Good," I replied, "where are they?"

"There," said he, pointing to his house.

"Very well—I have come home now, you may take them back."

He sprang up, and going on the top of his house he called several Indians together and gave them directions, when they went to work and in thirty minutes every box, every sack of flour, was taken out, and piled up precisely as they had found them in my house, and even a hatchet and a dozen nails were returned to me, unasked. The faithful Indian had removed them to his own house for safe keeping against straggling whites and vicious Indians. "Honor to whom honor is due."

I could relate many anecdotes of what transpired during my brief sojourn with the untutored savages which would present them in a favorable light, but it is probable the reader is already tired, and I forbear. I do not mean to appear as their apologist, but I do think that their character is not well understood by the mass of people, and that their good will might be gained by conciliation, kindness, and justice, if they can be kept free from malign influences, and that the principles of civilization may be instilled into their minds. But this will never be. Once in contact with the whites, they learn their vices without understanding their virtues; and it will not be long before intemperance, disease, and feuds will end in their extermination or complete debasement, and these once powerful tribes, like those upon the Atlantic shores, will have passed away, or be but a wreck of miserable humanity. They are already dwindling, for the fire-water and rifle of the white man are doing their work of death, and five years will not pass ere they will become humbled and powerless—a wretched remnant of a large population. I have been told that the valley of the Sacramento, fifteen years ago, contained from fifteen to twenty thousand, but a fatal disease breaking out, in one year destroyed many thousands—in fact, reduced them more than one-half; and this I think quite likely; for during a trip which I made last fall to the upper Sacramento, I passed a multitude of old deserted villages, which I was assured was caused by desolating disease. But the two races cannot exist in contact, and one must invariably yield to the other; and it was justly remarked by Governor Burnett, in his annual message of January, 1851: "That a war of extermination will continue to be waged between the two races, until the Indian race becomes extinct, must be expected. While we cannot anticipate this result but with painful regret, the inevitable destiny of the race is beyond the power or wisdom of man to avert."

Chapter 10*

I: *A Gambling Saloon* [37]

LAST evening I walked around to about fifty of the gambling tables. A volume could not describe their splendor or their fatal attractions. The halls themselves are vast and magnificent, spread over with tables and implements for gambling. The pictures which decorate them no pen of mine shall describe. The barrooms are furnished with the most expensive liquors, no care or attention being spared in the compounding and coloring of them. The music is performed often by professors, and is of the best kind. The tables are sometimes graced, or disgraced, by females, who came at first masked, and who are employed to deal the cards, or who come to play on their own account. The "Bank" consists of a solid pile of silver coin, surmounted by the golden currency of as many countries as there are dupes about the table. Often a sack

*For the editor's introductory note to this chapter, see Appendix, pages 366–67.

[37] Reprinted from Woods' *Sixteen Months at the Gold Diggings*.

or two of bullion, which has cost the poor miner months of labor, is placed upon the top of all. Sufficient money to send one home independent changed owners during my short stay. A boy of ten years came to one of the tables with a few dollars. His run of luck was surprising, and to him bewildering. In ten minutes he was the owner of a pile of silver, with some gold. In one minute more he was without a dollar. Thinking by one turn of the cards to double his profits, he lost the whole. The instances of great good luck on the part of the players are very rare. But they sometimes occur. A lawyer of this city recently swept three tables in one evening. A young man came from the States in one of the last steamers and was preparing to go to the mines. He borrowed ten dollars and went to one of the faro banks. During the night and a part of the next forenoon he had won $7000, when he made a resolution never to play more and returned home in the next steamer. Mr. Davidson, the agent of the Rothschilds, says that some of the professed gamblers send home by him to England the average sum of $17,000 a month. Many tricks are resorted to in order to bring persons to the table. An eye-witness assures me that he has seen the president of the Bank slip secretly into the hand of some one, employed for the purpose of decoying others, a quantity of coin. On receiving this he would leave the room, but soon return and present himself in a noisy manner at the table and boldly "plank down" the very money he had received. In five minutes the table would be surrounded by eager players.

As I entered one of the magnificent gambling saloons of San Francisco and proceeded from one table to another, I saw, to my surprise, a young man who had come from one of the most religious families in his native city placing down his money upon the table. I stepped to his side. In a moment the card was turned, and a small amount of silver was added to that already in his hand. He looked anxiously at me and said, "I would not have my mother know what I am doing for all the money in this room." "Why then do it?" I asked; "have you thought to what the first step may lead?" "But what can I do," he said, earnestly; "I came not here to gamble, but to find amusement; and can you tell me what other amusement is within my reach?" I think that was the first, and am sure it was the last time that my friend visited the saloons for the purpose of gambling. But it affords an illustration of the subject— the danger, in the absence of proper subjects of interest and amusement, of seeking these in wrong and sinful ways. Many a person in California becomes a professed gambler in consequence of taking the first step from desire of amusement. It can not be impressed upon your mind too deeply that the gambling table is the place of the greatest danger. It is one of the most ensnaring inventions of the great enemy of souls.

But how shall I speak of a kindred subject, so fraught with danger that numbers of our most gifted citizens have yielded themselves to it. I think intemperance may be named as, next to gambling, the most prevailing vice of California. They generally go hand in hand. In this country, where the common restraints are removed which formerly imposed a salutary check, this vice gains disgusting and dangerous prominence. All that it is in its secluded orgies, all that it becomes in its favorite haunts elsewhere, it is in California in open day. It blushes not to show itself in its most fearful forms even in the public streets. Many a poor miner who becomes discouraged and sinks down into gloom flies to strong drink as he would to a friend from whom he expects to receive

relief. Occasionally, the Daguerreotype
likenesses of dear friends at home, or the
sight of the neglected Bible—(for most
miners have both of these, almost their
only treasures)—or the reception of a letter,
the miner's only luxury, recalls him to his
better self, puts new hopes, new resolutions,
and new life into him. But gradually he
yields the ground again; again he stands on
slippery places, and soon he staggers into
his grave, for soon does vice of every kind
perfect its work here. Licentiousness, which
is so destructive an evil in large cities in
Europe and America, is found also in California, and there produces its bitter fruits.
Profanity—a kind of its own; a bold, independent, and startling profanity—is far too
common in the mines, as it is in the settlements. Several have told me that they have
fallen into this habit unconsciously, and in
some instances have asked, as an act of
friendship, that I would aid them in correct-
ing it. In one case, a company of young
men from New England mutually pledged
themselves to each other and to me to re-
frain from this habit. For the very reason
that it is so insinuating, and creeps so
gradually upon one, should it be more
sedulously avoided. In my own case, I
could perceive that the constant listening to

profane language produced a familiarity which continually lessened the sense of repugnance it occasioned. This would have been more and more the case had I not adopted an expedient which, while it aimed at the good of others, had the effect to guard my own mind against the moral contagion. The expedient which I adopted was this: when I heard a profane oath I accompanied it with a petition to Heaven in behalf of him who had uttered it.

No man, young or old, should go to California unless he has firmness of principle enough to resist, and forever hold at bay, all the vices of the country, in whatever disguise they may present themselves and in however fascinating shapes they may appear.

If I were asked what was the state of religion in the mines, I could only say, it is in no state. There are many men there who maintain their integrity and their piety. If there is preaching, it is well and respectfully attended. Many, perhaps most, occasionally read their Bibles or tracts. There is a respect for religion, as there is a respect for every thing which reminds one of home; but society must be in a very different condition—it must be settled, and have some elements of permanence—before a decidedly religious influence can be brought to bear upon it. When I say that the sound of the pick, spade, and rocker are seldom heard on the Sabbath—that the Bible is often and devoutly read—that often, from beneath some cluster of trees, the cheering sound of some hymn and the preacher's voice are heard, it is as much as can be said.

As to the operation of the laws at the mines and their effects upon the interests of the community, I can only give the facts in the case, without discussing the subject. When we first reached the gold diggings life and property were comparatively secure. Without law, except the law of honor; without restraint, except that imposed by the fear of summary punishment, which was sure to follow the only crimes cognizable under the new code—those of stealing and of murder—we were comparatively safe. If the way of the transgressor was hard, it was also speedily terminated. It was the reign of the rifle and the halter. And yet this was a people who had been accustomed to the laws of civilized countries, and who yet loved order. The principles of a republican government were only adapting themselves to a new and untried emergency. The crime was committed, and proved in the presence of a competent and impartial jury, who were also required to award the punishment. The sentence was pronounced by the alcalde, a grave was dug, the sharp crack of the rifle was heard, the body was buried, and every man proceeded silently to his own work. I have never yet heard of the case in which the verdict given under the first system was an unrighteous one, or the punishment inflicted undeserved.

But a change came; civil laws were enacted in the mines; and what was the result? Why, crimes of every kind were committed, and the very officers of justice were met by the taunt, "Catch me, if you can!" Seldom was the criminal caught; and when caught, more seldom was he brought to punishment. And there is but one opinion among the miners, that the system without civil law, but with summary justice, is, in the state of society which now exists in California, incomparably better than the system with such law, but without justice.

Ere long California will have a truly golden age, when law and justice and every moral and Christian virtue shall prevail.

II: *Bear and Bull Fight*.[38]

It was a beautiful Sabbath morning in November when the bells aroused me from a dreamy sleep; but before arising from my

[38] Reprinted from Helper, *The Land of Gold*, Chapter IX.

couch, being lazy and inclined to muse, I allowed my fancy to recall my departure from Carolina with all its attendant circumstances. The hour alone would have suggested such meditations, for it was on a dewy morning that I bade farewell to the loved ones of my far-off home. I recalled the yellow luster of the sun pouring his floods of golden light over the glistening tree tops; the tender adieus, the streaming eyes, the murmured blessing. I remembered the sadness of my heart as I thought of the distance that would soon separate me from the friends and companions of my youth, and the high hopes which soothed my pain.

As I was thus pondering I heard the sound of drum, fife and clarionet; and stepping to the window to ascertain what was the meaning of this Sunday music echoing through the streets of San Francisco, I saw a tremendous grizzly bear, caged, and drawn by four spirited horses through the various streets. Tacked to each side of the cage were large posters, which read as follows:

FUN BREWING—GREAT ATTRACTION!
HARD FIGHTING TO BE DONE!
TWO BULLS AND ONE BEAR!

The citizens of San Francisco and vicinity are respectfully informed that at *four o'clock this afternoon, Sunday, Nov. 14th,* at *Mission Dolores,* a *rich treat* will be prepared for them, and that they will have an opportunity of enjoying a fund of the *raciest sport* of the season. TWO LARGE BULLS AND A BEAR, all *in prime condition for fighting*, and under the management of *experienced Mexicans*, will contribute to the *amusement of the audience.*

Programme—In two Acts.

ACT I.

BULL AND BEAR—"HERCULES" AND "TROJAN,"

Will be conducted into the arena, and there *chained together*, where they will fight *until one kills the other.*

JOSE IGNACIO,
PICO GOMEZ, } Managers.

ACT II.

The great bull, "BEHEMOTH," will be *let loose in the arena*, where he will be *attacked by two of the most celebrated and expert picadors of Mexico*, and finally *dispatched after the true Spanish method.*

Admittance $3—Tickets for sale at the door.

JOAQUIN VATRETO,
JESUS ALVAREZ, } Managers.

Mission Dolores, the place where these cruel sports were held, is a small village about two miles southwest of San Francisco, which was first settled by a couple of Roman Catholic priests during the American Revolution. It is contended by some that this was the first settlement effected by white persons in Upper California. The buildings are but one story in height, covered with tiles, and are constructed of

297

adobe or sun-dried clay. With regard to the general aspect of the place, it is distressingly shabby and gloomy. For scores of years, the inhabitants, who are a queer compound of Spanish and Indian blood, have lived here in poverty, ignorance, and inactivity. But I am digressing. What was I to do about the bull-fight? I had never witnessed such an exhibition, and consequently had a great desire to see it. It was Sunday, however, and how could I reconcile the instructions of a pious mother with an inclination so much at variance with the divine command? Well, without entering into any thing like a defense of my determination, suffice it to say that I made up my mind to go, and went. Anxious, however, to moderate or diminish the sin as much as possible, I determined to hear a sermon first, and go to the bull-fight afterwards. For the sake of somewhat condensing the events of the day, I concluded to leave the city immediately and repair to the Mission, there to attend an antique Catholic church, which has been built nearly three-quarters of a century.

Starting off with this view, I arrived within hearing of the priests' voices about the time they began to chant the service, and on entering the rickety old church,

much to my gratification I learned that it
was an extraordinary occasion with them,
and that a deal of unusual display might be
expected. The rite or ceremony of high
mass was to be performed. Monks and friars
from the monasteries of Mexico were in
attendance; and the church was thronged
with a large and heterogeneous crowd.

Four o'clock, the hour appointed for the
fight between the bear and the bull, having
arrived, a few taps by the drummer and
some popular airs played by the other
musicians announced that the amphitheater,
which fronted the church and stood but a
few yards from it, was open for the reception of those who desired admission. I
made my way to the ticket office, and handed
three dollars to the collector, who placed in
my hand a voucher, which gained me access
to an eligible seat within the inclosure. I
found myself among the first who entered;
and as it was some time before the whole
audience assembled, I had ample opportunity to scan the characters who composed
it and to examine the arrangement and
disposition of things around me.

The seats were very properly elevated so
high above the arena that no danger was
likely to result from the furious animals;
and I suppose five thousand persons could

have been conveniently accommodated, though only about three-fourths of that number were present. Among the auditory, I noticed many Spanish maids and matrons, who manifested as much enthusiasm and delight in anticipation of what was to follow as the most enthusiastic sportsman on the ground. Crying children, too, in the arms of self-satisfied and admiring mothers, were there, full of noise and mischief, and a nuisance, as they always are, in theaters and churches, to all sober-minded people. Of men, there were all sizes, colors, and classes, such as California, and California alone, can bring together. There was but one, however, who attracted my particular attention on this occasion. I had no recollection of having ever seen him before that day. He sat a few feet from me on my left. There was nothing uncommon about his form or features. The expression of his countenance was neither intellectual nor amiable. His acquirements and attainments were doubtless limited, for he demeaned himself rudely, and exhibited but little dignity of manner. It was the strange metamorphosis he had undergone since the morning which won for him my special observation. Only four hours had elapsed since I saw him officiating at the altar and feasting upon a substance which he believed to be the actual flesh and blood of Jesus Christ, who died more than eighteen hundred years ago! In the forenoon of the Lord's day he took upon himself the character of God's vicegerent, invested himself with sacerdotal robes, assumed a sanctified visage, and discharged the sacred duties of his office. In the afternoon of the same Sabbath he doffed his holy orders, sanctioned merciless diversions, mingled on terms of equality with gamblers and desperadoes, and held himself in readiness to exclaim Bravo! at the finale of a bull-fight.

By this time the whooping, shouting, and stamping of the spectators attested that they were eager and restless to behold the brutal combat; and an overture by a full brass band, which had been chartered for the occasion, gave them assurance that their wishes would soon be complied with. The music ceased; the trap-door of the bull's cage was raised, and Hercules, huge, brawny, and wild, leaped into the center of the inclosed arena, shaking his head, switching his tail, and surveying the audience with a savage stare that would have intimidated the stoutest hearts, had he not been strongly barred below them. His eyes glistened with defiance, and he seemed to crave nothing so much as an enemy upon which he might wreak his vengeance. He contorted his body, lashed his back, sniffed, snorted, pawed, bellowed, and otherwise behaved so frantically that I was fearful he could not contain himself until his antagonist was prepared. Just then, two picadors—Mexicans on horseback—entered the arena, with lassos in hand. Taurus welcomed them with an attitude of attack, and was about to rush upon one of their horses with the force of a battering-ram, when, with most commendable dexterity, the picador who was farthest off lassoed him by the horns, and foiled him in his mad design. As quick as thought, the horseman from whom the bull's attention had been diverted threw his lasso around his horns also; and in this way they brought him to a stand midway between them. A third person, a footman, now ran in, and seizing his tail, twisted it until he fell flat on his side; when, by the help of an additional assistant, the end of a long log-chain was fastened to his right hind leg. In this prostrated condition he was kept until the other end of the chain was secured to the left fore leg of the bear, as we shall now describe.

Running a pair of large clasping-tongs under Bruin's trap-door, which was lifted

just enough for the purpose, they grasped
his foot, pulled it out, and held it firmly,
while one of the party bound the opposite
end of the chain fast to his leg with thongs.
This done, they hoisted the trap-door sufficiently high to admit of his egress, when
out stalked Trojan, apparently too proud
and disdainful to vouchsafe a glance upon
surrounding objects. He was a stalwart,
lusty-looking animal, the largest grizzly
bear I had ever seen, weighing full fourteen
hundred pounds. It was said that he was
an adept in conflicts of this nature, as he
then enjoyed the honorable reputation of
having delivered three bulls from the vicis-
situdes of this life. It is probable, however,
that his previous victories had flushed and
inspired him with an unwarrantable degree
of confidence; for he seemed to regard the
bull more as a thing to be despised than as
an equal or dangerous rival. Though he
gave vent to a few ferocious growls, it was
evident that he felt more inclination to resist an attack than to make one. With the
bull, the case was very different; he was of a
pugnacious disposition, and had become
feverish for a foe. Now he had one. An
adversary of gigantic proportions and great
prowess stood before him; and as soon as
he spied him he moved backward the entire

length of the chain, which jerked the bear's foot and made him rend the air with a most fearful howl that served but the more to incense the bull. Shaking his head maliciously, casting it down and throwing up his tail, he plunged at the bear with a force and fury that were irresistible. The collision was terrible, completely overthrowing his ponderous enemy and laying him flat on his back. Both were injured, but neither was conquered; both mutually recoiled to prepare again to strike for victory. With eyes gleaming with fire, and full of resolution, the bull strode proudly over his prostrate enemy and placed himself in position to make a second attack. But now the bear was prepared to receive him; he had recovered his feet wild with rage, and he then appeared to beckon to the bull to meet him without delay. The bull needed no challenge; he was, if possible, more impetuous than the bear, and did not lose any more time than it required to measure the length of the chain. Again with unabated fierceness he darted at the bear and, as before, struck him with an impetus that seemed to have been borrowed from Jove's own thunderbolt; as he came in contact with the bear, that amiable animal grappled him by the neck, and squeezed him so hard that he could scarcely save himself from suffocation. The bull now found himself in a decidedly uncomfortable situation; the bear had him as he wanted him. Powerful as he was, he could not break loose from Bruin. A vice could not have held him more firmly. The strong arms of the bear hugged him in a ruthless and desperate embrace. It was a stirring sight to see these infuriated and muscular antagonists struggling to take each other's life. It was enough to make a heathen generalissimo shudder to look at them. How ought it to have been, then, with enlightened civilians? This question I shall not answer; it was easy enough to see how it was with the Spanish ladies—they laughed, cheered, encored, clapped their hands, waved their handkerchiefs, and made every other sign which was characteristic of pleasure and delight. The contending brutes still strove together. Hercules quaked under the torturing hugs of Trojan. Trojan howled under the violent and painful perforations of Hercules. But the bear did not rely alone upon the efficacy of his arms; his massive jaws and formidable teeth were brought into service, and with them he inflicted deep wounds in his rival's flesh. He seized the bull between the ears and nostrils, and crushed the bones with such force that we could distinctly hear them crack! Nor were the stunning butts of the bull his only means of defense; his horns had been sharpened expressly for the occasion, and with these he lacerated the bear most frightfully. It was a mighty contest—a desperate struggle for victory!

Finally, however, fatigued, exhausted, writhing with pain and weltering in sweat and gore, they waived the quarrel and separated, as if by mutual consent. Neither was subdued; yet both felt a desire to suspend, for a time at least, all further hostilities. The bull, now exhausted and panting, cast a pacific glance towards the bear and seemed to sue for an armistice; the bear, bleeding and languid after his furious contest, raised his eyes to the bull and seemed to assent to the proposition. But, alas! man, cruel man, more brutal than the brutes themselves, would not permit them to carry out their pacific intentions. The two attendants or managers, Ignacio and Gomez, stepped up behind them, goading them with spears till they again rushed upon each other and fought with renewed desperation. During this scuffle the bull shattered the lower jaw of the bear and we could see the shivered bones dangling from their bloody recesses! Oh, heaven! what a horrible sight. How the blood curdled in my veins. Pish! what a timid fellow I am to allow myself to be agitated by such a trifle as this! Shall I tremble at what the ladies applaud? Forbid it, Mars! I'll be as spirited as they. But, to wind up this part of our story, neither the bear nor the bull could stand any longer—their limbs refused to support their bodies; they had worried and lacerated each other so much that their strength had completely failed, and they dropped upon the earth, gasping as if in the last agony. While in this helpless condition the chain was removed from their feet, horses were hitched to them, and they were dragged without the arena, there to end their miseries in death.

The second act of the afternoon's entertainment was now to be performed. It would be unnecessary, and painful to the feelings of sensitive readers, to dwell long upon this murderous sport. It was a mere repetition in another form of the disgusting horrors of that which preceded it. Fully satiated with the barbarities I had already witnessed, I am not sure that I should have staid to see any more, had it not been for the peculiar sensations which the cognomen of one of the actors awakened within me. By reference to the advertisement, it will be per-ceived that the two managers of this part of the proceedings were Joaquin Vatreto and Jesus Alvarez. The latter name sounded strangely in my ears. It occurred to me that it was peculiarly out of place in its present connection. What! Jesus at a bull-fight on Sunday, and not only at it, but one of the prime movers and abettors in it!

But now to the fight. All things being ready, the great bull, Behemoth, was freed from restraint and sprang with frantic bounds into the midst of the arena. He bore a suitable appellation, for he was a monster in size and formidable in courage. Two picadors, Joaquin Vatreto and Jesus Alvarez, mounted on fiery steeds, with swords in hand, now entered and confronted him. Behemoth looked upon this sudden invasion as an intolerable insult. His territory was already too limited for so powerful a monarch as he considered himself, and he could not think of dividing it with others. The sight of these unceremonious intruders inflamed him with such rancor that he could no longer restrain himself; but lowering his head and tossing his tail aloft, he rushed furiously at them. They evaded his charge. The horses were well trained and seemed to enjoy the sport, and to pride themselves upon their adroit ma-

neuvers. But both they and their riders
had enough to do to evade the fury of the
enraged brute. Each successive bout became more animated and fierce. The foil-
ing of the bull's purposes only exasperated
him the more. There was not room enough
in his capacious body to contain his effer-
vescing wrath. The foam which he spurted
from his mouth and nose fell upon the
earth like enormous flakes of snow. Faster
and faster, and with truer aim, he charged
his foes. At last one of the horses, in attempting to wheel or turn suddenly round,
stumbled, and the bull, taking advantage of
the event, gored him so desperately in the
abdomen that a part of his entrails pro-
truded from the wounds and trailed almost
upon the ground! This was truly a distressing scene. I could have wept for the poor,
innocent charger, but in this case tears were
of no avail.

One of the picadors now alighted and engaged the attention of the bull, while the
other led the two horses outside the inclosure. When this was done a man on foot,
called a matador, dressed in close-fitting,
fantastic garments, with a heavy sword in
his right hand and a small red flag in his
left, entered the arena and bowed first to
the bull and then to the audience. It was

now a matter of life and death between the
bull and the matador. One or the other, or
both, must die. If the bull did not kill the
man, the man would kill the bull; if the man
killed the bull, the man was to live, but if
the bull killed the man, the bull was to die;
so that death was sure to overtake the bull
in any event. The action commenced, and
waxed hotter and hotter every moment,
and it was only by uncommon skill and
agility that the matador could shun the
frenzied charges of the bull. Had it not been
for the flag which he carried in his hand, and
which enabled him to deceive his antagonist
by seeming to hold it directly before him,
when in reality he inclined it to the right or
to the left, as his safety dictated, the bull
would unquestionably have dashed his
brains out, thrown him over his head, or
gored him to death. Nothing could have
irritated or vexed the bull more than did
the sight of this red flag, and he made all
his assaults upon it, supposing, no doubt,
that he would strike the mischief behind it,
but the agile matador always took special
care to spring aside and save himself from
the deadly stroke. After tormenting, teas-
ing, and chafing him for about a quarter of
an hour in this way, six keen javelins or
darts, with miniature flags attached, were

handed to the matador, who ventured to face the bull, and never quit him until he had planted them all in his shoulders, three in each. Stung to madness, the animal reared, rolled, and plunged in the most frightful manner. Soon, however, he was on his feet again, pursuing his persecutor with renewed zeal.

The fates, however, were against him. He could not comprehend, and consequently could not foil the crafty designs of his adversary, who completely deceived him with the flag. Night was now coming on, and it being time to close the performance, the matador, placing himself in a pompous attitude near the south side of the arena, challenged Behemoth to the last and decisive engagement by waving the flag briskly before him. The bull, exasperated beyond description, needed no additional incentive to urge him to meet the enemy. With a force apparently equal to that of a rhinoceros, and with the celerity of a reindeer, he rushed at the matador, who, stepping just sufficiently to the left to avoid him, thrust the sword into his breast up to the hilt. The matador, leaving this sword buried in the bull's body, now laid hold of another which was on hand for the purpose, and stabbed him three times in a more

311

vital part, when down he fell at his victor's feet, dead. Then jumping upon the carcass of his slain rival, the matador brandished his sword, doffed his hat, bowed his compliments, and retired, amid the deafening plaudits of a wolfish audience.

III: *Sundays and Holidays*[39]

FROM OUR LOG CABIN, Indian Bar,
January 27, 1852.

I wish that it were possible, dear M., to give you an idea of the perfect Saturnalia which has been held upon the river for the last three weeks without at the same time causing you to think *too* severely of our good Mountains. In truth, it requires not only a large intellect, but a large heart, to judge with becoming charity of the peculiar temptations of riches. A more generous, hospitable, intelligent, and industrious people than the inhabitants of the half-dozen Bars—of which Rich Bar is the nucleus— never existed; for you know how proverbially wearing it is to the nerves of manhood to be entirely without either occupation or amusement; and that has been pre-eminently the case during the present month.

Imagine a company of enterprising and excitable young men, settled upon a sandy

[39] Reprinted from Dame Shirley's Letters, Number 12.

level about as large as a poor widow's
potato patch, walled in by sky-kissing hills
—absolutely compelled to remain, on account of the weather, which has vetoed in-
definitely their Exodus—with no place to
ride or drive, even if they had the necessary
vehicles and quadrupeds,—with no newspapers nor politics to interest them,—deprived of all books but a few dog-eared
novels of the poorest class,—churches, lec-
tures, lyceums, theaters and (most unkindest
cut of all!) pretty girls, having become to
these unhappy men mere myths,—without
one of the thousand ways of passing time
peculiar to civilization,—most of them living in damp, gloomy cabins, where Heaven's
dear light can enter only by the door,—
and when you add to all these disagreeables
the fact that, during the never-to-be-forgot-
ten month the most remorseless, persever-
ing rain which ever set itself to work to
drive humanity mad has been pouring doggedly down, sweeping away bridges, lying
in uncomfortable puddles about nearly all
the habitations, wickedly insinuating itself
beneath un-umbrella-protected shirt-col-
lars, generously treating to a shower-bath
and the rheumatism sleeping bipeds who did
not happen to have an India-rubber blanket,
—and, to crown all, rendering mining utterly

impossible,—you cannot wonder that even the most moral should have become somewhat reckless.

The Saturnalia commenced on Christmas evening at the Humboldt, which on that very day, had passed into the hands of new proprietors. The most gorgeous preparations were made for celebrating the *two* events. The bar was re-trimmed with red calico, the bowling alley had a new lining of the coarsest and whitest cotton cloth, and the broken lampshades were replaced by whole ones. All day long patient mules could be seen descending the hill, bending beneath casks of brandy and baskets of champagne, and, for the first time in the history of that celebrated building the floor (wonderful to relate, it has a floor), was washed, at a lavish expenditure of some fifty pails of water, the using up of one entire broom, and the melting away of sundry bars of the best yellow soap; after which, I am told that the enterprising and benevolent individuals who had undertaken the Herculean task succeeded in washing the boards through the hopeless load of dirt which had accumulated upon them during the summer and autumn. All these interesting particulars were communicated to me by Ned, when he brought up dinner. That distinguished individual himself was in his element, and in a most intense state of perspiration and excitement at the same time.

About dark we were startled by the loudest hurrahs, which arose at the sight of an army of India-rubber coats (the rain was falling in riversfull) each one enshrouding a Rich Barian, which was rapidly descending the hill. This troop was headed by the General, who—lucky man that he is—waved on high, instead of a banner, a live lantern, actually composed of tin and window-glass, and evidently intended by its maker to act in no capacity but that *of* a lantern! The General is the largest and tallest and—with one exception, I think—the oldest man upon the river. He is about fifty, I should fancy, and wears a snow-white beard of such immense dimensions, in both length and thickness, that any elderly Turk would expire with envy at the mere sight of it. Don't imagine that he is a reveler; by no means; the gay crowd followed him for the same reason that the king followed Madame Blaize, "because he went before."

At nine o'clock in the evening they had an oyster and champagne supper in the Humboldt, which was very gay with toasts, songs, speeches, etc. I believe that the company danced all night; at any rate they were dancing when I went to sleep and they were dancing when I woke the next morning. The revel was kept up in this mad way for three days, growing wilder every hour. Some never slept at all during that time. On the fourth day they got past dancing, and, lying in drunken heaps about the bar-room, commenced a most unearthly howling;—some barked like dogs, some roared like bulls, and others hissed like serpents and geese. Many were too far gone to imitate anything but their own animalized selves. The scene, from the description I have had of it, must have been a complete illustration of the fable of Circe and her fearful transformations. Some of these bacchanals were among the most respectable and respected men upon the river. Many of them had resided here for more than a year, and had never been seen intoxicated before. It seemed as if they were seized with a reckless mania for pouring down liquor, which, as I said above, everything conspired to foster and increase.

Of course there were some who kept themselves aloof from these excesses; but they were few, and were not allowed to enjoy their sobriety in peace. The revelers formed themselves into a mock vigilance committee and when one of these unfortunates appeared outside, a constable, followed by those who were able to keep their legs, brought him before the Court, where he was tried on some amusing charge and sentenced to treat the crowd. The prisoners had generally the good sense to submit cheerfully to their fate.

Towards the latter part of the week, people were compelled to be a little more quiet from sheer exhaustion; but on New Year's Day, when there was a grand dinner at Rich Bar, the excitement broke out, if possible, worse than ever. The same scenes in a more or less aggravated form, in proportion as the strength of the actors held out, were repeated at Smith's Bar and The Junction.

The Sabbath[40] in California is kept, when kept at all, as a day of hilarity and bacchanalian sports, rather than as a season of holy meditation or religious devotion. Horse-racing, cock-fighting, cony-hunting, card-playing, theatrical performances, and other elegant amusements are freely engaged in on this day. If I remember correctly, it was about two months after my arrival in the

[40] Reprinted from Helper, *The Land of Gold*, Chapter IX.

land of gold and misery that I had the misfortune to become acquainted with a renegade down-east Congregationalist preacher, who invited me to accompany him on the following Sunday in a deer chase. Throughout the country and in the mines shooting-matches and bear-hunting afford pleasant pastimes; gambling is also practiced to a considerable extent, though not so much as on other days. But we shall probably learn more of the manner in which Sunday is spent if we confine our attention to one of the larger cities, San Francisco, for example. Here regattas, duels and prize fights are favorite diversions; and the Lord's day seldom passes without witnessing one or the other, or both. Here, too, for a long time gaming was licensed on Sundays, as it is yet on week days; but recently the city fathers have passed an ordinance prohibiting the desecration, and I believe their example has been followed by three or four of the other cities. There is no state law upon the subject.

Connected with a tippling house on the corner of Washington and Montgomery streets there is one of the finest billiard saloons in the United States. It is very large and magnificently decorated, has twelve tables, and is furnished, I am informed, at a cost of twenty-five thousand dollars. To this place hundreds of infatuated men betake themselves every Sunday; and it is an unusual thing, at any time, to find one of the tables unoccupied. Every day of the week, from breakfast time in the morning till twelve o'clock at night this saloon, like many others of a like kind, is thronged; but the crowds are particularly large on Sunday, because people have more leisure on that day. Though, in this particular place, they are not allowed to gamble publicly on the Sabbath, they lose and win as much money in the way of secret wagers as they do openly on any other day.

What can we expect but an abuse of the Sabbath when we take into account the contrariety of characters, tastes, dispositions, and religions here huddled together? When we scrutinize society we find that some of its members, the Chinese and other pagans for instance, know nothing at all of our system or division of time and that they are, therefore, absolutely ignorant of the meaning of the word Sunday. There is no unity of thought, feeling, or sentiment here; no oneness of purpose, policy, or action. There is no common interest; every man is for himself, and himself alone. Society is composed of elements too varied and dissimilar; it is a heterogeneous assemblage of rivals and competitors who know no sympathy and recognize no principle save that of personal profit and individual emolument. Nearly all colors and qualities of mankind are congregated here. The great human family is, as it were, sampled and its specimens formed into one society, each communicating to the other his own peculiar habits and each contending for the same object—the acquisition of gold. It is manifest, therefore, that there can be but little concert or harmony of action. Masquerade balls, cotillion parties, and jig dances fill up the list of Sunday diversions. On Pacific Street alone, the most notoriously profligate thoroughfare in the City, there are from twelve to fifteen dance houses in which the terpsichorean art is practiced every night during the week, but usually with greater zest and animation on Sunday nights. These fandangos are principally under the superintendence or management of Mexican girls, of whom there is no small number in San Francisco and other cities of the State. Before I ever saw any of the Mexican ladies I had heard the most glowing descriptions of their ravishing beauty; but I must either discredit the accounts or else conclude that my ideas of female beauty are very imperfect, for I have never yet beheld one of them who, according to my standard of good looks, was really beautiful. Their pumpkin hues and slovenly deportment could never awaken any admiration in me, even in California.

Bonnets among them are quite unknown. Half the time they go bare-headed through the streets and to church, just as they do about their premises; but most of them have a long, narrow shawl, which is sometimes worn over the head, as well as the shoulders. This shawl is, in fact, an almost indispensable article of apparel, especially with the better classes, who never appear in a public place, whether in winter or summer, without it. They wrap it around their face, head, and shoulders so ingeniously that spectators can not obtain a glimpse of any part of their features save the forehead, eyes, and nose; the mouth, chin, and cheeks are cautiously concealed. There is a gross lack of consistency among these women. Notwithstanding they engage in the lowest debaucheries throughout the week, they are strict attendants of the Catholic church; and dozens of them may be seen any Sunday on their way to matins, mass, or vespers, clad in habiliments of the greatest possible variety. If they can only get one fine, fashionable garment they think it makes amends for the bad material and ill shape of all the others. Nor are they particular to have their whole person clothed at the same time. I don't think I have ever seen one of them fully attired in my life; something was always wanting. Sometimes they may be seen promenading the streets robed in the richest silks that were ever woven in Chinese looms, but when you gaze down at their lower extremities you discover them stockingless, their feet thrust into a pair of coarse slippers which expose to view a pair of rusty heels that look as if no ablution had been performed upon them for at least three moons. The Mexicans, however, in most cases are fond of aquatic exercises; and they have several bathing establishments in San Francisco for the accommodation of the public (at one dollar per head for each bath) as well as for their own convenience and gratification. Unless I have been misinformed it is a custom with the proprietors, when a gentleman retires to take his bath, to dispatch a female servant to his room to scour and scrub him off! As I resided near an American bath-house I always patronized it in preference, and did not acquaint myself with Mexican usages in this respect.

Lately, however, women of pure and lofty characters have emigrated to California, and, since their arrival there has been a gradual and steady improvement of morals among the people and the Sabbath is now much better observed than it used to be. Soon after their arrival schools and churches began to spring up and social circles were formed; refinement dawned upon a debauched and reckless community, decorum took the place of obscenity; kind and gentle words were heard to fall from the lips of those who before had been accustomed to taint every phrase with an oath; and smiles displayed themselves upon countenances to which they had long been strangers. Woman accomplished all this, and we should be ungrateful reprobates indeed if we did not honor, esteem, and love her for it. Had I received no other benefit from my trip to California than the knowledge I have gained, inadequate as it may be, of woman's many virtues and perfections, I should account myself well repaid; and I thank heaven that I was induced to embark in an enterprise which resulted in such a collateral remuneration. This I am constrained to say because I fear I should never have had a full appreciation of her merits had I not witnessed her happy influence in this benighted land.

It was only after leaving a home where her constant presence, her soothing and animating society, appeared as a matter of course, and removing to a sphere where she had a better opportunity of displaying her power, that I could estimate her real worth.

With the generous assistance and co-operation of the gentler sex the various religious denominations have succeeded in establishing for themselves suitable places of worship in most of the cities and larger towns throughout the State. San Francisco now contains fourteen churches, two of which are Presbyterian, two Congregational, one Unitarian, three Methodist, two Baptist, two Episcopal, and two Roman Catholic. The Swedenborgians, Universalists, Mormons, and sundry minor sects occasionally hold service in public halls; and, if I recollect aright, the Jews have two synagogues. There is also a pagan temple where the Chinese pay their adorations to Buddha, or to some other imaginary deity, whenever they experience a religious emotion.

Chapter 11*

I: *Articles of Agreement with the California
Company—Mar. 1849*

WE the Subscribers, of Madison Dane
County and State of Wisconsin, do
hereby form ourselves into a company for the purpose of going to California,
and for the mutual benefit and protection
of each other do adopt the following Laws &
Regulations, to wit—

Article I

This company shall consist of five or
more persons, and shall be known as the
Madison Wisconsin Mining Company. The
mode of conveyance shall be by mule and
wagon, and not more than five men to one
team of six mules.

Article II

The officers to consist of a Treasurer and
Secretary. The duty of the Treasurer to

*For the editor's introductory note to this chapter,
see Appendix, pages 368–72.

keep the money and common property belonging to the Company that may be paid into his hands from time to time, and pay the same out as the majority of the Company may direct, and report at any time the state of the funds, and keep a true and accurate account of the same. To direct said Company on the journey to California. It shall be the duty of the Secretary to take charge of and keep all of the records and papers belonging to said Company, and keep an account of the proceedings and transactions of the Company.

Article III

The officers shall be elected by ballot a majority necessary to a choice, and shall hold their offices for six months unless sickness or disability to discharge the duties of said office, in which case the Company may at any time elect another.

Article IV

The officers shall be strictly obeyed while in office by the Company. Each member of said Company to own an equal interest in the waggon mules & all the equipage necessary for the expedition, and have a certificate of the treasurer to that effect, filed with the Secretary.

Article V

Each member shall equip himself with a good rifle, pistol, and knife and one small axe or hatchet, which are to be his own private property, together with his clothing.

Article VI

Each member shall be provided with fifty dollars in gold, to be carried about his person, to provide against contingencies.

Article VII

No member is to lose anything on account of sickness or disability, but is to receive an equal proportion of the proceeds of said Company, and is to receive good care and attention during such sickness or disability.

Article VIII

Any member may be expelled from said Company on account of idleness by a two-thirds vote of said Company, but shall receive his portion of the avails up to that time.

Article IX

In case of the death of any member of said Company, the remaining Company shall be jointly bound to his heirs or assigns for his proportion to that time and shall forthwith transmit an account of the same to them by mail, signed by the officers.

Article X

No intoxicating drink shall be used by the Company except for medicinal purposes and no gambling is to be allowed.

Article XI

For the mutual benefit and protection of each to each, the pledge of our *Sacred Honors* not to leave a member in case of sickness or *danger of any kind* unless there is greater probability of losing our own lives than of saving his.

Article XII

These By Laws may be amended by two-thirds of the members at any time.

Signed	Abiel Easter Brooks	SS
	Peter Kavinaugh	SS
	James S. E. Brooks	SS
	S. R. Porterfield	SS
	Caleb E. Brooks	SS

Having arrived at the Gold mines in California we do mutually agree that the foregoing By Laws & Constitution of the Madison Mining Company is hereby canceled and the Co-partnership dissolved in witness whereof we set our hand and seal—

A. E. Brooks	S. R. Porterfield
Caleb E. Brooks	James S. E. Brooks
Peter Cavenaugh	

II: *Inventory of Equipment of Madison Wisconsin Mining Company*

Madison Wis. March 12, 1849.

At a meeting of the Madison Wisconsin Mining Company held pursuant to the Articles of Agreement, A. E. Brooks was chosen Treasurer and S. R. Porterfield Secy. The following property is Company property purchased up to this date.

6 mules (and expense going for them)	$480.50
1 Waggon and Cover	75.00
1 tent	10.00
Chains and Stretchers	6.70
Linch pins, Staples and hammer	5.00
1 Pair whiffletrees	3.00
Open rings	.50
4 Chains	2.50
1 saw	2.00
1 Chisel 75 file 50	1.25
1 Gross screws, gimlets & file	1.13
Ginger and spoons	.85
3 lines 45 Coffeepot 50	.95
Medicine Chest	20.57
Lumber and decking waggon	8.00
Pad-lock	1.45
2 Canteens	1.00

2 lb nails 20.	4 prs hames 3.00............ $	3.20
2 Brass kettles 2.25	1 Tin trunk 1.00......	3.25
1 Tin pan 31	2 augurs 1.13..............	1.44
2 Augurs 2.25	1 punch.................	3.00
5 Trace Chains.....................		2.50
Harness not purchased with Mules.........		30.00
1 Framing square......................		2.00
1 Hoe...............................		.50
1 Saddle and bridle....................		5.00
1 Scythe and Sneath...................		2.00
2 Bushels dried Apples.................		3.00
1 Drum of Figs.......................		1.60
7 Bags.............................		4.20
Keeping mules seven days..............		7.00
Blacksmiths bill......................		11.34

$703.43

The above is the amount up to this date
being for each share, One hundred and
forty dollars and sixty-nine cents

S N Porterfield   Sec.

The respective shares up to this time are
all paid in Madison March 12 1849

Abiel Easter Brooks   Treas.

III: *A Case of Theft* [41]

Sept 27 [1850] spent the forenoon repairing the upper dam and improvements.
Kept on mining until twilight had set in,

[41] From the diary of *Abiel Easter Brooks*. The pages
following the ones here printed, which presumably related the outcome of this trial, were missing when the
diary was copied.

when we returned to our several quarters. Our treasurer Mr Van Bergen carrying the proceeds of our afternoon's work in a common washing pan, that contained about two hundred & fifty dollars, he set it on the roof over the door to dry. It being nearly dark and supper to get, and all being tired and wet to the hips, the gold was neglected and left standing until one after another—after supper was over—had taken a turn at the fire, a few whiffs at the pipe, when we all retired, the treasurer going to bed last, at which time he said he looked over the door and saw the gold sitting there, and supposed it would be safe until morning. But such was not the case, for after breakfast when all were heading for the works, the clerk says to the treasurer "what was done with the gold last night, and where is the pan that contained it," Casting his eyes towards the spot where he set it, he replied some one has taken it away for I set it right up here over the door. Inquiry was immediately instituted among all hands, and each told his own story or what he knew about it, where they severally had been from the time of leaving the works until the present time. There was but one opinion as to who was the guilty man, but to recover the gold was quite another thing, than to find out who had stolen it. We determined, however, to go to work and repair the loss by digging more, and at noon would call a Court of Inquest and proceed with the case according to established usages. Accordingly at noon there was a Justice appointed whose name was John McCauley of Mansfield, Ohio the names to be presented were Ezra Bradner, E. O. McGee, A. E Brooks, Jas. S Brooks, Joseph Howrie, Cyrus McClintock, H McGee, Reuben Reynolds, C. R. Gardner—making ten in all. While the Court was putting up a suitable seat for himself, utilizing old kegs boxes and boards for seats, one of the party stepped aside, and gave James the wink to follow him, they went a few rods from the house when presently I went in the same direction James beckoned me to come to them and found the man's face suffused with tears. He said to me, "I have been talking to James about this inquiry, and he thinks you can stop it if you will, and if you will and save me and my family from awful disgrace and sorrow, I would sooner give $2,000 than have it known at home. This was the very vein to strike, if you want to strike the most vulnerable place in man's heart, talk of wife & children & home & friends. If that fails give him up. I replied to him by saying I was sorry to see him in such a plight, above all men present, for I placed great confidence in him and had spoken well of him to others, that this transaction was calculated to injure some for a long time, and it was only right that the offender should be known in order to clear the innocent. He replied that "he had told James all that he had to say about it and me and mine are at your mercy" to which I replied "go down to the river & wash up and appear as cheerful as possible, and I will befriend you, but do not confess any more to me, but keep silent. Here let me remark that we had one man in the crowd that was a lazy fellow and a good deal given to talk. I had dismissed him once and one of the partners had hired him again, in a case of necessity. According to previous notice all met around the Justice to prove himself clear of the charges proposed against him as his turn should come. The court proceeded in regular order—until the lazy man was put upon the stand. When he proved himself to have been in the Company of some of his mess from the time of leaving the works the night previous until the discovery that the gold was taken this morning except about ten minutes, which he could show to the satisfaction of all, that he was not occupied in taking the gold, then he stood aside. So one after another was tried until the guilty man took the stand, told his story and offered such proof as he thought would not injure his case. The Judge at my suggestion took until the next day to render a verdict when all hands returned to work, eight of the ten feeling the greatest assurance that some poor fellow would have to take a few lashes on the bare pelt and no mistake. This evening the gold was cared for in good earnest.

IV: *Regulations of Jacksonville placer Camp* [42]

Article I.

The officers of this district shall consist of an alcalde and sheriff, to be elected in the usual manner by the people, and continue in office at the pleasure of the electors.

Article II.

In case of the absence or disability of the sheriff, the alcalde shall have power to appoint a deputy.

Article III.

Civil cases may be tried by the alcalde, if the parties desire it; otherwise they shall be tried by a jury.

[42] Reprinted from Daniel B. Woods, *Sixteen Months at the Gold Diggings.*

Article IV.

All criminal cases shall be tried by a jury of eight American citizens, unless the accused should desire a jury of twelve persons, who shall be regularly summoned by the sheriff, and sworn by the alcalde, and shall try the case according to the evidence.

Article V.

In the administration of law, both civil and criminal, the rule of practice shall conform, as near as possible, to that of the United States, but the forms and customs of no particular state shall be required or adopted.

Article VI.

Each individual locating a lot for the purpose of mining, shall be entitled to twelve feet of ground in width, running back to the hill or mountain, and forward to the center of the river or creek, or across a gulch or ravine (except in cases hereinafter provided for); lots commencing in all cases at low-water mark, and running at right angles with the stream where they are located.

Article VII.

In cases where lots are located according to Article VI., and the parties holding them are prevented by the water from working the same, they may be represented by a pick, shovel, or bar, until in a condition to be worked; but should the tool or tools aforesaid be stolen or removed, it shall not dispossess those who located it, provided he or they can prove that they were left as required; and said location shall not remain unworked longer than one week, if in condition to be worked, otherwise it shall be considered as abandoned by those who located it (except in cases of sickness).

Article VIII.

No man or party of men shall be permitted to hold two locations, in a condition to be worked, at the same time.

Article IX.

No party shall be permitted to throw dirt, stones, or other obstructions upon located ground adjoining them.

Article X.

Should a company of men desire to turn the course of a river or stream for the purpose of mining, they may do so (provided it does not interfere with those working below them), and hold and work all the ground so drained; but lots located within said ground shall be permitted to be worked by their owners, so far as they could have been worked without the turning of the river or stream; and this shall not be construed to affect the rights and privileges heretofore guaranteed, or prevent redress by suit at law.

Article XI.

No person coming direct from a foreign country shall be permitted to locate or work any lot within the jurisdiction of this encampment.

Article XII.

Any person who shall steal a mule, or other animal of draught or burden, or shall enter a tent or dwelling, and steal therefrom gold dust, money, provisions, goods, or other articles, amounting in value to one hundred dollars or over, shall, on conviction thereof, be considered guilty of felony, and suffer death by hanging. Any aider or abettor therein shall be punished in like manner.

Article XIII.

Should any person willfully, maliciously, and premeditatedly take the life of another, on conviction of the murder, he shall suffer death by hanging.

Article XIV.

Any person convicted of stealing tools, clothing, or other articles, of less value than one hundred dollars, shall be punished and disgraced by having his head and eye-brows close shaved, and shall leave the encampment within twenty-four hours.

Article XV.

The fee of the alcalde for issuing a writ or search-warrant, taking an attestation, giving a certificate, or any other instrument of writing, shall be five dollars; for each witness he may swear, two dollars; and one ounce of gold dust for each and every case tried before him.

The fee of the sheriff in each case shall be one ounce of gold dust, and a like sum for each succeeding day employed in the same case.

The fee of the jury shall be to each juror half an ounce in each case.

A witness shall be entitled to four dollars in each case.

Article XVI.

Whenever a criminal convict is unable to pay the costs of the case, the alcalde, sheriff, jurors, and witnesses shall render their services free of remuneration.

Article XVII.

In case of the death of a resident of this encampment, the alcalde shall take charge of his effects, and dispose of them for the benefit of his relatives or friends, unless the deceased otherwise desire it.

Article XVIII.

All former acts and laws are hereby repealed, and made null and void, except where they conflict with claims guaranteed under said laws.

ABNER PITTS, JR., Sec'y.

Jacksonville, Jan. 20, 1850

V: *Narrative of Professor John B. Parkinson* [43]

There is said to have been a short time in California, immediately following the discovery of gold, when crime in the mines was almost absolutely unknown—when bags of "gold-dust" were left unguarded in tents and cabins while the owners were at work on their claims. This state of things was partly due to the rich surface deposits which were then rapidly discovered and to the consequent feeling that the supply was practically inexhaustible. It was easier

[43] Reprinted from *Wisconsin Magazine of History*, December, 1921.

to earn money than to steal it, and infinitely safer too. Miners at that time pitched their tents close together in clumps of chaparral and manzanita. The bonds of fellowship were strong and sincere. Leeches and parasites had not yet fastened upon the community. The wretch who could steal from his comrades in those busy, friendly camps was hopelessly hardened. An old pioneer speaking of these very early mining days once said: "In 1848 a man could go into a miner's cabin, cut a slice of bacon, cook a meal, roll up in a blanket and go to sleep, certain to be welcomed kindly when the owner returned." This Arcadian era lasted much longer, too, in the Northern mines, where the American element more largely predominated. When disturbances and conflicts did set in, their coming was often attributed to the influence of the lawyers. "We needed no law," many an old miner would say, "until the lawyers came"—a curious but very common confusion of ideas. As a matter of fact, there were plenty of lawyers all the time working as quiet citizens in the gulches, only waiting until there was a demand for their services. They made themselves known when wanted. Nine-tenths of the crimes and misdemeanors that appear on the docket of an ordinary criminal court were impossible in the mining camp, and a larger proportion of the ordinary civil cases were equally out of the question. The best of lawyers would have starved in such a community. But there was "law" from the beginning, and for the time and place it was the only serviceable kind. It was unwritten, simple, and went straight to the mark. And there was a court to enforce it—an assembly of freemen in open council. All who swung a pick or held a claim—boys of sixteen and men of sixty—took part in its deliberations. No more perfect democracies ever existed than these early mining camps. They had government, but its three departments were fused into one, and that one was administered directly by the people.

One of the best illustrations of the gold-miner's method of settling serious disputes occurred on Scotch Bar—a mining camp neighboring to my own, in northern California. A discovery of some very "rich gravel" or mining ground was made on this Bar, and in such a way that two equally strong parties of prospectors laid claim to it at the same time. Each group was entirely honest in believing its own claim the better one. The contestants at once began to increase their fighting numbers by enlistments from the rest of the camp, until twenty or thirty men were sworn in on each side. The ground in dispute was so situated that it was best worked in partnership, and thirty claims of the ordinary size took up all the territory in dispute. So here were two rival and resolute companies ready to begin work, and no law whatever to prevent a pitched battle.

It began to look very much like fighting. Men were asked to take sides and bring their bowies, revolvers, and shotguns. The two opposing parties took up their stations on the banks of the gulch. There was some further and very excited talk, and at last eight or ten shots were interchanged, fortunately injuring no one. By this time the blood of the contestants was fairly roused. The interests at stake were very large, and neither side proposed to yield. It now seemed that nothing could prevent a terrible hand-to-hand conflict. The next minute must precipitate it. But just at this crisis another power asserted itself—that which in every mining camp, and indeed in every pioneer Anglo-Saxon community, makes so forcibly for law and order. The very moment the first shot was fired, the camp, the neighborhood, the little community at large had taken the field. Dozens, hundreds of men who, five minutes before, were mere

spectators of the difficulty, now insisted
upon a parley, negotiated a truce, and urged
a resort to legal methods.

The moment this compromise was suggested, the combatants laid aside their weapons. They knew there was no legal authority within twenty miles, and no force,
even in the camp itself, able to keep them
from fighting. It was a victory of common
sense—a triumph of the moral principles
learned in boyhood in New England villages
and on western prairies. Men more thoroughly fearless never faced opposing weapons. But the demand for a fair trial in
open court found an answering chord in
every bosom. Both parties willingly agreed
to arbitration, but not to the ordinary arbitration of the miners' court. The matter
in dispute seemed too serious. They chose
a committee, sent it to San Francisco, had
three or four of the best lawyers to be found
there engaged for each party, and also engaged a judge of much experience in mining cases. It was a great day at Scotch Bar
when all this legal talent arrived. The
claims in dispute had meanwhile been lying
untouched by anyone, guarded by camp
opinion and by sacred pledges of honor, ever
since the day of the compact between the
rival companies.

The case was tried with all possible formality, and as scrupulously as if it had occurred within the civil jurisdiction of a district court. With a simple sense of fairness it had been agreed by the parties that the winners should pay all costs. When the verdict came, there was no compromise about it. It was squarely for one side and squarely against the other. The defeated party accepted it without a murmur. Neither then nor at any other time were they ever heard to complain.

An eyewitness, speaking of this celebrated trial, said: "The whole camp was excited over it for days and weeks. At last when the case was decided, the claim was opened by the successful party; and when they reached the bedrock and were ready to 'clean up,' we all knocked off work and came down and stood on the banks, till the ravine on both sides was lined with men. And I saw them take out gold with iron spoons and fill pans with solid gold, thousands upon thousands of dollars." On the banks of the river, with the hundreds of spectators, stood the defeated contestants, cheerful and even smiling.

In the early period, mining interests took precedence of agricultural in the entire gold-field. Law was made by the miners for the miners. Even the state courts at an early date decided that "agricultural lands though in the possession of others, may be worked for gold"—that "all persons who settle for agricultural purposes upon any mining lands, so settle at their own risk." The finest orchards and finest gardens were liable to be destroyed without remedy. Roads were washed away, houses were undermined, towns were moved to new sites, and sometimes the entire soil on which they had stood was sluiced away from grass roots to bedrock.

Down in Grass Valley, one of the rich placer regions, two men fenced in a natural meadow. They expected to cut at least two crops of hay annually, worth one hundred dollars a ton. But before a month had passed, a prospector climbed their brush fence, sunk a shaft, struck "pay gravel," and in less than twenty-four hours the whole hay ranch was staked off in claims of fifty feet square, and the ravaged proprietors never got a claim. Once grant that the highest use of the land was to yield gold, and all the rest follows.

But exceptions were sometimes as arbitrarily made and summarily enforced as the rule itself. In 1851 two miners began to sink a shaft on Main Street, in the business center of Nevada City. A sturdy merchant made complaint, but was promptly answered that there was no law to prevent anyone from digging down to "bedrock" and drifting under the street, and they proposed to try it. "Then I'll make a law to suit the case," said the merchant, himself an old ex-miner, and stepping into his store, he came out with a navy revolver and made the law and enforced it upon the spot, establishing the precedent that Main Street, at least in that city, was not mining ground.

Appendix

Appendix

Editor's Introductory Notes

Chapter 1

To California Via Cape Horn

Hinton Rowan Helper, from whose book, *The Land of Gold: Reality Versus Fiction*, the present chapter is reprinted, was an unusual man. He was born in December, 1829 in Davie County, North Carolina, the son of a small farmer. Davie County belonged to the upland section of the state where small scale agriculture was the rule and where widespread opposition to the institution of slavery existed. Helper was still but an infant when his father died, leaving to his mother the task of rearing a family of seven small children. In some fashion she succeeded, and Helper, youngest of the brood, grew up a backwoods youth inured to poverty, toil, and outdoor life.

Although he enjoyed but meager formal education he was blessed with a ball-bearing intellect. When he was twenty years of age he made his way to New York City, where a year later he embarked upon the voyage described in the present chapter. Three years spent in California were rewarded by much experience and but little gold, and in 1854 he returned to his ancestral homeland, ostensibly to resume the life of a farmer. In fact, however, he had long since planned to write a book recording his observations about the Land of Gold, and the resultant volume was published at Baltimore in 1855.

Its subtitle, "Reality Versus Fiction," sufficiently suggests the character of its contents. An observant reporter, with a marked taste for economic disputation, Helper found little to praise and much to deplore in California. If in the century that has since elapsed American Boosterism has found its most congenial home in California, the trenchant pen of Helper contributed nothing to this result.

To *The Land of Gold* he presently added a still more provocative volume. The decade of the fifties resounded with heated controversy over the slavery issue, the prelude to the Civil War of 1861–1865. To the volume of angry debate Helper made the most pungent single contribution by the publication in 1857 of *The Impending Crisis*, whose title was no less ominous than it proved to be prophetic. Helper detested the Negro (at a later time he coolly proposed that all Negroes who would not migrate to Africa should be massacred) and he viewed the institution of slavery as a millstone around the necks of the white race in the South, condemning the great majority to a state of economic misery and social ignominy. This demonstration was accompanied by an appeal to the class to which Helper himself belonged to strike off their shackles by destroying the hated institution.

The Impending Crisis intensified the sectional controversy which was already raging, and operated as a catalytic to crystallize the hatreds which were soon to be resolved on the field of battle. It immediately became a political issue, and Helper, as much as any one man, prodded the nation along its onward course toward Secession and Civil War.

His achievement is the more remarkable in light of the fact that in 1857 he was but twenty-seven years of age. The remainder of his long life was a sorry anti-climax. For many years, following the return of peace, he devoted his energy and his modest fortune to agitation for the construction of an All-America railroad from Hudson Bay to Patagonia. As yet the country had but little need for and less interest in such a project. At last in 1909, forgotten and poverty-stricken, Helper committed suicide in Washington. "He was a man of keen intellect," states his biographer, "with a touch of genius akin to madness."

Chapter 2

To California Via Panama

But scant information concerning J. D. Borthwick, the author of *Three Years in California*, whose first two chapters are here reprinted, has been obtained. The book was published in Edinburgh and London in 1857 and the April, 1857 issue of *Blackwood's Magazine* contains a long and favorable review of it. That the author was a Briton and none too familiar with the people of the United States is evident from his narrative. His family name is an ancient one in Scotland, and Borthwick Castle near Edinburgh was one of the older structures of its kind in that country. A painter of genre named J. D. Borthwick exhibited at the Royal Academy in the years 1860–70. Identity of name and calling suggests that he was probably our author, who drew portraits of miners, and the illustrations for his book.

Appendix

Chapter 3

To California Via Mexico

Although the journey to California by sea and across Mexico seemed comparatively easy, in the actual trial it proved far otherwise. The narrative of Daniel B. Woods, *Sixteen Months at the Gold Diggings*, from which the present chapter is reprinted, illustrates many of the hazards likely to be encountered. Concerning the author comparatively little has been learned. His own narrative discloses that he was an educated man and a member of the white collar class. It also discloses that he was a native of Massachusetts who had lived for some years in Philadelphia.

The Philadelphia directories for 1847 and 1849 list him as a resident of that city and a teacher. Allibone's *Dictionary of English Literature*, published in 1871, lists him with the title of "Reverend." Whether the editor deduced this from his narrative, which relates that in the course of the journey he was several times invited to preach, or whether he based it upon other information we are unable to state. Whether teacher or preacher—or both—his *Sixteen Months at the Gold Diggings* seems to be his sole literary work. His narrative of the 800-mile journey across

Mexico, followed by the sorry straits to which his party was reduced on the voyage from San Blas to San Francisco, affords a thrilling tale of travel and adventure.

Chapter 4

California in 1848

In June, 1846 President Polk authorized Jonathan D. Stevenson of New York to raise a regiment of volunteers for service in California in the war with Mexico which Congress had declared on May 12. The regiment, subsequently known as the First New York Volunteers, was mustered into service on August 1 and dispatched for California by sea on three transports, attended by the U.S. man-of-war *Preble*, on September 26.

The regiment arrived in California half a year later to find the fighting in California already ended. However, many of the men had enlisted with a view to remaining in California, and in the infancy of its American development they played a prominent role.

Thus it came to pass on April 1, 1848 that one of them who had been stationed at San Francisco, indited a lengthy communication to the editor of the New York *Herald* devoted to providing a comprehensive survey

Appendix

of the resources and state of development of California. Already, it is interesting to note, he had become a booster for his newly-adopted land and his account of its climate and resources does not suffer through understatement. Although it reports the recent discovery of gold, accompanied by the forecast that California would reap a "Peruvian harvest of the precious metals" as soon as men to mine them should arrive, this paragraph of his report failed to stand out from the accompanying mass of data. Indeed, the sapient editor of the *Herald* deemed it so little newsworthy that he neglected to give it place in the topical abstract which headlined the report. Such topics as "Religion," "the Press," and "cattle" were evidently regarded by him as more important.

The report of the *Herald's* unknown correspondent was reissued by Douglas McMurtrie at Evanston, Illinois, in March, 1943. His copy has been utilized for the present reprint, although with certain minor changes and corrections introduced with the purpose of clarifying the text.

355

Chapter 5

San Francisco in 1849

Bayard Taylor belonged to the select number of America's literary darlings. Born in 1825 to a Pennsylvania Quaker family, he very early manifested a taste for literature and an itching foot. Fortunately, too, he was equipped with a personality which charmed away all obstacles, permitting him to launch upon his career of traveler and writer before his twentieth year. A two-year European tour begun at the age of nineteen resulted in the publication of his *Views Afoot* in 1846 when he was still but twenty-one. It ran to twenty editions in less than a decade and gave him a literary vogue which was never lessened to the end of his life.

In January, 1848 Taylor was given charge of a Department in the New York *Tribune*. His disposition and his prestige as a traveler made it natural that upon the news of the discovery of gold he should join in the rush to California as correspondent of the *Tribune*. Sailing in June, 1849 and crossing the Isthmus of Panama, he spent five months in California and was back in New York in March, 1850. Apart from a series of letters published currently in the *Tribune*, the literary product of his tour was *Eldorado*, published in 1850.

Taylor was twenty-four years of age in 1849, with his intellectual curiosity still unsated and his physical vigor unimpaired. He was obviously a capital traveler, and his *Eldorado* confirmed and increased the popular acclaim as a writer which he had already won. Both for the contemporary public and for posterity it was a rare piece of good fortune that the well-nigh ideally equipped reporter should witness and describe one of the great migrations of historic times. Our present chapter reprints Chapter XII of *Eldorado*, describing San Francisco as he first saw it in September, 1849, and Chapter XX as he found it upon his return from the interior toward the close of October.

Chapter 6

The News Comes to Monterey

Like Bayard Taylor, Rev. Walter Colton was an experienced journalist and author. He graduated from Yale in 1822 and from Andover Theological Seminary in 1825. From then until 1830 he held a professorship in the Academy at Middletown, Connecticut, meanwhile dabbling in newspaper work.

In 1830 he became editor of a religious paper at Washington, devoted to opposing President Jackson's policy of removing the Indians from Georgia. Jackson succeeded, however, and the newspaper failed. Despite Colton's opposition to Jackson's Indian policy the two men became friends, and in 1831 the President appointed Colton to a chaplaincy in the navy. As a consequence of this connection he sailed on various cruises and industriously wrote books about them. In the summer of 1845 he was ordered to sea in the *Congress* which was bound for a cruise to the Pacific.

War with Mexico was imminent, and in fact was declared by Congress while the *Congress*, commanded by Commodore Stockton, was en route to the California Coast. Upon his arrival Stockton assumed command of the fleet of American warships in the Pacific and vigorously pressed the conquest of California. In July, 1846 he assumed control at Monterey and for lack of a better candidate appointed Chaplain Colton as Alcalde, or chief magistrate. Although Colton was a preacher with only a layman's knowledge of law, as Alcalde he found himself in possession of practically unlimited powers. The situation was, of course, anomalous, and he probably exercised his authority as well as any one else available could have done. He established California's first newspaper and built the State's first schoolhouse. He returned home in the summer of 1849 in failing health and as his last literary work wrote *The Land of Gold. Three Years in California, 1846–1849*, which was published in 1850.

Chapter XVIII of this work provides the material reprinted in our present chapter. Probably most readers have toyed with the idea of attaining sudden wealth and have pictured to themselves the use they would make of it. One would seek long in printed literature for any real-life parallel to Colton's recital of the consequences to an entire community of the realization of such a dream. His narrative affords food for reflection concerning the influence upon the individual of the acquisition of sudden wealth, as well as ample background material for the writing of numerous works of fiction.

Chapter 7

Three Weeks in a Mining Camp

The letters of Dame Shirley were first published in the *Pioneer*, California's first purely literary magazine. They began with the first issue, in January, 1854 and continued until the demise of the *Pioneer* in December, 1855. Had the venturesome editor done nothing more than preserve these letters for posterity he would have carved for himself a permanent niche in the literary history of California.

Dame Shirley was in reality a young matron whose more prosaic natal name was Amelia Smith. A native of Elizabethtown, New Jersey, she was orphaned in childhood and by her guardian was taken to Amherst, Massachusetts, where she grew to womanhood and obtained her education. Probably no more cultured community than Amherst in the middle years of the nineteenth century could have been found in America, and Amelia profited by it to become herself a highly cultivated woman. In 1849 she married Dr. Clappe, a physician, and sailed with him for California. Some months were passed in San Francisco when failing health induced Dr. Clappe to seek relief in the higher altitude of the Sierras, where he located in the mining camp of Rich Bar on Feather River.

In close proximity were other "bars," crowded with busy miners. Mrs. Clappe soon joined her husband and they procured a rude cabin on Indian Bar, which seems to have been a sort of adjunct to the larger Rich Bar camp. The scenes which transpired here during the three summer weeks beginning with July 4, 1852 are the subject of Dame Shirley's nineteenth letter, reprinted in the present chapter. All the letters (twenty-three in number) purport to have been written to a younger sister of the author at Amherst. The Editor of the *Pioneer* affirms that they were not intended for publication and that they were printed by him "with scarcely an erasure." Although all prior commentators, apparently, have accepted this statement as the literal truth, the present Editor is unable to do so. It was wholly conventional a century ago for authors to affirm that their books were prepared with no distant thought of publication, which latter step they had taken in response to the urging of their friends. Frequently, too, they were cast in the epistolary mold, which even yet writers of books sometimes elect to adopt. Whatever Mrs. Clappe may have written from her mountain fastness to her sister in distant Amherst, we find it easier to believe her communications as published in the *Pioneer* were the product of careful labor performed by the author with the goal of publication definitely in mind.

This question each reader must decide for himself, of course. Regardless of its merit,

posterity is deeply indebted to Mrs. Clappe
for her vivid recording of her observations
and experiences during the months of her sojourn at Rich and Indian bars. To the still
waxing flood of Gold Rush literature she
contributed one of the earliest and most valuable examples. If in her lifetime she endured many grievous frustrations, by her
Shirley Letters she achieved a permanent
hold upon fame. Recently when the Book
Club of California conducted a symposium
designed to obtain lists of the ten best books
dealing with some aspect of the Gold Rush,
thirteen of the sixteen recognized authorities
who participated in it included her *Letters*
in their lists. But two other works were
named by as many as half of the experts
consulted and only two more by as many
as one-third.

Readers of our present chapter may feel
assured, therefore, that it presents an au-
thentic picture of life in one well-known mining camp in the roaring days of the Gold
Rush. It need not be assumed, however,
that all camps, or even Rich and Indian bars
at all times, reveled in the uproarious scenes
the chapter depicts. Mrs. Clappe, herself,
indirectly implies as much. The people of
ancient Rome had their periods of Saturnalia. In her present *Letter* and in the one re-

printed in Chapter X Dame Shirley has elected to describe such a period in the life of the denizens of Rich Bar.

Chapter 8

How The Gold Was Mined

When the first rush was made to the mines in the summer of 1848 a good deal of gold was found with but little effort. The favorite equipment of many of the early miners, indeed, was a knife with which the precious metal might be scraped or dug from the rock crevices where it had been deposited. Employment of a pan for washing the gold, which meant separating it from the accompanying soil and gravel by whirling a pan of water in such fashion that the soil would be expelled while the heavier gold particles fell to the bottom, was perhaps the commonest method of operation during 1848 and 1849. Before long, however, the Long Tom, the cradle and other more complicated methods and mechanisms were adopted.

All this, and much else beside was carefully described by a veteran of the mines who contributed an article on *"How We Get Gold in California"* to the April, 1860 issue of *Harper's New Monthly Magazine.* The narrative, attributed only to "A Miner of the Year '49," was accompanied by a large number of illustrations which serve to clarify the narrative and to invest it with an aura of reality. Two of these illustrations are reproduced in our present chapter. To considerable degree the article provides a conspectus of the evolution of the mines and of mining operations during the dozen-year period which ended in 1860.

Chapter 9

Chinese, Mexicans and Indians

With fortune seekers from almost all over the world flocking to the mines, California quickly became a highly cosmopolitan community. Prominent among the early gold seekers were Kanakas from Hawaii, Sonorans from Mexico, and Chillenos and other nationals from South America. From the summer of 1849 onward citizens from eastern United States predominated both in numbers and in social and political arrogance. They very early assumed the attitude that California belonged to them and that all others, including even the native Californians, were foreigners, to be tolerated or driven out at their pleasure.

Appendix

Space is wanting to include in a single volume characterizations of all the racial groups which flocked to the mines. Our present chapter presents selections from J. D. Borthwick's *Three Years In California* (already utilized for the contents of Chapter II) picturing several racial elements, but more particularly the Mexicans and the Chinese; and from Alonzo T. Delano's *Life on the Plains and Among the Diggings*, first published in 1853, which supplies a sympathetic and enlightening characterization of the native Indian element.

A medical fad current a century ago is responsible for providing us with Delano's narrative. In the spring of 1849 a company of Gold Seekers from Dayton, Ohio rendezvoused at St. Joseph preparatory to launching upon the trek across the plains. Delano had no remote thought of becoming a gold seeker until ninety days before his departure from his home for the St. Joseph rendezvous. His health was bad, however, and his physician advised a change of scene to avert a fatal termination of his disease. In consequence he quickly decided to embark upon the overland journey to the mines. A physician who today would send a supposedly dying man upon such a journey would deserve to be debarred from the further practice of his profession. In the eighteen forties, however, it was orthodox procedure to send a patient upon a distant journey.

In Delano's case the treatment proved efficacious. In California he presently became a notable figure. Among other activities he became a gold seeker, mining superintendent, merchant, banker, writer, and theatrical manager. He also became much involved with fabulous Lola Montez, whom rumor credited with being his secret bride. Under the pseudonym of "Old Block" he wrote mining sketches which became widely popular, and his *Life on the Plains and Among the Diggings* still remains a classic of Gold Rush literature.

Chapter 10

Amusements of the Miners

Exiled from home and abounding in energy, it was inevitable that the miner should seek such means of recreation as he could find or devise. Everywhere the saloon and gambling place flourished, and to them most miners resorted, regardless of their habits and religious standards back home. Everywhere, too, dancing could be indulged in. Music and feminine partnership were of course, desirable for the pursuit of this recreation. In almost every group of men some one capable of providing music of a sort was found. If women were lacking, the want could be supplied by tying a bit of cloth around the arms of half the dancers, thereby designating them as women for the time being. Drinking, gambling, and dancing aside, theatrical entertainments were eagerly attended whenever the opportunity was presented. Less frequently, probably, the native Californians provided two kinds of show to which they had long been addicted: conventional bull fights and fights in which a bull was pitted against a grizzly bear. In the present chapter contemporary descriptions of bear and bull fighting, of saloons and gambling places, and of dancing are presented. The description of the bear and bull fight is reprinted from Chapter X of Helper, *The Land of Gold*; the accounts of gambling and drinking are taken from Woods, *Sixteen Months at the Gold Diggings*; the picture of dancing and Sunday activities is reprinted from the twelfth of Dame Shirley's *Letters* and from Helper, *The Land of Gold*.

Chapter 11

Argonaut Agreements and Mining Laws

Robinson Crusoe alone on his Pacific island could do whatever pleased him. When Friday arrived on the scene a unit of human society was created and rules and understandings governing the conduct of its members became necessary.

Practically no one journeyed to California alone, and those who embarked in companies commonly subscribed in advance of departure to a set of rules designed to govern their relations on the journey. These were more or less elaborate, varying with the circumstances and desires of those who drafted them. In many cases they were designed to continue in effect after the Land of Gold was reached.

At the time that gold was first discovered the mining country was chiefly a wilderness peopled only by its native Indian inhabitants. Before the close of 1848 several thousand fortune seekers had flocked into it, and by the end of 1849 their number had increased to perhaps 100,000. The years that followed were marked, of course, by further rapid increases.

In the absence of any established government, sheer necessity compelled the miners to improvise rules of conduct and agencies for their enforcement. Although the population of the mines was exceedingly heterogeneous, the native American argonauts from the eastern states promptly arrogated to themselves the dominant role in the country. Inheritors of the experience of generations of pioneering Americans and containing among their number many men of political experience and capacity, they were almost ideally fitted for the task of laying the foundations of the nascent commonwealth. Proof of their political capacity is the fact that in a relatively short period of time they evolved a body of mining law which subsequently received the sanction of the state and national governments and which today governs the procedure of all who undertake to find and develop mines on the public domain of the United States.

Basic to the entire system was the recognition of the principle of majority rule and the establishment of titles to holdings by right of prior discovery and appropriation. Each mining camp (the number of these eventually amounted to several hundred) became a separate social and governmental unit whose occupants in popular assemblies adopted regulations for the government of the camp. When the need arose, they assembled in larger or smaller numbers to constitute themselves a court for the trial of offenders, enforcing its decisions by the prompt application of the lash, the noose, or other penalty deemed most appropriate.

Practically all miners were squatters—usually on the public domain, but frequently on lands already in private ownership. The thirst for gold was overpowering and under its influence and that of the fluid state of society in the early years, much of injustice was wreaked both upon individuals and upon racial groups. Least capable of self-protection and most ill-treated were the Indians, who were maltreated and, frequently, massacred in ways which permanently disgraced the white invaders of their homeland. Perhaps next in order ranked the Chinese, the Mexicans, and the Spanish-Americans generally. But the dominant American group looked upon all others as foreign intruders, subjecting them to varying degrees of dislike and mistreatment.

In after years the Forty-niners were wont to believe that in the earlier months of the Gold Rush mining society exhibited a state of virtue and halcyon innocence such as mankind has for centuries associated with dreams of the Golden Age. Nostalgic dreams to the contrary, however, even-handed objective justice did not thrive in the atmosphere of the mining camps.

The agencies of justice civilized society affords are commonly far superior to the procedures dictated by the stark necessities of the mining camps, which amid the hurly-burly of the Gold Rush were frequently productive of injustice and absurdity. The miner who posted the notice, "Jim Brown of Missoury takes this ground, jumpers will be shot" was himself assuming the power of the State to defend his supposed property. It is obvious, however, that in the event of a dispute settlement of the issue by an established court of justice would have been preferable to the shotgun law enforced by Jim Brown.

In our present chapter three illustrative items are presented. The "Articles of Agreement" and inventory of equipment of the small overland company which went from Madison, Wisconsin to California in 1849 was copied for the present Editor from the diary of Abiel Easter Brooks over a quarter-century ago. Since then we have lost track of the original manuscript, which so far as our knowledge goes has never been published. From the same diary is copied the case of the theft of a pan of dust, and the court procedure which followed the discovery of the offense.

Appendix

The mining regulations adopted by the occupants of the Jacksonville placer camp, somewhat more elaborate than many other documents of the kind, are reprinted from Daniel B. Woods, *Sixteen Months at the Gold Diggings*. The reader will not fail to notice the provision excluding all foreigners from the camp, and the severity of the penalties prescribed for theft. The regulations were adopted at a meeting held "in front of Colonel Jackson's store" on January 20, 1850.

The final item is reprinted from the old-age recollections of Professor John B. Parkinson of the University of Wisconsin, published in the issue of the *Wisconsin Magazine of History* for December, 1921. The author joined the Gold Rush as a youth of eighteen in 1852 and spent three years in the mines of northern California. When the lament of his former professor that he had sacrificed his prospects for a career to become a gold miner was reported to him, he determined to return to Wisconsin and resume his interrupted education. His California narrative presents the old-age reflections of an unusually competent observer of mining life from 1852 to 1855.

Index

Index
